TEACHING
MUSIC

Raymond Elliott

Texas Technological College, Lubbock, Texas

TEACHING MUSIC

Methods and Materials for the Elementary Schools

Charles E. Merrill Books, Inc., Columbus, Ohio

Dedicated to Harrison and Luella Maxwell who, by their devotion and service to others, bestow honor upon their former teachers —one in particular.

First Printing .... *May, 1960*
Second Printing .... *April, 1961*
Third Printing ...... *December, 1961*
Fourth Printing ...... *September, 1963*

Library of Congress Catalog Card Number: 60–11334

Printed in the United States of America

Preface

Teaching Music attempts to present both the *how* and the *what* of music instruction at the elementary school level. Since music is not treated as an isolated subject, the outlook of the book is broad, presenting music as an integral part of the curriculum. Throughout these pages, emphasis is placed on the correlation of music with other subjects—not just *talk* about correlation, but the presentation of a wealth of material with specific suggestions on how this material can be related to other subjects. The purpose is not to "prop up" music or justify its place in the curriculum, but to increase understanding in all areas of study.

The book is specifically designed for three groups:

1. The regular elementary classroom teacher who desires material that will facilitate the preparation of units and lesson plans by bringing music and the social studies into a comprehensive and meaningful whole.

2. The prospective elementary teacher who desires to grow culturally through a better understanding and appreciation of music, and who wants to know the *how* and the *what* of music instruction.

3. The prospective music specialist who desires to broaden his horizons into other subject areas and thus be better prepared to present music to the elementary child.

Each of these groups needs to know how music relates to people and to other areas of study. To gain detailed information about these subjects would require extensive reading. Furthermore, these groups desire information concerning traditional tunes, such as Christmas and patriotic songs, and need aid in understanding the text of a song.

The book is in two parts, each closely related to the other. Part One deals with methods of presenting music to the child. In the interest of practicality, many actual teaching situations are presented in the sections titled "Teachers in Action." These illustrations also describe experiences of student teachers. The names are fictitious. A carefully selected list which is representative of the available teaching material is presented at the close of each chapter. This material is organized in compact form as an aid to teachers and students.

Special attention is directed to the section titled "For Further Development" at the close of each chapter in Part One. The suggestions given here are designed to aid teachers and college students in personal and professional growth and in the preparation of units of study and lesson plans.

Part Two deals with *material* closely related to Part One. This portion of the book is designed as a reference for both elementary teachers and college students. In its preparation the author was conscious of the college teacher's constant search for appropriate reference material for his students.

Part Two is arranged in chronological order. Periods of American and European history are paralleled and folk and art material associated with each is listed. A thumbnail sketch of the outstanding composers of each period is given. From such a presentation, the college student and elementary teacher may gain a panoramic view of music as it relates to history in general and to people in particular. Although much of the material in Part Two is applicable in the elementary grades, it carries the reader a step further than he needs to go in preparation for his elementary students and opens the door to greater cultural development. This presentation also lends itself to comments on Christmas, patriotic, and folk songs. Here, as in Part One, songs and records are listed so that teachers may extend their musical horizons. The over-all presentation is arranged in sections for easy reference.

The author hopes that this book will open new doors for learning and serve not only as a text but also as a reference for the prospective and the regular elementary teacher.

RAYMOND ELLIOTT

Acknowledgments

For their criticism and suggestions in the preparation of the manuscript, grateful acknowledgement is made to the following:

Mr. and Mrs. Charles Myres, Lubbock teachers; Mr. and Mrs. Charles A. Lawrie, Department of Music, Texas Technological College; Miss Katherine Evans, Department of Education, Texas Technological College; Dr. Gene Hemmle, Head, Department of Music, Texas Technological College; Professor Alice M. Snyder, Department of Music, San Francisco State College; and Professor Wayne Ramsey, Department of Music, Ohio State University.

Sincere gratitude is expressed to the following for permission to use the material described:

Capitol Records: recordings.
Chicago Musical Instrument Company: picture of MicrOrgan.
Conn Corporation: pictures of Conn rhythm, brass, and reed instruments.
Fawick Strings, Inc.: pictures of violin and viola.
Folkways Records: recordings.
Gamble Hinged Music Company: pictures of Gretsch Organ and Pianorgan.

Gibson, Inc.: picture of Gibson Guitar.

Everett A. Gillis, Texas Technological College: the poems "Jim Cooper, American," and "Cattle Drive."

Ginn and Company: the song "Playmates."

M. Hohner, Inc.: picture of M. Hohner Melodica.

The Kaleidograph Press: the poem "Jim Cooper, American."

Kay Musical Instrument Company: pictures of string bass and violoncello.

C. G. Martin and Company: picture of Martin Ukulele.

G. Ricordi and Company: the text of "Lane County Bachelor."

Oscar Schmidt-International, Inc.: picture of the Autoharp.

Walberg and Auge: picture of Song Bells.

David Wexler and Company: picture of Weiss Recorder.

The Wurlitzer Company: pictures of Wurlitzer Electronic Piano and Wurlitzer Chord Organ.

For their cooperation in obtaining needed materials, gratitude is expressed to the following: B. E. Adair Music Company; Earl Ray Band Company; Follett Publishing Company; Dr. Ishmael Hill, Assistant Superintendent of Schools, Lubbock, Texas; and Silver Burdett Company.

Finally, acknowledgement is due to David Buchan and Elizabeth Watson who illustrated the chapter-opening pages.

RAYMOND ELLIOTT

REFERENCE CODE

In referring to songs, the following code letters are used: G, Ginn and Company; S, Silver Burdett Company; F, Follett Publishing Company. The letters *a*, *b*, or *c* following a page number refer in that order to song titles on a given page. The letter *r* indicates that the selection is recorded by the publisher of the series.

Contents

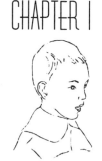

PART I Methods

CHAPTER 1

Prologue

Focus on Man

Music is neither a superficial whim nor a modern educational frill; it is a satisfying human experience as old, at least, as the recorded history of man. Nor is music a superfluous activity, separated from daily living. On the contrary, it has been so intimately and essentially a part of man that melody is interwoven throughout the variegated fabric of history. Furthermore, music has played a vivid and fundamental part in human development as an aid to observation, reflection, imagination, expression, and recreation. In these respects it is just as valuable today as it has been through the ages.

Why has man shown such interest in and devotion to music through the centuries? The answer is based upon man's nature and his needs. Man's threefold nature—physical, mental, and spiritual—gives rise to certain universal needs that music has always helped to satisfy. What are these needs and how has music contributed to their satisfaction?

3

Need to Make a Living. Man has always needed food, shelter, and clothing. Since early man had to make his living "by the sweat of his brow," he needed music to lighten the labor. The repetition of work activities suggested the rhythm pattern, and soon melody, however simple, emerged as an emotional expression relative to the task. Thus, working songs evolved. A wide variety of these will be referred to in this book.

Music meets man's present need in much the same way. The business or professional man, the housewife or the school child, who can sing a song, play a tune, or become absorbed in listening to music possesses something which makes a positive contribution to his daily living. Through its healing therapy, music can relax muscles, relieve tensions, and change unseemly and misshapen attitudes which the day's work may have induced. It was for such rewards that King Saul listened to young David's harp, and similarly, modern society, with its ever increasing pressures and tensions, needs and uses music. But music is not merely a retreat from the tensions of everyday living; it contributes positively to enrichment, to a fuller, happier existence. When the art of music is combined with the greater art of living, it becomes a most useful and practical subject.

Need for Peaceful Order—the Family and the Nation. Man was quick to sense the need for peace and tranquil order in his dealings with others; thus the family, the clan, the tribe, and the nation came into being. From such organized groups came the lullaby and the national anthem, musical forms that both express and encourage human solidarity.

One of the greatest joys of the American family used to be the piano or reed organ in the parlor. The family gathered around the instrument and joined in a unified expression of harmony and cooperation which bound the group together in a genuine feeling of oneness. There were guitars, fiddles, mandolins, harmonicas, and jew's-harps which formed a family musical ensemble. Today this kind of family activity is not as popular as it was, but the same unifying power of music is still felt in the school song, the church hymn, and the national anthem.

Need for Social Enrichment. To impart greater meaning and enjoyment to human relationships, man has always felt the need to beautify his social institutions and to enliven his social activities. Through the centuries, music has helped him to fill this need.

There is today a greater use of music in our social order than we may at first realize. For example, music comprises about one half of the worship service and approximately three-fourths of the marriage ceremony. In most of our social activities, from the cradle to the grave, music plays an important part. The banquet and the service club are not without the vitalizing and unifying spirit of song, and there would be no dancing without the irresistible rhythm of the band. We would sorely miss the enrichment that music gives to the home, the church, weddings, funerals, dances, and football games. We may conclude that music is the spice of all social functions and that it is highly valuable for social development and unity.

Need for Knowledge and Learning. The need for knowledge and learning became apparent as man fought against hunger, disease, and climate: the acquired skill, knowledge, and experience of one generation needed to be passed on to following generations. Knowledge required that man observe the world about him. In this process, he could not help perceiving the melody, rhythm, and harmony in nature. For music is probably the most natural of the arts and is most directly related to nature in that it lives, vibrating and pulsating with life itself. Thus music served as a means of interpreting the world of nature. As for its contribution to learning, music is related to so many other fields that through its study one is led into a consideration of history, art, literature, science, psychology, and sociology. For this reason it is a subject which can contribute to growth, not only throughout school years, but throughout the life span.

Need for Self-expression. Man has always felt a natural urge to express himself and has now learned that denying it often results in neuroticism, maladjustment, juvenile delinquency, and criminality. Man is by far the most versatile of all animals in his ability to express himself, and his creative impulse becomes so

great as to be an absolute necessity. For these reasons, he has
always responded to the beauty of his environment, leaving paint-
ings on the walls of his cave or pottery and jewels in his tombs. The
early Greeks left their architecture, sculpture, and poetry; the
Egyptians their pyramids; and all peoples have left their musical
instruments. Through music, man discovered a perfect medium
for expressing his threefold nature.

It behooves the modern school and teacher to provide wholesome activities through which children and young people may
express themselves. Music heads the list of subjects that make
this expression possible. For this reason, music education is concerned more with what music will do for the individual than what
the individual will do with music.

Need for Religious Expression. By nature man is religious, and
for centuries he has sought the answers to the "why" of life. He
has recognized a power, order, and intelligence beyond his per-
ception. Although beliefs have been widely diversified, most races
and creeds have agreed upon one thing: music is the perfect expression to accompany worship of the deity.

As stated earlier, about one half of the worship service consists
of music. Although the public school must generally avoid the
subject of religion, there are many songs with religious texts to
be found in the song series for children. Most of these have been
carefully written and edited to avoid offending any faith. Because
the very finest choral literature has been composed on religious
texts, a great deal of religious music is performed in the junior
and senior high school and in college.

Since music has, from the beginning, found its place in all of
the activities of man, helping him to meet the fundamental needs
of life, we should give it a greater part in our lives and encourage
our children to live a richer, happier, and fuller life through participating in musical activities. Our children will then be able to
lighten the burden of labor through song; use music in the home
for the development of beauty, harmony, and unity; thrill to
melody and rhythm in all sorts of social and community gather-
ings; learn and grow all through life through music's challenge to

the mind; and find mental, physical, emotional, and spiritual expression through this universal language. If we can give all this to our children, we will have made a distinct contribution to the exalting of life and of living.

Focus on the School

We now come to the question of *why, when,* and *how* music became a part of the school curriculum. In regard to the reason for its inclusion, it must be pointed out that at the time when music began to be widely admitted, the criterion by which each subject was judged was its *value and use in everyday affairs.* As we have seen from the foregoing discussion, music has for centuries been the companion of man in helping him to meet his basic needs. Measured by the yardstick of practical value, music therefore found great favor and wide and rapid acceptance. Furthermore, around the turn of the century, when the demand for music in the curriculum began to make itself felt, the philosophy of education was directed toward developing the whole child. Too much stress, it was felt, had been placed upon training the mind, and man simply was not all mind. Since music, from the beginning, had played such a prominent role in all man's activities and in expressing his threefold nature, it seemed wise to give it a place in child development and thus offer the opportunity for a richer, fuller, and more abundant life—for the present as well as for the future.

The ground-breaking ceremonies for the foundation of music education were conducted in Boston during the school year of 1837-38 under the capable leadership of Lowell Mason. Due, however, to numerous factors (including the western migration, the lack of musical organizations and publications, the rapid development of commercial and industrial activities, the building and growing pains of the new country, and the civil war and its aftermath), the foundations were not firmly laid until the closing years of the nineteenth century. Rapid strides were made during the first years of the twentieth century, but progress was retarded during World War I. Speed resumed during the twenties, and since that time continuous acceleration has been the rule. At the turn of the century, there were practically no organized school choirs, bands, and orchestras. Today there are literally thousands.

How music made its debut in the school room makes for an interesting story because the basic philosophy and instructional concepts of music education were established in the initial experiment. Actually, it was not as difficult as might be expected, for the ever popular singing schools of the day had already made a favorable impression on many prominent and influential people. An experiment or demonstration was all that was needed to prove its merits. Lowell Mason was the man of the hour and possessed the necessary training and interest to conduct such an experiment. In fact, Mason had already demonstrated the teaching of music to children in 1830, in connection with a lecture on the subject of "Vocal Music As a Branch of Common Education," delivered by William C. Woodbridge. A group of children trained and directed by Mason demonstrated the singing abilities of children. Woodbridge had only recently returned from Europe, where he had studied music instruction in European schools. In Switzerland, he had observed the work of George Nageli who was applying the new ideas of group instruction advanced by the influential educational reformer John Pestalozzi. Convinced of the practicability of these principles, Mason incorporated them into his *Manual of Instruction* and then proceeded to prove them in his work with children. Thus, the stage was set and the lights turned on in 1837, when the Boston Board of Education became convinced that music should be given a trial in the classroom. For some unexplained reason, the city council failed to appropriate the needed and expected money, whereupon Mason volunteered his services for the year. The experiment and spring concert were so electrifying that Mason was placed in full charge of music in the Boston schools. He continued until 1841, when he resigned in order to give full time to editing and composing.

Early Platform Established

The arguments of the skeptics during Mason's time were not unlike those heard today. Probably the most prominent of these arguments was based upon the traditional assumption that music was for the favored few—that only a small minority possessed God-given musical talents. Mason disproved this idea beyond question during his few years in the Boston schools. Strangely enough, the idea still persists in some areas today and has to be disproven by competent instructors. The truth of the matter, as presented in Boston, stands today: *what we call a musical ear is the result of cultivation, and the time to begin is in early youth.*

The answer to another objection of the skeptics became an important plank in the philosophic platform of music education. The objection concerned the impracticability, due to time and expense, of producing *a virtuoso musician.* The answer was that the aim was not to develop highly skilled professionals and that music should be given the same treatment as reading, writing, and arithmetic. It was pointed out that the aim in teaching grammar was not to produce poets. If now and then a professional poet or musician emerged as a result of instruction, well and good. Thus, from the very outset, *the aim of public school music education was crystal clear: the understanding and appreciation of music.*

Other ideas presented before the Boston Board of Education which have become embedded in our philosophy of music education may be summed up as follows:

1. Music, like some of the traditional subjects, is a discipline subject—discipline for the mind, ear, and eye.

2. The aim of group instruction is not merely to train the intellect; it is more important "to feel rightly than to think profoundly," a point that has never been questioned.

3. We all need amusements, and music serves this need.

4. Music is helpful training for a useful and happy adult life. It is one avenue to more abundant life in the present, and has strong carry-over possibilities for the future.

5. Music is a refining and elevating influence in the community. How true this is today, as school choirs, bands, and orchestras bring their contributions of culture to so many people so effectively!

Thus, the basic philosophy of the value and purpose of school music instruction was established. So profoundly true were these beliefs, and so basic in man's experience with music, that they have stood the test of time. They were proven in the first experiment at Boston. Strange as it may seem, it has been necessary to prove them over and over again, for the initial offering of music has always been considered an experiment. How often music has proved its manifold values can be measured by its growth in quantity and quality all over America.

What of the principles of instruction introduced by Mason? These, too, have become the foundation of instructional philosophy. The important ones may be summed up as follows:

1. Teach the sounds before the signs. Let the child experience tone and time before learning the notation representing them.

2. Cause the child to become active in his learning. Rather than first attempting to explain what he should do, lead him to observe what he has been doing.

3. Cause the child to understand music—its principles and theory—through music itself.

Although these three principles were set forth more than one hundred years ago, they have only in recent years been more fully practiced. The first one—teach the sounds before the signs—is precisely the procedure in learning our native tongue. First we learn to speak it by imitation and then learn the symbols representing the "stored" sounds. This principle, as it applies to music, was put into practice in a limited way around the turn of the century but only insofar as children were concerned. The impossibility of teaching a child to comprehend a beat and the relative note lengths was quite obvious, yet the child could feel and respond to them with little difficulty. It became the practice, therefore, to approach a knowledge and understanding of music by first doing things and then observing what had been done. This meant teaching children by ear and gradually leading them to an awareness of the symbols representing tone and time. Through such an approach it was possible to "store" in the mind and muscle many tonal and rhythmic patterns. When the child was ready for music reading, the "stored" patterns became the mental concepts which preceded the comprehension of symbols.

Learning music, then, is a process of *first experiencing and later explaining it*. Out of this approach grew the idea for the so-called song method, for many songs were needed for observation.

Focus on You

It is the first day of school. You are the teacher. Entrusted to you for their development are twenty-seven six-year-old human souls. They cannot read or write, count or measure, spell or sing. Your value to them is not necessarily measured by your proficiency in these skills, for although your knowledge is necessary, only your wisdom makes it effectual. The children may be led to understand things because they feel that *you understand them;* their attitude may be good because *your feeling toward them is wholesome;* they love school because *you love them;* they grow in self-confidence because *you have faith in them;* they develop initiative because *you entrust them with responsibility.* If you guide them wisely, the children will grow, and they will remember you. But if you "keep school" or "teach lessons," they may dislike school, may forget you, and may even forget the lessons. Nor should *you* forget *who they are.* Here is a doctor, and there is a nurse; here a minister, there a teacher; here a statesman, there a politician; here a banker, there an industrialist; here an artist, there a laborer; here a lawyer, there a criminal; and more important than all, here are husbands and fathers, wives and mothers.

In your role as teacher, you are not a domineering dictator; you are not master and they slaves. They are freeborn citizens and you are to help them remain worthy of the privilege. Although in extreme cases punishment may have to be imposed, it is self-control and self-discipline that form the ideal in democracy. For this reason, a democratic atmosphere must prevail and not a totalitarian dictatorship. The children cannot learn to think if you do it for them. Your role is that of a trusted guide, a wise counselor, a respected friend, an inspiring leader. You project "faith, hope and charity."

Nor should you forget that it is your attitude toward the children, their parents, and your colleagues that is the impelling and motivating spirit of the classroom. In your dealings with these people you are wholesome, pleasant, cooperative, and considerate without the suggestion of superiority. You are strong yet tender, firm yet pliant, loving but not affectionate, friendly but not familiar, sincere but not solemn. Your over-all attitude creates mutual respect, teamwork, and the desire to participate. Yet you avoid an appearance of coercion, for your leadership is not expressed by a commanding attitude. You, too, are but a student and your word is not infallible. Teaching is your chosen profession and you will be devoted to building the character and citizenship worthy of your calling.

To recapitulate, music has been, and is today, deeply engrained in our social and economic life. It is not a modern fad, for its activities in the modern school follow the selfsame paths that generations throughout the ages have traveled in their creative and recreative efforts. As a means of expression, it has more dimensions than any other media. It cannot be divorced from people and we entreat the reader to keep this in mind—*people and music, music and people.*

In the light of the foregoing discussion and in keeping with present-day educational philosophy, it is appropriate to state a general and a specific aim. The over-all aim in education should be: *To discover and offer opportunities for the development of abilities. The instruction necessary for this development should constantly give training in individual responsibilities, wholesome attitudes, good character, and the ability to think.* The specific aim for music should be: *"Music for every child; every child for music."*

For Further Development

1. Justify music in classroom instruction. In preparation for this read chapter 9.

2. Make a list of positive characteristics of a good teacher. In doing this, recall your experience in grade school, junior and senior high school, and college.

3. Discuss the general aim for education as stated immediately above. What would you add to it or delete from it?

CHAPTER 2

Voices to Sing

What about Singing?

No one knows how long man has been singing or why he first began to compose melody. Speculation has it that song might have come as a result of intense emotion that affected breathing and the vocal chords—screams of pain, cries of fear, ejaculations of delight, moans, sighs, murmurs, or the call of the lover. Nor is the nature of man's first melodies known, for music symbols as we know them did not begin to develop until about the tenth century A.D. The earliest singing was probably in unison, without harmonic effect except for the octave, which is the natural difference in pitch between the mature male and female voice. This supposition is based upon the fact that primitive tribes sing only in the unison and octave and that man's first attempts at writing music down were only melodic. Singing in parts came after the development of a system of notation.

Prior to this and for centuries after, songs were passed on from one generation to the next by ear. Our conclusion may well be that through the centuries song has been a companion of man, that people and song belong together—people and music, music and people.

Singing is a very satisfying, intimate, and personal experience, for it is not merely the voice that sings but the whole human personality—the body, the mind, and soul. When we sing, the song becomes a part of us, we a part of it. Saturated with its thought and feeling, it is as if the song—the idea—were born anew in us. Since the experience is so satisfying and its message so completely assimilable, it is an important agent for learning. For example, a historical, patriotic, religious, or poetic idea expressed in song makes a more lasting impression than the idea standing alone. It is through singing in particular and music in general that we may permanently fortify comprehension with impression.

Obviously, children should never be allowed to believe that singing is sissy. Such beliefs are held only by those who are ignorant of man's activities through the ages. Boys especially should be made to realize that until recent years it was the male who made the songs and sang them. And all should observe that there are bankers, lawyers, farmers, and teachers who enjoy singing. If singing is sissy, then members of Rotary, Kiwanis, and Lions Clubs are sissies. The wide participation in Barber Shop singing and college song-fests all over America is conclusive proof of the male's joy in singing and is a refutation of the stigma of sissiness.

Why Teach Singing?

An Expression of Feeling. We are all cognizant of the need for self-expression and its importance in human development. It has been said that *impression* without *expression* brings *depression.* In the development of the whole personality, the growth which comes through the expression of feeling should not be overlooked, for there is an interrelationship between mind, body, and emotion. Through individual participation in song, personality may be developed, and the individual may free himself of fetters as he gradually grows in self-confidence. Singing is not merely one means of self-expression, but is the ultimate outlet for the expression of feeling. All of the feelings experienced by the human race seem to converge in song, and when we re-express them, we become, as it were, more human.

A Sense of Belonging. Singing is a means for developing a sense of belonging and for experiencing group unity and cooperation. Through song we may identify ourselves with people—our people, with their various national backgrounds; other people in many lands, with their different customs and social patterns. We may learn about Indians, pilgrims, pioneers, cowboys, sailors, fishermen, miners, and lumberjacks. Then, too, we may identify ourselves with the geography of the land—with rivers, mountains, oceans, prairies, and deserts. Thus, we momentarily identify ourselves with the character of the song and grow in understanding. Yet singing also gives one a sense of individual satisfaction. Song is a companion of the individual alone—the cowboy, prospector, aviator. It is a means whereby each man may express himself as an individual apart from the group. Thus, singing serves both "togetherness" and "apartness" and in this way appeals to, and reveals, the two components of man's nature—his social self and his individual self.

An Aid to Observation. Much of man's development has come about through observation. Every song that man has made has necessitated observation of himself or of the things about him. The child is born into a world of sound and motion, and at birth he begins the process of discovering these in himself and in the world about him—clouds and stars, sun and moon, land and sea, bugs and birds. Thus, through the intimate experience of singing, he is led to make observations about his environment and learns in an absorbing way about himself and the world of sound and motion around him.

Singing Is Fun. If singing were not a satisfying and joyous experience, man would have ceased the activity centuries ago. Make no mistake about it, through the ages man has sung for the complete joy of it. There have always been nonsense songs which existed solely for relief of tension and diversion from activity. This diversion is one of the values of singing in school. By nature, the child has a "playboy" complex. Songs with a play and fun motif, based upon everyday experiences, delight children. Such songs often act as "ice-breakers" for the timid child and as an escape for others.

Carry-over into Adulthood. As John Keats said, "A thing of beauty is a joy forever." Singing is one of the beauties that may be enjoyed throughout one's life—in grade school, junior and senior high school, college, the church choir, and the community chorus. The power of the carry-over depends a great deal upon the personal satisfaction derived from experience on each preceding level. This, of course, places grave responsibility upon the teacher. Each of us needs some avenue of escape, something to recharge his spiritual battery. It may be a hobby—reading, or listening to or participating in music. The time to develop such interest is during the formative, impressionable years.

How To Teach Singing

The Child Voice

The child is vocally a miniature adult, for the range of the average child's voice is about the same as that of the average adult. The real difference is one of quality, since the smaller instrument of the child produces a lighter sound. Furthermore, the child's voice is about as flexible as the adult voice and as capable of expressing various moods. Nor is there one technique for the child and another for the adult: the proper physical position and muscular action are the same at any age.

Teaching Vocal Habits

Good vocal habits are taught, like songs, by imitation. The teacher who sings as he speaks, in a natural, relaxed style, teaches by precept and example. The children, for the most part, will imitate the quality, posture, and vocal habits of the teacher. This does not imply that the teacher must be a "trained" singer. On the contrary, the dramatic, "arty" type of voice is undesirable in the elementary classroom. All artificial and so-called popular styles should be avoided. Vibratos, especially those of the wide, slow variety, are likewise highly objectionable. It is enough that the teacher sing with good diction; a relaxed manner with no tension in the jaw, tongue, or throat; and with the "half-voice" which approximates the child's voice. Above all, the teacher should avoid the use of the heavy quality in the lower range. The use of this quality sets up a barrier to the upper range in either the adult or child voice.

It is of primary importance that the child understand the text of the song. Since body and voice respond automatically to feeling, he should also become aware of the mood of the song. This is not accomplished by lengthy discussion, but by brief statements, suggestions, pictures, the selection of songs which are related to other activities of the grade level, and by the music itself. The first step in establishing the mood is motivation, which will be discussed presently. Most important is the teacher's understanding of the song and his ability to convey its meaning and feeling to the children through singing. We may well conclude that good vocal habits are not established by formal presentations, but by imitating the teacher and by instinctive response to the emotional content of the song.

Protecting the Child Voice

As stated earlier, it is not merely the voice that sings but the whole child—the personality. In fact, voice and personality are so closely related that an injured voice is a permanent handicap to the whole person. For this reason, the child should be cautioned even against practices which may impair the effectiveness of his speaking voice. He should be cautioned against loud talk and excessive yelling on the playground or at athletic events. When singing, he should avoid heavy quality, extreme high and low pitches, hushed and forced tones, and full volume. The ideal is a natural, easy tone of medium volume.

One of the great tragedies in the American school is the assumption that excessive yelling at athletic events and pep rallies is necessary and that moderation shows a lack of school spirit. The team, while supposedly developing courage, self-confidence, and self-reliance, resorts to savage techniques of frenzy, and those on the sidelines join in fanatically. Paradoxically, those who foster such wild emotional excitement frown on any form of refined or civilized expression of feeling. They would make stoics of us all except at the ball game or school assembly. The team or individual athlete who must have such artificial stimulation is certainly lacking in qualities which make for great sportsmanship.

The vocal teacher who tries to obtain certain choral effects by forcing young voices or by encouraging a hushed tone injures voices and contributes to permanent personality damage. Visible manifestations of the forced tone may be observed in a wincing of the face muscles, blood rushing to the face, and distended neck muscles. The breathy tone quality so prevalent in adolescent and adult voices is a result of hushed singing.

Teaching the Song by Ear

This is often referred to as *rote* singing. The song is learned through the ear by hearing it as many times as necessary. It was by this method that the child learned to speak, and by this method that man, before the development of music symbols, learned and preserved his songs from one generation to the next. The teacher selects a song which he likes and believes the children will enjoy and understand. After memorizing it, he sings it for the children using good diction and expression, but without affectation. His manner is natural, his mood enthusiastic, and his style simple. He repeats the song on several successive days, giving the children a purpose for active listening with each repetition. When the children are ready to participate, they merely join with him. As their confidence increases, he moves gradually into the background vocally. The whole process is one of informality and enjoyment.

Learning to sing by rote measurably contributes to the over-all development of the child. In order to learn a song, he must give full attention, concentrate, and observe—disciplines which are necessary in all learning. From a musical standpoint, he is receiving valuable ear training which may contribute to his general development. Music educators have often repeated the truism that "The child first learns to listen, and then listens to learn."

Motivation

Authentic information about the composer or the composition can be a motivating factor. This is particularly true of patriotic songs and those which bear some relation to history. The extent of the information should be determined by the probable interest and comprehension of the children. Unfortunately, the term motivation has been so overemphasized that some teachers think it necessary to give each song or instrumental piece a big verbal build-up. Some have even assumed that there is a literal story for each song. It must be emphasized, however, that a song tells its own story. If it is a good song, it can stand on its own merits. Interpretative remarks which clarify the meaning or show the depth of feeling are usually sufficient.

The composer's general purpose in all songs is the same: to communicate ideas clothed in feeling—words and music. The story behind the creation of most compositions is as simple as this: the composer has an urge to create and something to express; his medium of expression is music; and so he writes a song. If it is good, it does not need a crutch.

Miss Scott, a student teacher, introduced a song as follows: "Children, I'm going to sing a song for you, it's one you should know. I want you to sit still and listen as I sing."

The children obeyed and sat still, but they simply were not interested in hearing Miss Scott sing a song which was supposed to be good for them. They tuned her out with less effort than would be needed to turn a radio dial. Miss Scott realized that her first attempt had been a failure. First she blamed the song, then music in general, and finally she doubted that the children were interested in singing. But knowing that other children enjoyed such activities, she concluded that it was *she* and not the children who had failed. She selected a new song, and asked herself, "If I were a child, what would cause me to want to sing this song?" Suddenly, the answer was simple. She made careful plans and got completely satisfying results from the following:

"Children, I know a song about boys and girls. After hearing it, tell me how many children are in this song" (purpose for listening).

Playmates[1]

Mary Jason   (Rote)   *English Folk Tune*

With spirit

Jon - a - than is tall - est, Bet - sy is the small - est,

Tom is a boy with brown eyes: _ _ _ _

Jon - a - than is jol - ly, Bet - sy has a doll - y

Tom has an air - plane that flies. _ _ _ _ _

"How many children were in the song? Hold up the right number of fingers. Do you like the song? I like it too. We'll hear it again tomorrow."—Not, "I'll sing it." "Who remembers something about the song *we heard* yesterday?" Knowing that the children are not ready to sing "Playmates"—the melody, rhythm, and text are not yet familiar—and realizing that several repetitions might be tiring for both herself and the children, Miss Scott diverts attention to the song they heard yesterday.

The second day, Miss Scott begins, "Who can tell me how many boys and girls were in the song *we heard* yesterday? Three is correct. As we listen today, let's learn their names." Thus a new purpose is given for listening. She sings the song, and then asks, "What are the names of the children?"

---

[1] From *Tuning Up* of the "World of Music" series, published by Ginn and Company, owners of the copyright. Used by permission.

At the next singing, Miss Scott leads the children to recall the song by asking review questions concerning the number and names of the boys and girls, and suggests that they now listen to learn something about each boy and girl (new purpose for listening.) She sings the song, using her hand to indicate the up-and-down movement of the melody, and then asks, "What do we know about Jonathan?"

Class: "Is tallest."

This is true, but not complete, and Miss Scott takes advantage of the opportunity to repeat the passage "Jonathan is tallest." Several children join with Miss Scott and she nods approval.

Miss Scott: "What do we know about Betsy?"

Class: "Is smallest."

Again, Miss Scott *sings* the complete passage "Betsy is the smallest."

In like manner, Miss Scott tests for content understanding and makes the necessary correction by *singing*. Judging by class attention and response, Miss Scott feels that the entire class is now ready to participate and asks the children to sing with her. As an aid to recall, she uses her hand in gestures to suggest "tallest," "smallest," "dolly," and "airplane that flies." As the children grow more confident of the song, Miss Scott fades into the vocal background. On another day, when the song is sung, Miss Scott adds the piano accompaniment to heighten interest and to give added hearing experience.

To recapitulate:

1. Miss Scott motivated the children and arrested their attention with one brief, simple statement: "I know a song about boys and girls."

2. She gave them a purpose for listening.

3. She sang the song in its entirety.

4. On the second and third singing, she continued to hold their interest by giving new purposes for listening.

5. She sang for the children, but she did not continue to dominate the scene after the children could successfully carry the melody.

6. She rewarded the children with the added coloration of piano accompaniment.

The Whole Method

Miss Scott used the *whole method* in presenting this song, a method which should be employed on short songs and which embodies a principle applicable to all songs. Although Miss Scott repeated parts of the song, this was not in her original plan. She did so because of the somewhat incomplete replies to her questions. As is evident in Miss Scott's presentation, the value of the whole method of learning lies in establishing the logical order of sequence.

The Part Method

The term *part method* is a misnomer, for there is actually no such method. A better term would be the "whole-part" or the "whole-part-whole" method. As suggested above, emphasis should be on mastering the whole concept. Had Miss Scott been presenting a longer song, perhaps one with four phrases, she would have sung the song in its entirety on several successive days. At the time for class participation, she would have again sung the whole song, then the phrases one by one, inviting the class to repeat these after she had sung each one. Finally, she would have again sung the entire song before asking the children to sing it.

Actually, the use of the so-called part method is diminishing. The reason may be found in our own adult experiences in learning a song. We are attending a party when the group begins to sing an unfamiliar song. We join in gradually, perhaps first by humming and then by singing a few words here, a few words there. In the final analysis, we learn the song by the whole method through participation almost from the outset. This is similar to Miss Scott's presentation. If we learn by doing, why delay the activity until some prescribed moment?

In this connection, it seems unwise to repeat a song until the teacher feels the entire class is ready to respond. Some children are ready before others and should be allowed to sing along with the teacher or the record. Early participation will be a strong incentive for others to join in. Otherwise, the tempo of learning may be set by the slowest members of the class, and the interest of the brighter students may be stifled.

Singing with the Children

It has long been the practice to sing *for* but not *with* the children. However, the preceding discussion suggests a balance between the two methods. If the teacher never sings with the children, they are apt to believe that she does not enjoy joining with them or that singing is for groups of adults alone and groups of children alone. Actually, singing knows no lines of color, race, creed, class, culture, or age. In this respect, all who join in the activity are on the same level. Singing with the children is an excellent indication that the teacher is an enthusiastic member of the group. On the other hand, if the teacher always sings with the group, she will become a crutch and the children will not develop confidence and self-reliance.

The Uncertain Singer

Some first grade cherubs sing like archangels while the performance of others seems to be of the fallen angel variety. The teacher's duty, in the spirit of the guardian angel, is to lead, guide, inspire, and develop each cherub and seraph in the use of his wings of song. Certainly in no area are individual differences more glaringly apparent than in singing, nor are more understanding and patience needed. Although we may know of corrective devices, we are often inclined to avoid aurally distasteful tasks. The difficulty, then, is not necessarily in the lack of "know-how" but in the lack of patience.

As stated above, many six-year-old children cannot sing—that is, not according to adult standards. By this we mean that such children are unable to reproduce a given melody at a given pitch level. A minister jokingly described his vocal handicap in these words: "I can 'carry a tune' all right, but I have difficulty in unloading it." This perfectly describes the child's vocal problem, for he can and does sing in his own way. Although his vocal utterances may be similar to man's earliest attempts, described in chapter 1, they may be considered as a form of song. This kind of singing may or may not be based upon previous experience. It may be heard on the school ground or during any play activity. Some teachers attempt to capitalize upon these short vocal utterances as an aid to the vocally inhibited child. In this respect, child readiness is not as strong a consideration as teacher readiness.

Children who cannot at first reproduce a prescribed melody have, in the past, been labeled as monotones, non-singers, listeners, defectives, and uncertain singers. If such children must be labeled, only the two latter terms should be employed and then only in the mind of the teacher. Since children at this age cannot read, should language teachers label them as non-readers and hope that they will, in some miraculous way, gain something by listening to others read? Unfortunately, some music teachers have been guilty of similar sins in asking the defective singer to listen.

Musicians agree that monotones are extremely rare. The author has tested literally hundreds of defective singers, both children and adults, all of whom had serious difficulty in hearing and reproducing a single tone or a series of tones. Eventually, however, everyone of them was able to follow a melody. Actually, a true monotone would have no inflection even in his speaking voice. He could not aurally or vocally distinguish differences in pitch. The author has been unable to find even one adult or child, among the hundreds tested, whom he would label as a monotone.

There are, however, many uncertain or defective singers at the first grade level. A defective singer is one who is vocally inhibited, an impediment which may stem from one or more of a number of sources:

a) Lack of musical background in the home and church. Neither the father nor the mother sings, and there is no musical instrument in the home. The general attitude of the parents toward music is a strong influence.

b) Innocent remarks by parents and relatives such as "Johnny takes after his father, he can't sing a note," or "Mary can't sing as well as her older sister Jane." Such remarks often cause a psychological block toward music.

c) Lack of social and emotional maturity. Such a child is usually withdrawn and timid and cannot be coerced into singing. A clever teacher can indirectly involve him in rhythm activities such as those found in singing games, or group swinging or swaying motions.

d) Attempting to sing in the low pitch level of the speaking voice. In other words, the child simply has not found his singing voice. Most problem singers belong in this category.

e) Lack of tonal memory, that is, the inability to recall even short tonal groups long enough to reproduce them.

The two latter causes are the most serious and are so interrelated that it is often difficult to determine which weakness is the greater. Psychologically they may bear some relation to one or more of the other causes listed above. Regardless of the problem, however, it has been proven again and again that through active participation, creative activities, patience, encouragement, and careful selection and treatment of material most children can eventually find their singing voices. The problem is usually personal and does not originate in lack of ability or vocal technique.

At any rate, the first grade teacher may expect to find a normal curve in singing ability in the average heterogeneous group. This would include a few who can sing well; a few who, at first, cannot sing at all; and a larger group who are dependent upon others. But, as in all school activities, teacher planning should provide group opportunities for the development of all the children.

Vocal Orientation for the Uncertain Singer

The first step in vocal orientation is to lead the child to an awareness of the vocal sounds he makes, for he has never heard or been conscious of the sound of his own voice.

The second step concerns developing an awareness of the oneness of tones in unison, for the defective singer has no idea of the sensation of his voice when matched with another tone.

These two problems are basic with most defective singers, and each is related to hearing. Since vocal control and hearing are so closely related, there can be no real progress without the aid of the

ear, for the ear is the singer's guide. The first task, then, is to arrest
the ear by developing an awareness of the vocal sounds the child
makes in speech, in play activities, and with the melodic fragments
he utters. In developing this awareness, we imitate him; we sing
his song, as we shall presently see.

The second task is to develop an aural awareness of prescribed
tones and to lead the child to reproduce like sounds. In doing this
the process is reversed; the child imitates us, he sings our song.

This game of imitation played by the children and the teacher
can be an interesting and certainly a creative activity and is
basic as a corrective measure.

As stated earlier, all children sing bits of melody in their play
activities. Hearing one of these utterances, the alert teacher repeats the passage and invites the class to join in on Mary's song.
In all probability, Mary is unable to repeat her melody without
aid. But repetition of her melody by the teacher and the group at
her own pitch level is a creative approach to orienting Mary and
other vocally handicapped children. In this respect, the teacher
may encourage all the children to sing in connection with their
various activities. Since the teacher is an important member of
the group, he may encourage this sort of expression by singing
short passages which the children may want to repeat. Such creative activities are particularly valuable in helping the defective
singer to experience his own voice in harmonious agreement with
others. Mary was able to experience this for the first time because
her melody was heard inwardly and outwardly, and not because
she was asked to match a prescribed melody, a task quite impossible for her. The teacher simply began at Mary's vocal level.

The present trend is away from isolated tone-matching drills
which are separated from melody or song and confined to the defective singers. Such procedure is impractical from the standpoint
of time and psychologically undesirable in that it emphasizes a
defect which causes Mary to feel that she is different. Even in
tone-matching drills, the teacher usually has to find the child's
pitch, for the child cannot match the teacher's. For example, if
Mary is asked to match F (first space), she will probably sing D,
C, or B-flat below, each of which is a tone in the harmony of F.

We tell her to sing higher, but this has no meaning for her and she continues to sing *her* tone. Finally, in despair, we play her tone and for the first time she experiences a unison sound.

Mary's tone is undoubtedly from the lower range of her speaking voice. Since she has not found her singing voice, the most practical procedure is to move to her range, changing the key of the song which she is attempting to learn to a lower pitch. This suggestion raises the question of injury to the child voice. Although care of the voice is desirable at all times, singing in a natural, easy tone with medium volume is not harmful. No vocal injury will be inflicted by singing too low (or too high) if the voice is not forced or, on the other hand, suppressed to produce a devitalized tone. In fact, the child's voice is not as delicate an instrument as some have assumed, as attested by the cacophony on any playground.

As stated earlier, the average child voice is similar to the adult voice in range, but not in quality. The child must not be allowed to imitate the heavier, fuller quality of the mature voice. Without doubt, the child can sing high. So can adults, but each is apt to grow tense when the pitch lies too high. Although the average voice range is considered to be from around Middle C to F (fifth line), D and E-flat (fourth line and space) are far more comfortable. Occasional skips up to F, however, are not objectionable. E-flat (first line) to B-flat and C above is a very comfortable range for the beginner. In this connection, the teacher should examine the range of songs in *The Kindergarten Book,* Ginn and Company; *Music 'Round the Clock,* Follett Publishing Company; and *Music Through the Day,* Silver Burdett Company.

The piano is exceedingly valuable in vocal orientation and in training the ear. This is particularly true with regard to the tendency of some chords to progress to others. For example, the tones of the dominant seventh chord, when sounded together, have a strong tendency to progress toward the tones of the tonic chord. Although unaware of it, the child has heard the dominant seventh to tonic progression many times over radio and television, for most compositions end with such a cadence.

Miss Allen, a first grade teacher, used these chords as an ear training aid for the entire class. Knowing that several of her uncertain singers could not produce pitches above Middle C, Miss Allen used this pitch as the dominant tone and played the following melody. She asked the children to tell her what the tune reminded them of.

After the second hearing, a girl, one of the "singers," said it reminded her of a clock—*tick, tock;* a boy thought it sounded like a bell—*ding, dong.* Miss Allen complimented each of the children and agreed with them. She then invited the class to listen to the song of the clock as she played the following, letting the melody predominate.

She repeated it again as the children listened to the song of the bell, and then asked, "What words does the clock seem to sing? What words does the bell seem to ring?" Eventually, the class agreed on the following:

> *Tick, tock, tick, tock sings the clock.*
> *Ding, dong, ding, dong rings the bell.*

The song captured the children's imagination, and they heard and sang it with genuine enjoyment on several successive days. One day they bent forward, letting their arms swing like the pendulum of the clock and the clapper of the bell. This gave the children another opportunity to hear the melody and its compelling harmonic background. On another day, the children used rhythm sticks and wood blocks to make the sound of the clock and, on another day, the triangle to make the sound of the bell.

In time, some of the children learned to play the melody on resonator bells, melody bells, and piano. The crowning reward came when all of these instruments were combined to play the song. Knowing that correct hearing precedes vocal control, Miss Allen began each daily repetition by first playing the melody and then adding rhythmic or instrumental activities. Singing came next. Then, as the children became increasingly confident in vocal control, Miss Allen transposed the song to higher keys.

Thus, Miss Allen patiently provided many opportunities for hearing and singing. Although the repetitions were necessary, they were not boring, for a new activity was introduced each day. At no time did Miss Allen single out a defective singer. In time, the melody became so familiar that a few of the uncertain singers could sing it independently; others still needed the support of the piano or the class; a few continued to drone along on Middle C. Miss Allen was not overly concerned about the latter group, for they were "in tune" on a tone common to both chords and were, therefore, experiencing the unison sound. Since they could participate in all activities connected with the song, they had no reason to feel inferior, and their attitude toward music remained good.

On subsequent days, Miss Allen selected songs of limited range, some of which employed only the four tones of the above melody. She found good examples in G. *The First Grade Book*, page 26, "Bounce Ball," and page 14, "Tiptoe Song." She continued to play the chords as an aid to hearing and to establishing a feeling for tonality, and invited the children to suggest rhythmic and instrumental activities as the songs were repeated.

All song series for children contain tone-matching material in song form. Some of this material has a very limited range. The teacher should feel free to lower the pitch to match the speaking voice of the child, gradually raising it as a melodic passage becomes increasing familiar. Furthermore, the melodic idea of some songs is based upon a familiar children's play song:

The teacher may interest the children in creating words for this melody in keeping with their everyday experiences. For example, "Johnny has a birthday," "Johnny has a new bike," or "It is cold this morning." Certainly such activities are not to be confined to the melody above, but may be employed with any of the tone-matching songs listed in the various song series or any bit of melody which children sing in their play activities. When the children have had wide experience in such tonal games, songs may be introduced which contain the same or similar tonal passages. For example:

G. The First Grade Book, pp. 34b, 77br, 5, 39, 154
F. Music 'Round the Clock, p. 38r
S. Music Through the Day, pp. 36a, 64b, 94b, 130
CALLS
S. Music Through the Day, p. 74b
F. Music Round the Town, p. 5
SONGS WITH LIMITED RANGE AND REPEATED IDEAS
G. The First Grade Book, pp. 14ar, 165b, 178r
F. Music 'Round the Clock, pp. 11r, 30r, 56r
S. Music Through the Day, pp. 45r, 72r, 76a, 80b
F. Music Round the Town, p. 21
SONGS WITH OCCASIONAL WIDE SKIPS
G. The First Grade Book, p. 43a
SONGS EMPLOYING IMITATION
G. The First Grade Book, p. 68a
SONGS WITH WHICH INSTRUMENTS MAY BE USED
F. Music 'Round the Clock, pp. 14r, 34

In concluding the discussion of the defective singer, it must be emphasized that separating the children according to singing ability is most discouraging for the uncertain singer. If the defective singers hinder the remainder of the class in learning a new song, the teacher may select them to do rhythmic activities until the song is under way. This gives ample opportunity for the defective singer to become aurally oriented to the melody, and again it must be remembered that hearing and vocal control are closely related. When the song has been fairly well mastered, the key may be lowered and all invited to participate by singing.

Many teachers prefer the song approach stressed here to isolated, cut-and-dried drills, such as "too-too-too." They believe equal results may be obtained by using a train song in which a "choo-choo" pattern is repeated. Imitating the sound of a siren or whistle also may be used as effectively in songs. The purpose is the same as in drill: to help the child find his singing voice by experiencing pitches above the low level of his speaking voice.

Use of Records for Teaching a Song

Although the teacher is the best agent for learning a song, there are many splendid recordings which may be used. These are particularly valuable for the instructor who feels inadequate as a singer and should be used occasionally even by teachers who sing well. The criteria for selecting a record are the same as those for choosing any song. One should avoid overly dramatic voices, poor enunciation, and accompaniments which overshadow the voice.

Before presenting a recorded song, the teacher should be thoroughly familiar with it. After the children have heard the song two or three times, they may be encouraged to sing along with the record until it is learned. As the children gain confidence, the volume may be reduced, letting the voices of the children predominate. Finally, the children should sing the song without aid from the record. If the song is recorded in a key which is uncomfortable for the children, it may be changed when the record is no longer needed. When the children are able to read, the words may be written on the chalkboard, or song books may be used. In either case, the teacher should help the children to follow the words and encourage them to "tip" their fingers to the rhythm. As in the personal presentation, rhythm activities may be employed, and purposes for listening should be given.

Records are particularly valuable for introducing songs by the great composers. Since these songs were not written for children, the range is often a barrier to child participation. However, the children should have opportunities to hear and follow the music and text of such songs as Handel's "He Shall Feed His Flock" and Schubert's "Ave Maria." After singing folk, patriotic, or

Christmas songs, or songs of great tradition, the children should follow the text and music as they hear good recordings of them. Many of the songs from the various music series are recorded and may be obtained from the publisher of each series. A list of these is given at the close of the chapter.

Choosing Songs

One of the teacher's most important duties, and it can be a pleasant one, is selecting songs for children. Surely, no teacher should merely turn the page to find a song for tomorrow, but should search through the book for one which is appropriate to the musical needs and personal interests of his class. The music specialist should be familiar not only with material in current series but also with that of earlier series. ("Playmates," for example, is from one of the older song series.) Using the appropriate song will create infinitely more interest and make a more lasting impression than any number of stories, speeches, and discussions. Appropriateness in itself is an excellent means of motivation. The over-all criteria for selecting songs, then, are appropriateness and interest, considering the teacher as well as the children. This, of course, raises the question of what is appropriate and interesting. Appropriateness will be considered presently. As to what is interesting, we all are inclined to like those things which relate to our own experiences. With children, this would include both animate and inanimate objects which they have observed or encountered in play activities—dogs, birds, crickets, dolls, trains, swings, kites, and, in later years, mountains, oceans, rivers, stars, and clouds. Of particular interest are people, especially those of our own age. Children, for example, are most interested in children and their activities. They like the song "Playmates" because it relates to people of their own age—Jonathan, Betsy, and Tom are in their classroom. By nature, the child is self-centered. His is a small world and all things revolve around him. With the gradual expansion of his horizons, he becomes increasingly interested in things about him and in other people. It is well to include in classroom planning those songs which will help the child to broaden his horizons. Although a certain amount of child-centered emphasis in planning is both good and necessary, this should not be the whole purpose of curriculum planning and execution.

Interest also may be aroused by relating the song to school subject matter—something the children have studied in numbers, reading, or art. In fact, most songs found in the song series may be correlated with social studies. This enhances the students' appreciation of both music and other subjects. Such songs would certainly include patriotic, historical, work, Indian, and cowboy songs, as well as spirituals and ballads. Occasional information about songs, or interpretations of their texts, will result in better understanding, with consequent stimulation of interest.

Appropriate and interesting songs may be found in the broad classifications which follow.

Songs for Fun. As has already been stated, man has sung through all the centuries past. Much of this was for pleasure—for the sheer joy of singing. Songs for fun and recreation may not have any other value and may even be nonsense songs. But the relaxation they afford is valuable in itself. Songs in this classification include singing games, play songs, and those of a make-believe type.

Songs about Home. First grade children are adjusting from home to school. Songs that relate to father, mother, brother, sister, pets, playthings, or any home activity are interesting and valuable.

Songs about School. School is a new and exciting experience for children. Songs relating to any school function or to playmates make a strong appeal.

Songs with Religious Texts. Home, school, and church are considered to be the institutional core of society. All song series contain songs with religious texts. For the most part, these have been carefully edited so that selections may be made which are not objectionable to any faith. As may be seen in examining Part Two of this book, religious songs are related to the people and to the history of America. This is one of the reasons for including them in the song series.

Traditional Songs. These include such songs as the Stephen C. Foster melodies, Christmas carols, and patriotic songs. Detailed information concerning the most widely known traditional songs is given in Part Two of this book (see specifically chapters 9, 11, and 12).

Songs of the Seasons. The children are becoming more aware of the days of the week, the months, and the various seasons of the year. Closely associated with the seasons are special events such as Halloween, Thanksgiving, Christmas, Saint Patrick's Day, Saint Valentine's Day, Easter, Arbor Day, and Independence Day. Songs about these can heighten the child's awareness of his country, its people, its traditions, and its customs.

The Country and Its Heroes. School boards and leaders throughout the country often express concern because so many young people know little about the history of their country and its people. This concern is shared by teachers in general and particularly by instructors in history and government. It is our conviction that singing patriotic songs, songs about national heroes, songs of the North and South, songs about people and their occupations, songs relating to geography—rivers, oceans, mountains—can aid materially in giving young people a better understanding of, and feeling for, their homeland.

Songs of Other Lands. One of our greatest international problems is the lack of understanding between nations. Efforts have been made to correct this situation through student exchange programs and through cultural exchange. Music is one of the media for better understanding, and its use in this connection should begin in the early grades. National music of various countries is listed in Part Two.

Songs of Lasting Value. Although not usually appropriate for singing in the elementary grades, great songs of the ages may be introduced by means of recordings. Many of these, such as Handel's "He Shall Feed His Flock" and Bach's "Jesu Joy of Man's Desiring," are entirely within the grasp of the child. The same is true of many ballads, folk songs, and art songs.

Folk Songs. In folk songs we find the heart and soul of any people. Here is their reaction to what they have observed, thought, and felt, about themselves and their surroundings. Someone has said that folk songs reflect, like a mirror, the kind of life a people live. Of equal importance, is that we find *ourselves* as a part of that reflection—find ourselves in the tide of human thought and feeling, walking, talking, agreeing with the people of yesterday—find ourselves in the midst of our history and heritage. These songs are the bedrock of culture. The simplicity, directness, sincerity, and wide range of human experience expressed in these songs open up new horizons of understanding for both adults and children. In addition to expressing human nature, these songs demonstrate the flavor or temperamental color of a people. A more complete picture of this type of song is to be found in the illustrations woven through various chapters of Part Two of this book.

Songs through Which We Learn. As suggested elsewhere in these pages, a song is not necessarily an end in itself. Glancing back over the categories above, one is made to feel that singing may indelibly stamp impressions on many areas of learning. Through feeling, it adds color to fact. Suffice it to say that much general learning is possible through the singing activity. In addition to the song classifications above, the following should be mentioned:

1. *Learning about music.* This includes responding to melody and rhythm, learning about instruments, and learning to read and understand the language of music.

2. *Learning about nature.* The various song series are resplendent with songs which excite imagination and wonder about nature—clouds, stars, frost, snow, and the seasons.

3. *Learning about other things.* These would include songs about animals, insects, farm life, occupations, transportation, and safety.

It should be observed, too, that songs in all of these categories are of interest to both children and adults. This is as it should be, for the child is not a world unto himself nor one apart from adult thought, feeling, and influence. In fact, child development is dependent upon adult influence, guidance, leadership, suggestions, encouragement, and discipline. Music is one means of bridging the gap between child and adult thought and feeling. Through singing, child and adult may better understand each other.

Teachers in Action

Miss Bennett engaged the children in a tone-matching audition. Several children who were able to match her tones were classified as singers and placed at the back of the room. A large number who indicated some difficulty in vocal control were classified as uncertain singers and were placed in the center of the room. Others who had no apparent control over their voices were classified as defective singers and placed at the front of the room. This seating arrangement was used for the following reasons:

1. The "good" voices from the back of the room would carry forward as an aid to the less accurate singers.

2. The defectives at the front of the room could hear Miss Bennett better, and she could help them occasionally.

3. Miss Bennett could give special drills to each group according to its need.

From time to time, Miss Bennett let the defectives imitate a siren, a train whistle, the wind, the meow of a cat, the bark of a dog. But they were not allowed to sing with the other children, for their "monotones" hindered the learning of a melody. At times, Miss Bennett let the children speak the words in the rhythm of the tune.

Miss Collins, in like manner, classified the children according to singing ability, but avoided isolated tone-matching drills. Instead, she taught the entire group many of the songs recommended for defectives in the teacher's manual. These were always sung in the key in which they were written. In order to hold interest, maintain a good attitude, and give the defectives something to do, she let them participate in rhythmic and instrumental activities used in connection with the songs. They were not allowed to sing with the group until the rest of the class had learned the song. For special help, Miss Collins selected short tonal patterns from familiar songs—patterns which often occur on such words as "hello," "good-by," or "good morning" and drilled the defectives on them. She indicated the relatively high and low pitches with corresponding levels of the hand and encouraged the children to do likewise. This helped the defectives to picture the melody in their minds. Moreover, it would help all the children later when they began to observe relative arrangements of notes on the staff. In this activity Miss Collins was using the sense of sight as an aid to hearing.

Miss Dodds, knowing that singing is as natural as speaking and that children have been singing their own songs since they started cooing in their cradles, used still another approach. She encouraged children to sing about their various experiences—the vocal utterances she had heard them use on the playground or in classroom activities. In order to stimulate this sort of creative activity, Miss Dodds occasionally sang statements made by the children. For example, when James told her that his dog had puppies, she asked the dog's name and whether James could sing "Collie has some puppies." James sang his song, Miss Dodds repeated it, and soon the entire class joined the chorus. Although James could sing his melody, his defect in tonal memory might have defeated his efforts to repeat it. But Miss Dodds repeated it at his own pitch and the class gave it further emphasis.

Continuing in this manner, Miss Dodds discovered that many of her defective singers were actually experiencing melody in their own way and eventually were able to sing the melodies of other children. Observing this, Miss Dodds presented short songs with limited range and at pitch levels that enabled all the class to participate. As the children grew in confidence, the pitch was gradually raised.

Carolyn, who was doing practice teaching in the third grade, surprised the children one morning by playing and singing "Are You Sleeping?" (S. *Music Now and Long Ago,* p. 75.) No introduction or motivation was necessary, for attention and interest were stimulated by Carolyn's use of the French text. Immediately, the children wanted to learn the song in French; Carolyn taught it to them.

A week later, Carolyn explained that the song was a round, and they attempted to sing it as such. After two or three disastrous attempts, Carolyn realized that the children were not quite ready to sing both an independent part and different words at the same time; they needed additional experience in hearing the combined melodies. To correct this, Carolyn played the second entrance of the melody against their singing. When the class indicated ability to carry their part independently, Carolyn asked a group to hum along with the piano. The words were finally added and the class experienced a minimum of difficulty.

Judy, who was doing practice teaching in the second grade, was asked by the regular teacher to present the first verse of "America the Beautiful." Judy realized that its poetic expressions must be made comprehensible to the children. As she slowly read the words to herself, she observed that she was picturing "amber waves of grain" and "purple mountains." Pictures—that was the answer! She found six beautiful pictures: ripened grain, mountains, fruit trees in blossom, Uncle Sam kneeling in a prayer of gratitude with hands clasped in front of the world globe, and a beautiful scene of the sea. Each picture was revealed as she sang the song. The children learned the meaning of such words as *spacious* and *amber* from the pictures. In the process of learning the song, the children revealed the appropriate pictures as the words were sung.

The following term, Judy did practice teaching in the fifth grade. The regular teacher asked her to review some patriotic songs. Recalling the impression pictures had made at the second grade level, Judy decided to use them again. Placing them where all could see, she told the class that the pictures were about a patriotic song, and asked the students to identify it. Then the class sang the first verse.

The following day, Judy told how Katharine Lee Bates had been inspired to write the song while on top of Pike's Peak. The class found a map of Colorado, located Denver and Colorado Springs, and pin-pointed Pike's Peak. After singing each verse, Judy asked for the meanings of such expressions as *flaw, self-control in a democracy*, and *liberty in law*.

The children indicated a renewed and genuine interest in learning more about their country. They had learned a song, and they had learned some of the basic principles of their country and its government.

For Further Development

1. Discuss and evaluate the presentations of Misses Bennett, Collins, and Dodds, and Carolyn and Judy. Which of these approaches do you prefer? State your reasons.

2. Various class committees select one of the following: (These activities may be spread over a period of two or three weeks depending upon the size of the class and the amount of time allotted to the singing activity.)

a) Select three different types (see "Selection of Songs," this chapter) of first grade songs. Teach them by rote to the class as if it were a first grade group. Class evaluate the technique used.

b) Select three different types of recorded first grade songs and teach to the class (using the record) as if it were a first grade group. Class evaluate the presentation.

c) Select three different types of third grade songs and teach by rote to the class as if it were a third grade group. Class evaluate the presentation.

d) Select three different types of recorded songs for the third grade. Teach each to the class as if it were a third grade, using the record. Class evaluate the presentation.

e) Select six songs appropriate for defective singers. Explain to the class the basis of each selection and indicate how each song is to be used to aid the uncertain singers.

f) Select the songs and recordings for a Christmas unit—third grade. If possible, duplicate copies of your material so that each member of the class may have one. Class evaluate the material. (See "Christmas Songs," chapter 9.)

g) Select the songs and recordings for a patriotic unit—fifth grade. Relate to social studies. Prepare as suggested at *f*. (See "Patriotic Songs," chapter 11.)

h) Select songs and recordings for an Indian unit—third grade. Relate to social studies. Prepare as suggested at *f*. (See "Before the Pilgrims," chapter 10.)

i) Select songs and recordings for a Pioneer unit—fourth grade. Relate to social studies. Prepare as suggested at *f*. (See "The Common Man," chapter 12, and "Jim Cooper," chapter 13.)

j) Select songs and recordings for a river and/or mountain unit. Relate to social studies. Prepare as suggested at *f*. (See various song series.)

3. Arrange for at least one listening period each week in order to hear:

a) Recordings for various song series.

b) Representative recorded material listed in chapters 9 and 10. Make a list of your favorites which you would like for your personal record collection and another list which you could use in your classroom.

Recordings

Ginn and Company recordings for "Our Singing World" series.

Silver Burdett Company recordings for "Music for Living" series.

Follett Publishing Company recordings for "Together We Sing" series.

RCA Victor Basic Record Library for Elementary Schools contains four albums of songs plus an album of Christmas songs and one of patriotic songs.

"TOGETHER WE SING" (Follett Publishing Company)

REPRESENTATIVE SONGS	Music 'Round the Clock	Music 'Round the Town	Music Through the Year	Music Across Our Country	Voices of America	Voices of the World
Songs for Fun	35r, 40r, 48r, 53r, 54r	64, 96, 101, 109, 122r	15r, 82, 109	24a, 48r, 68, 104b, 112, 130, 131r	22, 23r, 28r, 29, 41, 42	
Songs about Home	11r, 13r, 14r, 15r	22, 124r, 127r, 128r, 131	29, 74r, 128r, 136r	25b, 31r, 84, 115r, 160r	67, 79, 168	
Songs with Religious Texts	70r, 71	68r, 70, 71r	26r, 39, 43, 51, 84, 107r, 129r	74a, 99, 148, 170	36r, 172, 184, 186	9, 79, 88, 183, 188
Traditional Songs	4r	106	76b, 116b	76, 77, 101, 142r, 143	26a, 26b, 27, 30, 35, 60, 62, 98, 133	10, 34, 72, 182
Seasonal Songs	18r, 68r, 69r, 74r, 78r, 79r, 80r, 81r	78r, 80r, 85, 88r, 91	6r, 7r, 14r, 30r, 34r, 40r, 48r, 54r, 58r, 63r, 65, 72r	25r, 90r, 91a, 109, 152, 153, 164r	74r, 109r, 190, 191, 192	55, 59, 110, 111, 144, 146
The Country and Its Heroes	65, 66	48, 50	38r, 46r, 84b, 88, 89r, 150	4, 6, 7, 54r, 94, 126, 165r	6, 7, 8, 10, 11, 84r, 161, 162, 164, 165a, 165b, 194	190
Folk Songs	26, 39, 88r	7, 24r, 26r, 29, 32r, 41r, 46r, 53, 62r, 74r, 104	9r, 11r, 16, 23, 32r, 44, 68, 83, 92, 125r, 141, 155	12r, 13r, 15r, 19, 22r, 29, 39r, 66r, 67r, 74b, 87, 118r	13r, 20r, 44, 49, 50r, 63, 71, 72, 80r, 112r, 116, 119, 144	14, 18, 21, 37, 38, 50, 57, 86, 107, 108, 118, 122, 126, 128
Songs of Nature	10r, 87r	93r	103r, 122	9, 35r, 60r, 70r, 106	64r, 89br	174
Songs of Animals and Insects	21r, 23r, 24r, 31r, 33r, 34, 41r, 45, 56r	21, 42r, 60r	31r, 123, 134	40, 41a, 41b, 42r, 58, 108a, 166, 169	143r	112

"MUSIC FOR LIVING" (Silver Burdett Company)

REPRESENTATIVE SONGS	Music Through the Day	Music in Our Town	Music Now and Long Ago	Music Near and Far	Music in Our Country	Music Around the World
Songs for Fun	10ar, 14a, 15r, 68a	18b, 44r, 59, 94, 109, 133	4, 10, 17, 34r, 122	25, 38, 136, 143, 144r	34, 35, 43, 157	52, 133
Songs about Home	25, 27, 28ar, 33b, 35ar	4r, 6r, 8, 10r, 27	90b, 92b, 107	151	118, 168b	2
Songs with Religious Texts	114a, 119b	28, 56, 138a, 143r	1, 148	1, 56r, 88r, 162	25, 48r, 110, 204, 205r, 215r	22r, 24a, 24b, 25, 79, 154r, 155
Traditional Songs	118, 124b	58, 61	72, 73, 75, 129r, 155	112, 121, 123, 140, 156, 168, 169, 174	105, 112, 136	10, 48, 152
Seasonal Songs	60br, 110ar, 111a, 113a, 121, 126a, 128r, 130	122, 132r, 135, 136r, 137, 142, 144ar, 144b, 146, 151r, 152r	145, 150br, 153r, 154, 158, 159r, 160, 163r, 165r, 167, 168r	2ar, 7, 10, 11, 158, 166r, 170r, 173r, 175, 179r	56r, 210r, 211, 216r	34rb, 80, 85, 86, 87r, 93, 125, 136a
The Country and Its Heroes	124a, 125	57	128, 161, 164	176, 180	1, 26, 122, 126, 128r, 130, 131, 132, 134r, 138, 141, 144	73a, 73b, 76, 96, 98
Folk Songs	3b, 5r, 10ar, 11r, 38r	14, 24r, 31, 38, 64	3, 29, 56, 84r, 92b, 94	4r, 13r, 29r, 40, 44r, 46, 48, 60br, 68, 111r, 141r, 145, 160	6, 12, 14, 20, 22, 38, 41r, 63, 66, 79, 109r, 151, 156r, 164	3, 5, 8, 12r, 17r, 53, 57, 61, 67r, 70, 103r, 116, 199
Songs of Nature	20a, 49r, 64ar	30, 124r, 134br, 149r	40, 142ar, 142br, 143	5r, 9, 20b, 82r, 153	2, 3, 4r, 70, 196, 214b	23, 29, 37, 44r, 46r
Songs of Animals and Creatures	38r, 43r, 53r, 54, 62r, 65, 106br	15r, 16, 19, 20r, 43, 66r, 98, 101, 113r, 120r	12, 21, 50r, 90ar, 101r, 110r, 114, 152r	14r, 21	54r, 58, 145	105, 119, 148r, 221

"OUR SINGING WORLD" (Ginn and Company)

REPRESENTATIVE SONGS	The First Grade Book	Singing on Our Way	Singing and Rhyming	Singing Every Day	Singing Together	Singing in Harmony
Songs for Fun	4a, 11a, 17br, 43a, 59a, 81ar, 46a	16, 20, 22ar, 27, 52r	16, 19a, 32b, 35r, 163r	29r, 30r, 31r, 45r, 50, 81, 155r	16ar, 23r, 24ar, 24br, 25r	33, 34r, 45
Songs about Home	54a, 54b, 55b, 56b, 57a, 57br, 60b	48b, 49, 51ar, 54, 57, 60br	59, 69b, 70ar, 72a	62, 63, 65	70, 76a, 77r, 79, 80r, 81b	85a, 85br, 88b, 89
Songs with Religious Texts	66a, 67a, 90b, 91b	61a, 62a, 62b, 75r	73a, 73b, 74a, 74c, 75, 83	73a, 75br, 88r	85ar, 86, 88, 89, 90a	99, 100r, 102, 104r, 105r, 107b, 108r, 133br
Traditional Songs	95a, 95b, 99, 103, 104, 105, 107b	42, 85, 87a	12b, 27a, 56, 65, 87	35r, 68a, 77r, 79	22r, 183r	91, 135, 140
Seasonal Songs	128ar, 130br, 131br, 133, 137br, 139ar	71ar, 76r, 79r, 112b, 115a, 116br, 119ar	81r, 116r, 119ar, 122, 127ar	95r, 97, 99r, 107, 108, 135r, 140, 147rb	108, 109, 110r, 117, 118r, 123, 151r, 157r	143, 144r, 151r, 181, 188, 195r
The Country and Its Heroes	106a, 106b	86, 87b, 88, 89r, 90	78, 95, 96a, 96b	110a, 110b, 112	124, 126r, 128, 129	132, 152, 153, 154, 156
Folk Songs	49b, 50br, 52a, 55a, 57a, 57br, 151b	7, 22br, 31r, 34r, 46rb	18ar, 38, 40r, 44r, 55r	37br, 38r, 39r, 40r, 47r, 51, 55r, 59, 78	19b, 20r, 21, 31r, 42r, 45r, 58r, 91r	7, 23, 34ar, 38r, 41r, 46r, 50, 52r, 59r, 62r
Songs of Nature	117r, 119a, 124b, 127cr, 132b	103a, 106a, 107, 108br	106ar, 107a	118r, 121, 123r, 126r	139, 140r, 142r	175, 178r, 192ar
Songs of Animals and Insects	143a, 144, 146a, 149a, 157b, 159ar, 159br	12, 13, 123a, 125r, 136b, 137b, 140br	128, 129, 132, 136r, 143r, 146ar	154r, 157b, 158a	165br, 174ar, 176	

CHAPTER 3

Feet to Pat

What about Rhythm?

Rhythm is fundamental in music. It was probably the first of the elements of music to develop. Early man surely felt rhythm as a manifestation of the pulsating life within and about him. His breathing, the beat of his heart, the ebb and flow of the tides, changes in the moon, and the cycling seasons were constant reminders of its existence. Realizing that he and all life about him were governed by a great unifying force, man merely got in step.

Rhythm and gesture have long been media of expression for man. It has been speculated that his first expression of rhythm took the form of beating on a hollow log which served as a means of tribal communication or perhaps to accompany crude forms of dance. A later and more organized expression of rhythm was that of beating the drum to accompany tribal ceremonial dances. Rhythm and gesture were employed in the Greek curriculum under such scholars as Aristotle. Miriam, sister of Moses, danced to the music of the trumpet. David danced before the Ark of God. Both song and dance were used in processionals to temples and holy places. In more modern times, the European nations developed characteristic folk dances. A number of these crystalized into standard musical forms as composers refined them and brought them into the concert hall. Among these important dance forms are the morris, hey, allemande, courante, saraband, bourree, gavotte, minuet, loure, waltz, polonaise, rigaudon, gigue (or jig), and bolero. These and other traditional dances are discussed more fully in Part Two.

Rhythm is design in accent, motion, and time. It is the pulsating framework on which tonal beauties are hung; through its accents, melodic and harmonic elements are organized into orderly form. It would be difficult indeed to recall the tones of a melody if they were taken out of their rhythmic setting.

Basic design in music is set forth by regular recurrences of strong and weak accents, or pulsations, which produce *meter*. Each accent is given a count, or a *beat*. Beats are arranged in groups of two or three, or combinations thereof. Meter, then, concerns the scheme of accents which sets up a *fundamental rhythm*. The meters most frequently found in the song series are illustrated below, along with their schemes of accents which correspond to those in poetry. The accents are indicated as follows: — strong; ‿ weak; \ medium strong. The latter is a strong accent, although somewhat weaker than the initial accent, and it initiates an additional group of two or three. The grouping of the accents is indicated by the measure bar.

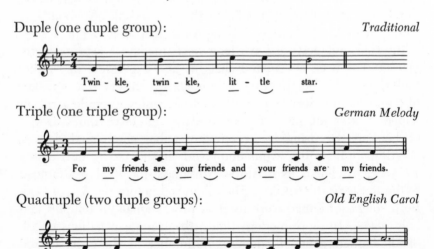

Duple (one duple group):   *Traditional*

Twin - kle,   twin - kle,   lit - tle   star.

Triple (one triple group):   *German Melody*

For   my friends are   your friends and   your friends are   my friends.

Quadruple (two duple groups):   *Old English Carol*

God   rest you mer-ry   gen - tle-men. Let   noth-ing you dis - may.

Sextuple or compound duple (two triple groups):

In addition to the basic meter produced by the recurrence of these groups of *accents*, there is another kind of rhythm which is governed by the arrangement of various *note lengths* such as half notes, quarters, and eighths. We often refer to this as the rhythm of the melody or, in the case of a song, the rhythm of the words. Such arrangements of various note lengths within the metric pattern are illustrated below.

Yankee Doodle
Traditional

The Star-Spangled Banner
John Stafford Smith

Battle Hymn of the Republic
William Steffe

Silent Night
Franz Gruber

There are, therefore, two elements in rhythm: one which is produced by the regular recurrence of strong and weak pulsations, and a superimposed one which is produced by the arrangement of the various note lengths. The first is usually referred to as *meter* and the second simply as *rhythm*.

Why Teach Rhythm?

Musical Organization. As we have already noted, rhythm brings order to music and gives design to melody. Without the organization which rhythm provides, it would be difficult to remember a melody. Therefore, learning to feel and respond to rhythm is essential to all music instruction and learning.

Self-expression. As is true of singing, responding to music in the various rhythmic activities is an excellent means of self-expression. Such response is valuable in freeing children from inhibitions. Those children who, at first, have difficulty in singing often find responding to rhythm particularly rewarding. Any feeling of self-consciousness or inferiority which may be associated with singing can often be offset by a sense of belonging when the child participates in rhythmic activities.

Ear Training. The rhythm activity is an excellent approach to ear training. Before responding to the music, the child must first listen to it. By listening, he may become aware of tempo, dynamics, mood, and so on. Learning to listen is highly important for the young and inexperienced child and measurably contributes to all phases of his musical growth.

Feeling Rhythm. It is through the various rhythmic activities that the child develops a feeling for, and response to, the rhythm of the melody and the fundamental rhythm produced by the recurrence of the strong and weak pulsations. This feeling and response are essential to musical growth.

Feeling the Phrase. Responding physically to music is an excellent means of perceiving the phrase and distinguishing between unlike passages.

Muscular Co-ordination. Another value of rhythmic activities is the development of muscular co-ordination, so essential for mastery of any skill.

Understanding Symbols. Finally, responding to rhythm is basic to an eventual understanding of the musical symbols which represent the response. Learning to feel rhythm, then, is an important experience for the child who has not yet learned to read music.

How to Teach Rhythm

Teaching children to respond to the rhythm of music should proceed according to the sequence followed in man's musical development—that is, first by ear and then by notation. The first physical responses are based upon familiar child activities such as walking, running, and clapping. Many rhythmic activities may be employed in developing a feeling for and response to music. Free rhythmic play; action songs; singing games; dances; rhythm instruments; galloping, swaying, swinging, skating, walking, running, and skipping; impersonation, pretending, imitation, and dramatization—all may be used in eliciting responses to rhythm. Here, as in all music learning, discriminative listening is a necessary part of the learning process.

There is a wide diversity of opinion concerning the proper approach in developing a physical response to music. These opinions range from stereotyped responses, which fall into patterns prescribed by the teacher, to creative bodily movements which, unhampered by any guidance or control, freely express the children's feelings. The first approach recognizes that music exists in prescribed rhythmic patterns and seeks to develop exact responses to them. The second seeks bodily response, with or without regard for the prescribed rhythmic patterns. A third approach combines the best features of these two extremes. These three different approaches are discussed below. Each has its strong and weak points, and the reader is asked to judge for himself which is most valuable in child development in general and rhythmic development in particular. His judgment should be governed by

immediate and ultimate goals and how he may best utilize the
various rhythmic activities in the attainment of these goals. It
might be well to keep the following question in mind: What are
the general and specific aims in rhythmic development?

The Controlled Response

As someone has said, music is not just motion; it is design in
accent, motion, and time. Music exists in prescribed patterns of
meter and rhythm. We must firmly establish correct responses to
these patterns, so that later the child may be led to translate them
into music symbols as an aid to reading music. The first step is to
develop a vocabulary of pattern responses. Since some of the
children cannot walk, run, or skip in time to music (some cannot
skip at all), they must be informed as to what the music tells
them to do. They are then drilled in these responses, for it is
highly important that their muscles be disciplined in conforming
to prescribed patterns. For, as we all know, music is prescribed
and the ultimate goal is an accurate reproduction in both tone
and time. Once these responses are established, they are available
for immediate use in all rhythmic activities.

Criticism of the controlled response approach stems from the
fact that, however worthy its goal, it lacks originality, imagination, and creativity. Even though music does exist within the
framework of conventional meter and formal patterns of rhythm,
there is no real justification for such rigid presentation. The
teacher must never assume that "telling" assures learning. Children should learn to use their own minds. They should therefore
be interested, stimulated, drawn out, and encouraged to *discover*
things for themselves. Telling them what and when to do everything may have some value in initial efforts, but this must not be
practiced after the orientation period. Extreme control is as
stereotyped as meters and rhythms are said to be.

The Creative Response

The basic goal of this approach is an unhampered, creative
expression of emotion through bodily movements. No suggestions

are made to the children, and there is no attempt to control or guide the expression. The emphasis is placed upon complete freedom of movement. Nothing is said about walking, running, or skipping. There is no *correct* response. Although the children may not be able to walk or skip to the music, any guidance in these actions would stereotype both the music and the expression. There is, then, a vast difference between free rhythmic play and controlled response. It must be emphasized that free rhythmic response is an expression of feeling and is excellent for the release of tension and excess energy but is not necessarily guided by the music.

There are strong arguments which teachers use against this approach. Although creative expression is healthy and necessary, the ultimate goal is not clearly defined, for certainly the abandonment of all inhibitions is not a desirable goal for the present or the future. A man and wife live creatively and happily within self-imposed limitations; children in the home impose additional restrictions on the parents. People live creatively and peaceably within the limits of their self-imposed rules—freedom under the law; and fortunately, people are inhibited by traditions and conventions of social behavior. Wild animals that seem completely free must learn to exist within the limits imposed by the law of the jungle. Even the saying "as free as a bird" is misleading, for the bird is confined to his own territory, his tree, and his flight lanes. The inventor and the scientist create within the limits of known laws and forces, and the history of any science is the story of the evolutional processes from the simple to the complex. The universe itself is the very essence of law and order, rhythm being one of its controlling forces.

As we are not completely free physically and mentally, so we are not always free to express our emotions. For example, if anger, fear, jealousy, hatred, worry, and anxiety are not controlled, they disturb the normal functioning of body and mind and may eventually cause serious physical and mental disorders. There is a definite relationship between mind, body, and emotion; and discipline is necessary in the development of each. In this connection, music is not merely the expression of great emotion or the great expression of emotion; music is also the product of *disciplined*

minds. In their effort to escape the conventional, the extreme
advocates of the creative approach avoid any form of stereotyped
expression. Yet the music which produces the desire for free
expression is cast in formal molds. It must be remembered that
for centuries music has been bounded by conventional meters and
rhythmic patterns, but that within these limitations composers
have found almost inexhaustible possibilities for creativeness.
Similar creative possibilities exist in regard to the expression of
feeling through rhythm.

Controlled Creativity

It should thus be apparent that one cannot abandon all control
merely to gain freedom of expression, for complete freedom is
neither wise nor desirable. This does not mean that creative efforts should be stifled, but rather that they should be encouraged
*within the orderly patterns which produced the desire for ex-
pression.*

Specifically applied to music, this means that though the
teacher does not tell the children what to do, he does lead them
in discriminative listening and aids them in making wise choices.
The children listen in order to determine what it is that the music
tells them to do, and their clue to the mood is in the rhythm.
After sharing their opinions through discussion, the children listen
to the music again. They may experiment with their ideas as
a means of determining which one is most expressive of the music.
Although it is seldom necessary, the teacher may ask questions
which help them to make a wise choice: does the music make
you want to walk, run, or skip?

These, then, are three approaches to the expression of music
through rhythm. We shall see later how the three philosophies
may be applied in instruction.

The Fundamental Movements

As has already been noted, rhythm was probably the first
element of music to develop. It is also the easiest and most natural

musical response for the child. Even before he can walk, the child moves his arms and legs in patterns that suggest walking, running, skipping, and jumping. It is with such familiar, large-muscle activities as these that the child first begins to respond to rhythm. Thus, the child will learn to respond physically to music through activities which are natural and already highly developed: walking, running, skipping, clapping with the hands, tapping on the desk, and "tipping" with the fingers. Without developing some such response to music, further musical progress would be retarded.

Regardless of the approach which different teachers use in developing a feeling for rhythm, all teachers agree that emphasis in the primary grades should be upon feeling and responding to rhythm rather than on the symbols. Only when a feeling for basic rhythms, as expressed in the strong and weak pulsations of duple and triple meters, has been established and when the children can respond to the various note lengths through such activities as walking, running, and skipping, will the introduction of music symbols have meaning for the children. This phase of develop-ment—translating movement into symbols—is treated more fully in the chapter on music reading.

The constant reference here to meter and rhythm may cause the inexperienced teacher to ask, What meter and/or rhythms suggest certain patterns of response? The suggestions which fol-low may serve as an answer.

Duple and quadruple meters:

walk, walk   run, run, run, run   skip-ty, skip-ty   The fundamental rhythm
walk-ing   run-ing, run-ing   is marching or walking.
           trot-ing, trot-ing

Triple meter:

The fundamental rhythm is swaying or swinging. Rhythmic patterns are the same as in duple and quadruple meters.

Sextuple meter:

Gal-lop-ing, gal-lop-ing   Skip-ping, skip-ping   walk, walk   The fundamental rhythm
                                                     walk - ing   is swaying or swinging.

When the children begin to observe visually the symbols which represent the various note lengths, they may notice that running and galloping notes are alike in appearance but different in feeling. The teacher may explain this by stating that running notes may tell us either to trot or gallop. Skipping music is made of both walking and running notes, for when we skip, we seem to be half walking and half running.

As we have already observed, teachers use different procedures in developing a feeling for rhythm. In the controlled response, the teacher may begin by leading the children as they chant such words as *walking* and *running*. When the steady rhythm of the chant has been established, the children clap, walk, and run to the rhythm. The teacher then adds appropriate music by singing, playing the piano, or using a record. Or the teacher may begin by leading the children to imitate a trotting or galloping horse and adding appropriate music. If he begins with a song or a record, he simply tells the children what to do.

Some teachers believe that this is the proper approach, especially at the first grade level. The children do not know what to do and have no background for creative efforts. For example, some cannot walk in time to the music and others do not know how to skip. So they are first taught these activities and the music is added. Responding to conventional or prescribed rhythmic patterns is new to the children and they enjoy it.

Those who favor the creative approach object violently to such rigid control. They maintain that there is no *correct* response. Their purpose is not to get *the* response to prescribed patterns but *any* response which allows freedom of expression. After all, some children have difficulty in responding to prescribed rhythms just as they do in reproducing prescribed tonal patterns. They express rhythm in their own way.

Other teachers combine these two approaches. Although the teacher encourages creativity, he believes that his wider experience should be used in guiding children toward desirable goals. After learning a song, the children clap to the rhythm of the words as they sing; the words guide the children in their response. After becoming familiar with the music of a record, the children contribute various ideas, and the teacher guides them by asking whether the music is loud or soft, slow or fast, sad or happy, and whether the music makes them want to walk, run, or skip. This teacher believes that the children will eventually develop more rapidly and naturally in free and creative rhythmic responses by first laying a foundation in fundamental movements. So he guides the learning situation, and leads the children to relate familiar physical activities to the music they hear.

Another teacher uses Mother Goose rhymes as an aid to feeling rhythm. While repeating the rhymes, the children clap, skip, or walk, to such rhythms as are shown below; well known melodies are added later.

Hickory, dickory dock. The mouse ran up the clock

Bob-by Shaftoe's gone to sea, silver buckles at his knee;

Another teacher sets the names of the children to tonal and rhythmic patterns. When the children are familiar with their musical names, a game is played in which the children identify each name by its tonal pattern as it is played on the piano or other melody instrument, or as it is sung on a neutral syllable. Another game involves the children in identifying a name by its rhythmic pattern, which they clap. As examples, a few names are given below.

At various times, the teacher leads the children in creating combinations of these patterns, which they also clap.

The Rhythmic Defective

There are a few children who, at first, have no sense of rhythm and cannot feel the beat. This means that they cannot respond to the prescribed patterns of rhythm set forth in music. The reason for this may be that music has not yet arrested their attention or that mind and muscle are not yet working together as a team. But whatever the cause, insisting upon *correct* responses to prescribed rhythmic patterns is apt to develop a sense of inferiority in regard to rhythm activities. Many teachers provide opportunities for free rhythmic play which, in addition to being a face-saving device, is also a means of developing co-ordination and a feeling for rhythm. Other aids for these children are as follows:

1. The children hold hands in a row or a circle and swing their arms together to swinging music.

2. The teacher, or a student with a strong feeling for rhythm, plays pat-a-cake with rhythmic defectives.

3. The children join hands and move their arms in a rowing action to galloping rhythm.

4. The children form a line of "cars," join hands to elbows, and play train as their arms move together. Sliding feet for a "choo-choo" effect may be added later.

5. Two children play a ringing-rope type of church bell to music in duple or quadruple meter.

6. Couples march shoulder to shoulder.

7. Couples facing each other join hands in a pushing and pulling motion.

As may be observed, these activities do not single out the rhythmic defective child but involve him in group activities which control his movement. In addition to this, the senses of sight and hearing act as aids for the defective.

Rhythmic Orientation

As suggested above, some children have difficulty keeping time to the music. Generally speaking, such children are usually shy, inhibited, and undeveloped emotionally and socially. They should not be singled out but should be involved in activities such as those suggested below. As an initial step to orienting such children in responding to rhythm, many teachers prefer to begin with movements which children use in their regular play activities. Observing the children swinging, one teacher used the rhythm of this play activity as a starter. Couples faced each other, joined hands, and moved their arms in the rhythm of the swing. The group chanted the word *swing*. When the rhythm was established, the teacher began to play the "Man on the Flying Trapeze" in time with the children. Another teacher observed the children on the playground chanting "run, Philip, run." The rhythm was quarter, two eighths, quarter. Upon return to the classroom, the teacher led the class in rechanting the phrase. The children clapped and stepped to the rhythm of the chant. The following day, the teacher played the first four measures printed below as the children clapped and stepped. On another day, she added the last four measures, asking the children to do what the words and music suggested.

Free Rhythmic Activity. Free rhythmic activity involves letting the children do what they think the music suggests. Such free play is valuable as initial experience, especially for those who find it difficult to respond accurately to prescribed patterns, such as skipping. With individual initiative unhampered, the child is free to listen and respond to the rhythm of the music. When the teacher predetermines the response, attention is diverted from the music to pleasing the teacher. Teachers who provide many early experiences in free rhythmic play find that the children are soon able to respond to prescribed patterns. Moreover, children who are weak in rhythm will learn from other children by imitating them. Many teachers are convinced that learning under such conditions is faster than when the teacher directs.

Impersonating. Closely related to free rhythmic play is impersonation. Children love imitative play in which they impersonate the movement of animate and inanimate objects—a horse, an airplane, a flying bird, a train, and so on. Some teachers add appropriate music after the rhythm has been established. Others prefer to let the music suggest the rhythm. Whatever the approach, teachers should take advantage of the child's joy in imitative play as a means of orienting him in rhythmic response.

Action Songs. Action songs are those which involve the children in responding by appropriate movement. They may be taught before fundamental movement to prescribed patterns has been established. Although they elicit a definite response to the music, the process is not as exacting as responding to prescribed patterns. Action songs are therefore valuable in developing active listening. Creative teachers stimulate the child's imagination by adding appropriate action to many songs whether or not they are classified as action songs.

Singing Games. Singing games, like action songs, are not as exacting as responding to prescribed patterns. They are particularly valuable during the orientation period. First attempts should require very simple motions. Directions for the games are usually given in a footnote to the songs, or in the teachers' manual, or, in the case of a recording, on the record cover. Teachers who feel inadequate in this activity may find it beneficial to work with the physical education instructor. Only two suggestions seem necessary concerning singing games:

1. Verbal explanations are usually time-consuming and difficult for the children to follow. Many teachers prefer leading the group through the game routine. When the routine is learned, the children are encouraged to add their own creative elaborations.

2. As a rule, those who take part in the game should not sing. This is particularly true with games requiring considerable action. Groups should alternate in singing and playing the game. Those who sing may engage in such activities as clapping. (A list of singing games is given at the close of this chapter.)

Dances. Dancing as such is not begun until the children have had wide experience in various rhythmic activities and can respond almost automatically to the pulsation of music. For this reason, emphasis on dancing is usually reserved for the intermediate grades. First attempts should require very simple step patterns such as those used by American Indians. Problems are minimized if the children have had wide experience in singing games. Directions for dances are sometimes recorded with the music or given on the record cover or in the teachers' manual or teachers' guide. General information concerning traditional dances, including their national origin, is given in Part Two. Such information may be used in connection with social studies.

Dancing of even the folk type is frowned upon by minority groups in some communities. In extreme cases, any form of rhythm activity is interpreted as dancing. Other groups may permit rhythmic activities but object to dancing *per se*. Actually, any physical response to music, even patting the foot, is a form of dance. The difference in interpretation seems to be based upon whether one sits and pats his feet, stands and pats his feet, or moves forward and backward on his feet. The first is not dancing, but the last is. At any rate, teachers should respect the rights of objectors and not require their children to participate in activities which are considered objectionable.

Rhythm Instruments

To give the child further experience in rhythm, to sustain his interest, and to create an early interest in musical instruments, rhythm instruments are sometimes employed to accompany songs, dances, and instrumental music. The stick, drum, and rattle were among the first instruments used by man and are easiest for the young child to manipulate. Many rhythm instruments are similar to those used in symphony orchestras and bands—drums, triangles, cymbals, bells, castanets, or tambourines.

The rhythm band (or *toy orchestra* or *rhythm orchestra*, as it is often called) is diminishing in popularity and can hardly be justified if its only purpose is to develop a feeling for rhythm, for this can be done by the other activities discussed in this chapter. However, the use of such rhythm devices can stimulate an early interest in musical instruments. Another value of rhythm instruments is that they encourage discriminative listening. To play the right instruments correctly at the right time, the children must listen to the music creatively. They must determine which instruments best express its mood, distinguish between like and unlike phrases and sections, and identify passages as loud or soft, fast or slow. Such listening is essential in developing musical taste and the power to interpret.

Like other specific activities in music, the rhythm band as such may be stressed to the detriment of the over-all musical development of the child. A few teachers who have little else to offer, or who lack patience in developing the child in other phases of musical growth, have overemphasized the rhythm band, exploiting the children and deceiving the parents. Lured by attractive costumes and by the fact that children are naturally "cute," the public may be deceived into believing that the children who are able to strike, shake, rattle, or ping at the right instant are really learning. In fact, it is quite possible to train children to respond like animals in a circus, with very little resultant learning. In a few isolated areas, city and county contests are held. The teacher plans the score, spends a great deal of time training the group, and wins first place at the contest. In such cases, the winners are surely the losers.

There is a difference of opinion on methods of orienting the children in the use of rhythm instruments. One approach is to let the children play when and as they please, gradually leading them, through discriminative listening, and eventually bringing some semblance of order out of the chaos of sound.

Another approach is based upon the assumption that the introductory activities, at least, should be directed by the teacher, who explains exactly how and when each instrument is played. As the children gain knowledge of the sounds produced by the various instruments, they are led to discriminative listening and encouraged to use their own judgment in choosing instruments for various sections of the music.

A third approach is based upon man's early use of instruments in connection with singing. The teacher introduces one instrument at a time in connection with a song. Each child is given an opportunity to play this instrument and thus becomes thoroughly familiar with its sound. By this approach, interest may be sustained over a long period of time, giving each child a familiarity with each instrument. Thus, the children gain a background for making good choices. One teacher begins by introducing the less appealing rhythm sticks. A pair is available for each child. All the sticks are placed on a table and the children march by (to music) and each selects his pair. No one plays until the entire group is ready to perform. Since the children are not aware of the existence of other instruments, they are, for a time, satisfied with sticks. After several days, the teacher separately introduces drums, triangles, or other instruments. Each child has an opportunity to play the *new* instrument before another is introduced. The use of sticks diminishes in proportion to the number of other instruments in use, but they are never entirely eliminated. Thus, rhythm instruments are very appropriately used to accompany singing. Modern song series contain many suggestions for using instruments in connection with songs.

Rhythm instruments are also employed to accompany dances. The children should become thoroughly familiar with the music before attempting to use instruments. After two or three hearings, they should discuss the nature of the music and suggest instruments which best express its mood. After playing, they should be led to question their choice of instruments and encouraged to experiment with various combinations of instruments for the various sections of the dance.

The heavy, low-pitched instruments such as drums usually play on the first beat in duple and triple meters, on the first and third beats in quadruple meter, and on the first and fourth beats in sextuple meter. Lighter sounding instruments may play on each beat, and others may follow the rhythm of the words or melody. Agitated passages in which faster notes are employed suggest the use of "shaking" instruments.

Phonograph records for use with rhythm instruments are available from the publishers of the various song series. The RCA Victor Library for Elementary Grades contains one album for the rhythm band.

Rhythm instruments may be purchased, made, or "procured." Children of low economic status prefer "store-bought" instruments, while those who have everything often enjoy making their own. The local junk yard, mother's old pot and pan department, and dad's workshop are excellent sources. For example, sections from discarded baseball bats, broomsticks, or bowling pins are excellent hardwood material for wood-block effects. Doweling sticks, which may be purchased from a lumberman, make good rhythm sticks. Horseshoes suspended by wires make excellent triangles, and reinforcement steel of various sizes makes superior gongs as do brake drums and brass trays. Gourds and various other containers filled with peas, shot, rice, small gravel, and the like, are good "shaking" instruments. Pots and pans and their lids produce a variety of sounds. Wooden kegs or metal cans may be converted into drums by stretching portions of inner tubes or drum-head material over the open ends.

Teachers in Action

The following are actual examples of teachers in action and represent different approaches. Each may have its strong and weak points. The reader is asked to study each approach carefully and decide for himself which is best.

Miss Elson, who has already taught the first verse of "Clap Your Hands" (p. 20a, G. *The First Grade Book*), begins, "Boys and girls, today we are going to learn to clap our hands to the song we sang yesterday." She chants and claps in a steady one-two rhythm, accenting the first count; the children imitate her. When the children are clapping together, Miss Elson sings or plays the melody of the song. On another day, she teaches them in a like manner to clap to the rhythm of the words, which involves quarter, half, and eighth notes. On still another day, the children are taught to walk and run to the music.

This is accomplished by first chanting the word *walk* in a steady rhythm or by repeating "right, left," as a guide for the feet. When the children are responding together, Miss Elson adds the music. On another day, the children chant the words of the song, which involves them in both walking and running notes. The words serve as instructions for the feet.

Doris, a student teacher who has taught the first verse to the same song, begins, "Boys and girls, do you remember the hand-clapping song we sang yesterday? It went like this." She sings the first verse, clapping in a steady one-two fashion. Some of the children begin to imitate her clapping, and she smiles her approval. Without a pause, Doris continues with the second verse, but claps to the rhythm of the words (quarter, half, and eighth notes). She asks, "Did you notice any time difference in the way I clapped?" One child observes the change and Doris sings the song again so that all may make the observation. More children join in the rhythm activity. On another day, Doris plays a record of the song above (Ginn and Company) without a word of introduction. The children recognize the song immediately. Doris asks if they heard any clapping in the song. As the children listen again, they discover that the clapping was the same as Doris had done the day before, and they join in singing and clapping.

Betty, a student teacher in the second grade, introduced by rote "Running and Walking" (p. 17, G. *Singing on Our Way*). After learning the song, the children clapped the meter and the rhythm of the words as Betty sang. They also walked and ran as the words indicated. Betty led the children in a game of counting "one, two" as she played the song. In order to have a word for each note, Betty suggested that they count "one and two and" on the running notes. The children observed that on running notes they took two steps for each step on a walking note.

On another day, books were distributed. The children found the song on page 17 and for the first time saw a musical score. Betty explained that music was written on five lines and spaces—the staff—and that the round characters on the lines and spaces were notes. She also explained that the words were written under the notes and that at the end of a line one skipped to the words under the next staff. After singing the song, Betty led the class to observe different notes. Some were black with a stem; these were walking or quarter notes. Some were white with a stem; these were step-point or half notes. Some were black with a stem and a flag; these were running notes. Although Betty realized that the children did not understand the terms *half, quarter,* and *eighth,* she believed it expedient to associate the correct terms with familiar experiences. She justified her use of these terms on the premise that our understanding of words is a developmental process and recalled how her own comprehension of the term *mother* had changed through the years.

Betty wrote the melody of the song on the chalkboard, naming each note and describing it—walking or quarter note with stem; running or eighth note with stem and flag. She sang the song and pointed to each note. Then a child pointed to the notes as Betty played, and the class clapped to the rhythm of the pointer. Since the melody is the same for each phrase, the girls sang the second phrase as the boys sang the first. At a later date, they clapped the rhythm of the two phrases simultaneously. In a similar manner, they walked and ran to the rhythm. This sort of game was always played in connection with notation.

Some weeks later, Betty introduced "Skipping and Galloping," which is directly underneath "Running and Walking." She played it, and the children observed both familiar and unfamiliar aspects. They compared the notation of the two songs and concluded that although the notes were on the same lines and spaces, the walking and running notes were arranged differently. Betty sang the new song as the children clapped; they also skipped and galloped to its rhythm. Skipping music (quarter notes followed by eighths), Betty explained, seems to half walk and half run, just as we skip. Galloping notes looked like running notes but "felt" different— some running notes seem to make us want to run, whereas some make us want to gallop.

A boy who was taking piano lessons asked why the numbers at the beginning of the two songs were different. Betty explained that the figure 2 in "Running and Walking" meant that we should count "one, two" as we had already done, and the class played the counting game again as the melody was played. They discovered that the count *one* always came after the line across the staff (measure bar). Betty wrote the counts above the notes. The figure 6 in the second song, Betty explained, meant to count six. They counted "one, two, three, four, five, six" to the second phrase, as Betty played; the counts were written above the notes. Betty also reminded the children that running notes went twice as fast as walking notes, and that we could therefore have two counts for each of the quarter notes in the first phrase. At any rate, there were six counts between measure bars. Since no one asked about the bottom figure in the time signature, Betty did not mention it.

Beverly, a student teacher, begins, "Children, today we are going to learn a singing game. I need six children: a lassie, a laddie, a farmer, a soldier, a cowboy and a fireman. Which of you wants to be one of these?" The children are selected and Beverly tells each what to do. Beverly plays the record of "Did You Ever See A Lassie?" (Victor Singing Game Album).

Miss Grimes, an experienced teacher, uses the same recording in this manner: "Children, we are going to hear a song and play a game. After you have listened to the record, tell me the names of all the people in the song." The children listen and recall a farmer, a soldier, a cowboy, and a fireman. Miss Grimes sings the phrases in which the words *lassie* and *laddie* are mentioned, and explains their meaning. She plays the record again, suggesting that the children guess how the various people in the song would act, and then says, "Let's choose Mary to be the lassie, Henry for the laddie, Frank for the farmer, Billie for the soldier, Earl for the cowboy, and let's see—who wants to be the fireman? All right, Albert." The children form a circle and each child acts out his part as his name is mentioned. On another day, six other children play the game. On still another day, the children decide what other characters they would like to be. In all the repetitions, all the children participate by singing and acting out the character parts.

Miss Johnson, a regular second grade teacher, after playing the recording of "Amarillis" (Victor Rhythm Album Four), distributed the rhythm instruments and indicated which instruments should play during each part (ABC) of the music. The children played as instructed.

Miss Hillard used the same recording, but in a different way. After hearing the recording two or three times, the children observed that there were three tunes—A, B, C. They discussed the mood or character of each part and expressed their feeling for each in free rhythmic activities. Miss Hillard made no suggestions as to what the music told them to do. When the children were thoroughly familiar with the composition and its various parts, rhythm instruments were distributed to them and the children decided on the combination of instruments to be used for each part. Miss Hillard, who was not a strong teacher in music, observed that the children were not using the instruments suggested in the album. She asked the children to try the suggested instruments. They experimented with other combinations and discussed each. The whole purpose was to develop discriminative listening.

Roberta, a student teacher in the first grade, used "Flying Birds" (Victor Rhythm Album One). During the first three playings, the children were asked to listen and decide what the music told them to do. A brief discussion was held after each hearing. Noticing that one of the girls was moving her arms in a swinging motion, Roberta asked her to do what the music said. The child continued her arm movement and moved forward with sliding feet. A boy moved a step forward, a step backward, in time with the music. A small group of children began to sway to the music. A few of the children, however, apparently had no feeling for the rhythm, and one inhibited boy indicated no interest at all in responding. Roberta had the children form two rings, join hands, and swing their arms in and out to the rhythm of the music. In this way, Roberta involved all members of the class in the activity, and the strong helped the weak without attention being directed toward either.

For Further Development

1. Discuss rhythm as a unifying force in the universe.

2. Discuss rhythm as a basic design in music. See "National Characteristics," chapter 9.

3. Discuss the presentations of Misses Elson, Johnson, and Hillard and of Doris, Betty, Beverly, and Roberta. Indicate the strong and weak points of each approach.

4. Various class committees select one of the following for class demonstration:

a) Select three action songs; teach them to the class by rote. Encourage the class to originate the actions, adding yours as a rewarding experience.

b) Select three singing games; teach them to the class by rote, including the game. Indicate how you would involve the inhibited child in the games.

c) Select three recorded singing games; teach the songs and games to the class. Indicate how you would involve the inhibited child in the games.

d) Select three different types of dances for the fifth grade and teach them to the class. You may use the piano or recordings. Indicate how you would relate the dances to social studies.

e) Make a list of devices for aiding the rhythmic defective. Demonstrate their use.

f) Select three songs (one for each of the first three grades) in which a limited number of rhythm instruments may be employed. Teach these to the class, using the instruments.

g) Arrange for a listening period to become familiar with the rhythm material recorded for children and with the national dances listed in chapter 9. Make a list of your favorites which you would like to add to your record collection.

Recordings

RCA Victor Basic Library for Elementary Schools. This library contains six rhythm albums, one for each grade, an album of singing games, and an album for rhythm band.

RCA Victor, "Let's Square Dance." Album No. 1 is designed for grades three and four, and Album No. 2 for grades five and six.

Square Dance Associates, 33 So. Grove, Freeport, New York. This is a course in square dancing arranged in four albums.

Ruth Evans Records, 326 Forest Park Ave., Springfield, Mass. The eight albums contain a wide choice of rhythmic activities including singing games, fundamental dance steps and formations, and one album of European folk dances.

Bowmar Records, H 921 Santa Monica Blvd., Los Angeles 29, Calif. Of particular interest for use in connection with social studies are Singing Games and Folk Dances, Folk Dances of the World, American Folk Dances, and Latin American Folk Dances.

Follet Publishing Company recordings for "Together We Sing" series.

Silver Burdett Company recordings for "Music for Living" series.

Ginn and Company recordings for "Our Singing World" series.

"TOGETHER WE SING" (Follett Publishing Company)

Rhythm Activity	Music 'Round the Clock	Music 'Round the Town	Music Through the Year	Music Across Our Country	Voices of America	Voices of the World
Action Songs	17r, 42r, 70	71r, 102, 122r	70, 81, 105br, 133	20, 86r, 112, 139r	92r	
Singing Games	35r, 36r, 38r, 39, 40r	7r, 46r, 76r, 95, 97, 98, 101, 106, 107, 122r	15r	24ab, 48r, 95, 105, 125r, 139r	57b, 99	
Dances		99, 100	20r, 25, 35, 64r	33br	63, 58, 110r	150,185
Galloping, Swaying, Swinging, Skating	26, 30r, 53r	23r, 41r, 44, 63r, 66, 74r, 96, 127r, 128r	19r, 40r, 48r, 76r	56r, 123		15,180
Running, Trotting	24r, 51r, 53	24r, 42r	15r, 32r	80, 83		117,122
Walking, Marching	11, 48r	6, 13r, 22, 39r, 40r, 103	84b, 90, 109, 116a, 150	4,126	13r, 16, 20r, 161, 164	
Impersonation, Pretending, Imitation	15r, 18r, 47r, 56r	16r, 21, 36r, 73r		94	14ar, 49	
Skipping		23r	11r	82r		
Instruments	7, 24r, 36, 48r, 49, 54r, 61r	36r, 53, 74r, 78r	33r, 40, 71, 82, 118, 126	25ar, 32r, 33br, 35r, 38, 39r, 46r, 84, 92, 132b, 158	44r, 49, 52, 57a, 77, 80r, 81r, 92r, 126, 129r, 193	10, 22, 96, 103, 108, 124, 127, 134, 162, 166, 167, 169

"MUSIC FOR LIVING" (Silver Burdett Company)

RHYTHM ACTIVITY	Music Through the Day	Music in Our Town	Music Now and Long Ago	Music Near and Far	Music in Our Country	Music Around the World
Action Songs		2, 3, 7b, 34, 47r, 84, 103, 109	8, 14, 17, 36, 63	10, 25, 68, 106a, 111r, 145	96	93
Singing Games	6, 14b, 15r, 17, 60a, 69	65r, 68r, 69, 119r	25, 24r, 95, 118r, 121, 125, 137r			
Dances			21, 124r	6, 34r, 36br, 38, 40, 42, 154r	42r, 61r, 74r, 84r, 93, 114, 156r, 194r, 198r	184, 181r, 185r
Galloping, Swaying, Swinging, Skating	38r, 51, 64b, 65, 102b, 105r, 111a, 113a, 132a, 137	90, 94, 95, 86r, 87r	10, 14, 64, 90b, 143, 156	2b, 3, 36r, 44r, 67b, 69, 79, 143b, 145	7r, 72, 79, 158, 176, 196	10, 57, 202b
Running, Trotting	7, 10br, 65, 118b	12r, 61, 101	12, 51, 92b, 129, 149	16ar, 20a	43, 214a	
Walking, Marching	3b, 10ar, 11r, 20b, 49r, 99r, 131	35, 38, 61, 69, 135	7, 15, 28, 60, 71, 75, 103r	60a, 147, 167r	3, 42r, 116, 128r, 172, 132, 134r, 138	76, 155
Impersonation, Pretending, Imitation	19, 21, 42, 57r, 37, 39r, 62, 76a, 95r, 106br, 111a, 139b	1r, 16, 18b, 21r, 37, 46r, 80, 98	10, 18, 34r, 49, 87r	32, 122, 134r, 138, 161, 163	64, 80, 96, 174r	26r, 44r, 99, 111r, 215
Skipping	9r, 10ar, 11r, 50r, 68a, 132b	4r, 29, 38, 81r, 131, 133	122, 124r, 125, 160	7, 38	20, 27	46r, 138
Instruments	10ar, 20ab, 21, 37, 43r, 76a, 89a, 90r, 128a	17, 50r, 73, 78r, 109, 110r, 127	6, 10, 12, 13, 17, 29, 58r, 64, 116r	3, 9, 10, 11, 27, 67a, 79, 87, 99, 120	6, 14, 73, 92, 131, 146r, 153r, 155, 172, 188	61, 82r, 100, 110r, 132, 194r, 198

"OUR SINGING WORLD" (Ginn and Company)

Rhythm Activity	The First Grade Book	Singing on Our Way	Singing and Rhyming	Singing Every Day	Singing Together	Singing in Harmony
Action Songs	7ab, 21b, 34ab, 44br, 59a, 60a, 78c, 105, 125ab, 159ar, 171ar	26r, 42, 43, 45br, 54, 55b, 153r	9, 10, 24r, 28r, 60r, 161r, 165	7, 17r, 22br, 56r	66b, 123, 148	35, 38r
Singing Games	45, 46ab, 47ab, 48r, 50ar, 50br, 51, 52ab	7r, 9r, 31r, 32r, 34r, 35ab, 36, 37r, 39r, 144r	11, 13, 16ar, 41r, 42r, 44, 45r, 46ar, 48br	45r, 46r, 47r, 49ar, 51r, 52r, 53, 57, 61r, 158br	29r, 30r, 32r, 34r, 35r, 186r	39, 44
Dances				12, 54r, 59	31r, 33r, 40r	37r, 40r, 41r
Galloping, Swaying, Swinging, Skating	22ab, 24arbr, 28arbr, 30arbr, 31db	29r, 118r, 22br, 24b, 26r, 27a	9, 23r, 61, 148	19, 20	13, 14, 16ar, 18b, 23r, 42r, 45r, 73b, 154, 181	13, 23, 41r, 69, 88a
Running, Trotting	11br, 12ar, 12br, 13a, 14arbr, 23arbr	55a	20ar, 20b	27, 51r	49, 186r	45, 174a
Walking, Marching	9, 15b, 36a, 36br, 38ar, 40r, 41	28, 158a	27ab, 49ar, 51a, 64b, 82b, 164	112, 170r, 178r	60b, 65, 128, 129, 153, 189	17r, 152, 156
Impersonation, Pretending, Imitation	18ar, 22b, 30br, 33r, 35a, 36br	22ar, 23r, 25a, 105a, 119b	60r, 160, 161r		68r	50
Skipping	18ar	20, 24a, 63r, 68a, 116a, 136a	16ar, 21ar, 21b	50b, 172ar	16r, 36, 44br, 9	31r, 160
Instruments	134b, 173r, 174ab, 175, 176ab	46br, 50r, 78, 101r, 103b, 155b	154ab, 155br, 156, 160, 164, 165a, 68arb	43, 55, 170r, 172arb	45r, 48r, 59, 92, 138, 139, 188, 189	7r, 38r, 40r, 43r, 52r, 62r, 68, 200r

CHAPTER 4

Ears to Hear

What about Listening?

Ear training is involved in every step of musical growth and is, in fact, directly related to musical development. For this reason, listening should not be isolated from other music activities: yesterday we sang, today we dance, tomorrow we listen. Regardless of the activity—singing, reading, creating, or responding to rhythm—the aural experience is the initial and principal consideration. The ear is the musician's compass, directing every phase of musical growth. As treated in this chapter, however, listening refers specifically to what is usually called *appreciation*. In other words, the listening activity is for aural exploration of music. It should never stray from active listening. Although it should be a pleasant experience, it should also be stimulating, imaginative, and creative.

The foregoing paragraph suggests many questions. What is *appreciation?* How does one learn to appreciate? These are difficult questions, for many considerations are involved—native capacity, environment, interest. One thing is certain: the response to music is both intellectual and emotional. It is therefore difficult to distinguish between appreciation and enjoyment. To suggest that the enjoyment of music is purely an emotional response and that appreciation is an intellectual response is to sever the relationship between mind and emotion. This cannot be done.

Appreciation and Knowledge

It has been suggested by some teachers that in order to *appreciate* fully one must know the facts and understand the labels associated with a subject. But Webster defines "appreciation" as follows: "To set a just value on; to esteem fully the worth of; to be sensitive to the aesthetic value of; as, to appreciate music." He goes on to say that to, "appreciate, in discriminating use, implies sufficient understanding to admire or enjoy a thing's excellence, but in looser use, may imply merely warm admiration or enjoyment." This definition is broad enough in its implications to embrace varying degrees of musical knowledge and background. It is perfectly possible to enjoy or appreciate a thing without being completely conscious of its technical or formal aspects. For example, one may thoroughly enjoy and appreciate Milton's "Sonnet on His Blindness" without a knowledge of its technical form. One may equally appreciate Beethoven's *Fifth Symphony,* which might be called an "epic on his deafness," without a conscious knowledge of the sonata-allegro form. One's appreciation grows with his experience and with his feeling for Milton and Beethoven, sonnets and symphonies.

The same is true of labels or names. One may thoroughly enjoy or appreciate a literary work without being completely conscious of the author's use of figures of speech. Similarly, he may thrill to a great work of music without a technical knowledge of tempi, form, counterpoint, or harmony. Valuable as such terms are, they add to one's knowledge but not necessarily to his understanding. Labels merely provide names for things with which we are already familiar. This may be easily illustrated. A child speaks kindly to his dog; the dog responds with a wag of his tail. Later the child learns that these acts are called stimulus and response by the psychologist. Thomas Edison is said to have remarked, after reading *Elbert Hubbard's Scrapbook*, "He taught me things I knew, but I didn't know I knew them."

Appreciation and Analysis

Analysis is another question frequently raised in connection with music enjoyment or appreciation. Some people have analytical minds whereas others do not. It seems quite safe to state that those who have analytical minds enjoy and gain emotional satisfaction through such mental activity. To them, there is a particular beauty in logic itself. On the other hand, to the illogical mind, any attempt at analysis destroys the over-all beauty of an effect and actually obstructs appreciation. Consider the contrast, say, between two opera enthusiasts. Each week, two men sit in the balcony of a New York theater attending performances of a series of Gilbert and Sullivan operas. One knows practically nothing about the operas; the other is an authority on the subject. The latter follows a conductor's score and with critical attitude intently observes each detail of the performance. The other, in relative ignorance, watches and listens with delight. Which of these men gets the most from these performances? Considering their backgrounds, is it not possible that the purchasing power of their take-home pay is the same? Stated another way, although their purses are different in size, each is filled. Some will argue, of course, that the authority would *enjoy* the performance more if he were not so analytical and critical, and that the other would *appreciate* the works more if he, in the words of Webster, "had sufficient understanding to admire or enjoy."

All of this leads us to emphasize a point that is too often overlooked: understanding is not limited to the intellect, for, to a degree, one may understand through feeling. A dog understands your "puppy talk" to him and probably breaks out in "goose pimples" as you speak, but he does not comprehend the words you speak. His understanding is through feeling, a response to mood. Each of us understands more through this medium than we may realize. *It is probable that the greatest attainment in appreciation is reached when intellect and emotion unite to enhance understanding.*

Whatever degree of intellect or feeling is involved, each individual comprehends his environment in his own way. Your understanding differs from that of another person for your mind and feeling are peculiarly your own. With this in mind, we must not be guilty of attempting to impose our understanding upon another, for our intellectual and emotional garments are tailor-made. Just as we react differently to various drugs, so we vary in our response to stimuli.

Influence of Environment

We must consider, too, that our concept of beauty at any level of development is influenced by environment. A barbarian girl with greasy hair, an ornament in her nose, the absence of a front tooth, and beaded scars on her chest and back may be the belle of her village, but she is hardly your idea of a "Miss America." Our idea of feminine beauty is largely conditioned by movies, television, and advertising. With the impact of environmental influence in mind, it is easy to understand why one child reacts enthusiastically and another with apathy to what his teacher calls beautiful music. One child is constantly exposed to beauty in his home; his parents like and listen to music; they have good pictures on their walls and good books in their bookcase; they attend concerts, lectures, and art exhibits. The environment of the other child is devoid of these influences. This reminds one of Ulysses' statement in Tennyson's poem, "I am a part of all that I have met."

Appreciation and Aptitude

We should not assume that one must possess some sort of special aptitude in order to appreciate music. One acquaintance of the author's is a brilliant and highly educated lady, a teacher in the first grade. Her culture is genuine, and not a veneer for meretricious show. She knows nothing at all about the technical aspects of music and actually claims to be tone deaf because of her difficulty in "carrying a tune." She does not play an instrument. Her only means of participation is through listening. Yet she thoroughly appreciates the best in music and is, with Shakespeare, "moved by concord of sweet sound." One would believe that she was personally acquainted with each composer and lived during his time. She loves opera and knows its characters. She loves all forms of instrumental and vocal music and responds to delicate shades in tone color, tempi, and dynamics. Her enthusiasm for music is genuine, for she wants to share new records with her friends. Her record collection is finer than that of many musicians, and she spends more time actively listening to music than does the writer.

It should be evident that music appreciation for the child must begin with response to mood. Through mood he can gain the import of the message of music. Understanding first comes through feeling. Music speaks first to the heart and then to the head. As has been said so many times, we first learn to listen and then listen to learn. Be all of this as it may, every person is an artist by nature and each brings his individual cup to be filled at the fountain of beauty. If we must measure appreciation, it must be according to cup overflow and not according to the size of the cup.

Why Teach Listening?

Active Listening. Educators are becoming increasingly concerned because their students have not been taught to listen. Businessmen complain that their young employees do not hear instructions accurately. Their hearing is passive, not active. Although educators and schools are blamed, the weakness may result partially from the multitude of aural distractions in modern society. We hear so many commercials, announcements, songs, and sermons that we develop the habit of passive hearing. As one minister expressed it, "Words as used in speech seem to have no barbs— nothing sticks any more; words go in one ear and out the other."

How many of us have turned on the car radio to hear the weather forecast and immediately forgotten it? This habit of passive hearing presents a challenge to all educators, and especially to those who teach music, for learning to listen to music is by far the best means of developing accuracy in general hearing. As has been pointed out many times, the general medical practitioner and the heart specialist in particular have long recognized the value of musical training, which is to say ear training, as a distinct asset in stethoscopic diagnosis.

Music in Everyday Living. Aside from the reason that listening in general should be improved, we teach listening to music in particular because every phase of life is colored by musical sound —through the radio, television, concerts, the church, weddings, theaters, dances, football games, and military reviews.

Leisure Time Activity. More important than these values is the opportunity music listening presents for profitable and wholesome use of leisure time. Young people, as well as adults, will seek out activities of some sort for their leisure time. Unless we provide for wholesome outlets, their choice may well be degrading.

Therapeutic Value. The therapeutic value of music has long been recognized. With the increase of emotional disturbances has come the use of music as a healing balm for the mind. Its calming and soothing influence may restore the listener to emotional composure.

Equilibrium. Man has gone far in the development of science —much further than in human relations. In science we find the expression of man's search for accuracy and efficiency. This is good except that, standing alone, it makes a robot man, insensitive to an equally important part of man's nature, the emotional, and indeed to the real nature of the world about him. To be blind, deaf, and insensitive to the beauty of the earth and man's attempts to reach perfection in the expression of beauty is certainly not in the interest of equilibrium. Music is one of many media for developing a normally balanced individual.

Broader Interests. Most important of all is that music, being related to so many areas of human endeavor, can lead one to investigations of man's efforts in other fields—psychology, sociology, science, literature, history, art, architecture. When we really listen to music, we communicate with the heart and mind of man through the ages.

How to Teach for Music Appreciation

From the Known to the Unknown

Arresting attention—a "lend me your ears" attitude—is the first consideration in guiding the child to an appreciation of music. When this is done, the music can speak for itself. A very excellent way to arrest the ear in the early listening experiences is to play a recording of a familiar song or one which is being learned. Another source of familiar material recommended for kindergarten and first grade are Mother Goose rhymes. Little or no comment is necessary. The children's familiarity with both words and melody, coupled with the surprise of hearing "their song," is immediately provocative. This approach may be used at any grade level, employing a reading song or a patriotic, Christmas, or traditional melody. For additional practice in learning to listen, the children should learn several songs each semester by listening to records. This idea should be carried over into the upper elementary grades by having children follow the *notation* of familiar songs as they listen to the recordings.

The familiar song approach is also an excellent bridge to instrumental music. For example, the children will listen actively to an instrumental recording of "Country Gardens" or "Jesu, Joy of Man's Desiring," after having learned the melody through song.

Song: "Come, Let's Be Merry" (G. *Singing and Rhyming*, p. 18)
Recording: Victor Rhythm Album Six
Song: "Jesu, Joy of Man's Desiring" (G. *Singing Together*, p. 98r)
Recording: "Our Singing World series, Ginn and Company.

Correlation

Another means of gaining immediate attention is to use recordings which are related to other classroom activities. For example:

Indian Music—American Indians
Early American Music—Pilgrims or Colonial days
Cowboy Songs—Western movement
Songs of the Forty-Niners—Gold Rush
Songs and dances of any country being studied

Closely allied with this is correlation with specific subjects such as English, geography, art, history, and foreign language. Such tie-ins may be achieved by reading a poem or story, by showing a picture to set an introductory mood, or by association with textbook material and outside reading. Correlation with other subjects enhances both areas and tends to stimulate wider interest. Furthermore, it provides a definite purpose for listening, and gives a stronger impression of people and times.

The Role of the Teacher

The teacher who grades papers, makes out reports, fidgets with desk material, or gives his attention to other things during the playing of a record may expect inattention on the part of the class. The teacher should guard against too much talk or suggesting too many purposes for listening. A single purpose for listening is sufficient for each hearing. Any information concerning the composition or the composer should be carefully selected and presented in keeping with the interest and comprehension of the children. The teacher should vary the introduction and the presentation in order to hold attention from day to day.

Little comment seems necessary regarding the suggestions made thus far. However, giving information which aids in creating an interest or suggesting a purpose for listening is not only permissible but desirable. The information might relate to activities or experiences of the children, a group of people, a custom, a period, a historic event, an instrument or group of instruments featured in the melody, a composer, a type of composition, form, or mood. Such information is often more effective when woven into the class discussion following each subsequent hearing.

Selection of Material

Selection of material is highly important in listening sessions. The problem is minimized if the teacher uses recordings prepared for the various song series or such albums as the RCA Victor Record Library for Elementary Schools. Such material is classified according to grades. This is a distinct aid to the regular classroom teacher. Selection of recordings, aside from these carefully prepared programs, should be made with discrimination. The following suggestions may prove helpful.

1. *Wide choice of material.* The student should become acquainted with a wide variety of media and styles of expression. He should hear selections which feature various voices or instruments and their combinations. The teacher should avoid limiting the selection to his favorite compositions.

2. *Good tone quality.* Children are generally impressed by good tone quality and respond to this element of beauty even though they may be otherwise unimpressed. It must be remembered that growth in appreciation is a matter of acquiring aural taste. If time is to be spent on listening, then only the best should be used. This reference is not to what many people call "arty" or "long hair" performances, but rather to good taste in tone quality and performance. Bear in mind that expression follows impression and that early impressions are often lasting ones.

3. *Music associated with great events or heroes.* The Star-Spangled Banner; The Marseillaise; Erie Canal; When Johnny Comes Marching Home; Old Chisholm Trail; Tenting Tonight; Casey Jones; We Gather Together (Thanksgiving); The Landing of the Pilgrim Fathers; and He Is Born, the Holy Child, are songs of value and interest to children because they deal with important historical events.

4. *National music.* Music is a universal language and through it we may better understand other peoples of the earth. The use of national music in connection with social studies and foreign languages in the upper elementary grades is an especially effective means toward such understanding.

5. *Avoidance of popular music.* Education is associated with growth and change in the acquisition of taste. How may one's appreciation grow and how may one acquire a different taste except by tasting? The adult who still claims "Humpty Dumpty" as his favorite poem has not developed. Yet many adults remain at the Humpty Dumpty level in their musical development. It must be emphasized that growth demands effort and challenge. The athlete who runs only until his breathing is slightly accelerated will never make the team. He must run until he feels he can't go any farther and then keep on running. This does not mean that comparable effort is necessary for growth in all areas, but it does suggest that learning and growth demand challenge and effort. It simply is not all fun, for thinking is hard work. At any rate, we grow in appreciation in proportion to the reach above and beyond our level. The wise teacher is one who helps his students to move their goals constantly forward yet never allows the goal to be completely out of reach. The goal for learning should be constantly moved up so that the seeker must stretch to reach it but never so far ahead that he must jump in an attempt to catch an always elusive star.

This seems to imply a strong criticism against so-called popular music although it is not intended to be derogatory. It is perfectly natural and normal for young people to like the music of their day. But much of the music in this idiom has *no lasting value,* and is abundantly available on radio, television, and at the movies. Since it can be heard any time or place, and since it has no educative value, it has no place in an educational institution. We do not refer here to semi-popular or "pops" music such as that composed by Jerome Kern, Sigmund Romberg, Cole Porter, George Gershwin, and Victor Herbert.

Other general criteria for the selection of material may be found in chapter 2 where the selection of songs is discussed.

Some Important Questions

Questions frequently asked in the college classroom are given below. It is hoped that the answers will help the teacher in listening to music and at the same time suggest ways of approaching listening for children.

1. *How may we understand the message of the composer?*
The composer does not try to impress us so much with *his* thought as with our own. In a sense he says, "I'll create a mood in which you may cradle your own thoughts. Give me your most noble thoughts, and I'll try to crown them with splendor. Relive your most exalted feelings, and I shall try to clothe them in garments of sublimity." So the composer only sets the stage, creates the situation; we act out the character parts. He gives only in proportion to our ability to receive, for his message is echoed in our hearts and minds.

2. *But doesn't the composer deal with ideas?*
Yes, *musical* ideas—tone and time. These are his technical language. Since techniques are in themselves incapable of expressing concrete ideas; we must rely upon our own imagination. This is precisely what the composer did in creating, and we must re-create with him. He has provided the framework, we must complete the structure. We echo his message in proportion to our level of thought, feeling, experience, and imagination, for he speaks to us through *our own* voices. When we have assimilated the full import of his message, we say, "This is exactly the way I feel, and a perfect way to express it."

3. *Isn't there some reason why the composer wrote this piece?*
Yes, he is a creator and he must create or perish. For him, to live is to create. Thomas Edison spent the greater portion of his life in the laboratory. Did he love his work more than wife or family? Was he self-centered, and did he seek fame and fortune? It is highly probable that he was guiltless in these respects. He was merely true to himself and answered the call from within, the inner urge to seek the answers to many questions. He could not have done otherwise. So he gave himself to himself. Composers and all creators are like that. The point is this: we must dispel any idea that a composer must have a specific reason for writing a piece—that he must have a "glorious experience" or have experienced great inspiration. There are, of course, instances of these experiences, but for the most part the composer writes to

satisfy an inner creative urge. There is much truth in the statement that composing (or creating) is about ten per cent inspiration
and ninety per cent perspiration.

4. *Doesn't the music tell a story, doesn't it describe something?*
It is well to rid ourselves of the erroneous idea that there must
be a story behind a piece of music. If we must have a story, then
perhaps we love stories more than we love music. When we can
allow the music to speak for itself without props of any sort, we
will cease to place limits on our listening and begin to approach
maturity in our ability to appreciate music.

In another sense, all music is descriptive; it describes a general
mood. Some music is purposely designed to describe a series of
events such as a storm and the calm following it. Such music is
called *program music*, for it follows a program of events. But even
here the description is general. If we were not told the story or
the program, we might not even guess that there was one, or,
surmising it, we might make up one as appropriate as the original.
For example, the growling of the bear in MacDowell's "Of a
Tailor and a Bear" has been guessed to be a lion, an elephant,
a fight, a conflict. As far as the music is concerned, any one of
these is correct. However, only the bear is in keeping with Mac-
Dowell's title. Since this is true, the bear should eventually find
his rightful place in the story. If this piece is presented to children without first telling the story, as it should be, no child will
suffer damage or disappointment upon learning that "his" animal
was not a part of the story. On the contrary, he is usually delighted to learn that the animal was a bear. After hearing the
story, one little girl who had made up her own story said, "But
I like my story best." The teacher replied, "Remember your story,
Carol; it's as good as mine, but let us also be sure to remember
MacDowell's title." To recapitulate: all music is descriptive; some
music attempts to describe a series of events; it is not wrong to
know and follow these events so long as they do not limit imaginative listening. With this caution in mind, it is probably best to
listen to program music before learning its program.

5. *But can we get a clue to the composer's intent through the
title of the composition?*

The answer is yes and no. In such pieces as "Of a Tailor and a Bear" we could; in others, such as "Sonata," we could not. The yes-and-no answer is better understood when we realize that a title may be chosen before or after the piece is written, the latter probably being the most likely. After finishing a composition, a composer may consider several titles which seem to suggest the general mood of his work. The next time you hear an unfamiliar piece, try to select a title for it. You, like the composer, may consider several and the one you choose may be as appropriate as the one selected by the composer.

On the other hand, the title may be highly significant in that it may help us gain a deeper feeling and understanding for the work. A good example is *Peer Gynt Suite*. Although another title might be selected, the suite would lose its significance by being dissociated from the Norwegian playwright Henrik Ibsen and the principal character of his play *Peer Gynt*. Although Beethoven removed the dedication to Napoleon from his *Eroica Symphony*, the title ("Heroic") is significant in the light of Napoleon's place in history.

The conclusion is that we must neither wholly rely upon nor completely disregard the title as a clue to the composer's intent.

6. *Since you suggest that we discard our crutches, what can we rely upon? Shall we turn to facts about the composer, his life, his style, and shall we analyze the music in terms of these facts?* You can rely upon the music; listen to it. If at first you need crutches, use them, but discard them as soon as you can stand alone. When first hearing the music, relax; let yourself go. Don't try so hard to *appreciate* that you forget to *enjoy*. After you have learned to enjoy the music, you will want to learn more and more about it. You can then begin to gather facts about the music and the composer.

Concerning analysis, it must be pointed out that only trained musicians are capable of analytic listening in the real sense of the word. For the child or the lay listener the goal is not to be able to identify a rondo or a theme and variation, or to follow the sonata-allegro form. There are, however, some things which may aid listening. A few of these follow:

a) Listen to determine the mood—whether the music is joyous or somber.

b) Listen to the rhythm, which gives a clue to the mood.

c) Listen to the tempo—fast or slow.

d) Listen to simple melodies and their recurrence. Later, there may be simple variations of a melody.

e) Listen to voices—soprano, alto, tenor, bass, and their combinations.

f) Identify the instruments by sight and sound.

g) Identify choirs of instruments, and special sound effects from such sources as the harp, the celeste, and the percussion group.

A judicious observance of these matters will enhance listening and sustain interest without cluttering the mind with matters beyond the comprehension of most of the children.

By and large, however, the over-all stress in the listening activity at the grade school level should be upon the relationship between music and people. Consequently, emphasis throughout these pages is on the ties between music and social studies. It is indeed unfortunate if the technical aspects of listening to music receive the principal emphasis at a time when the child is being introduced to the peoples of the earth. As repeatedly pointed out, music is definitely related to all human endeavors, and the initial presentation should be done with this in mind. Zoo animals are presented in their natural habitat. Why not present music in its natural environment—people and music, music and people?

Directed Listening

Since there is already much passive listening in modern society, the listening experience in school should not be left to chance. Attention should be drawn to the melody, mood, tempo, instruments, voices, text, like and unlike passages, and so on. Concerning these aspects, some teachers believe the children should be prepared to listen for something specific. In order that the listening may be guided and yet not completely influenced, the children are given a choice of several moods, tempi, instruments, and so on. They listen and make a choice. Other teachers prefer to avoid any suggestions prior to hearing a composition, and to point up its characteristics through discussion following the hearing. Still other teachers are violently opposed to any suggestions by the instructor. They play a composition and ask for student opinion. Any opinion is acceptable, for the teacher must not influence the student's opinion. Most teachers, however, do not approve of this latter approach. They believe that neither the layman nor the professional should form an opinion after one or even several hearings. They maintain that snap judgments are a most dangerous influence. As one teacher phrased it, "Withhold judgment until all the evidence is in."

Music, a Temporal Art

Music lives and comes into being through vibration and pulsation. We cannot arrest it and listen to it as we might focus on the general or detailed aspects of a painting. What we momentarily hear is related to what has gone before and to what follows. Since this is true, a composition should be heard again and again, so that one can, from any aural point, remember what has gone before and anticipate what is to come. Then, too, many different things are going on in music at the same time: one or more melodies, rhythms, harmonies, instruments or voices—all cast in the framework of musical form. During different hearings, we may wish to concentrate on one or more of these at a time. Furthermore, a composition should be heard over and over so that the organizations of tone and time may be grasped. How readily one grasps these organizations depends upon his physical, mental, and emotional make-up, his total life experiences, and his specific music experiences.

With these thoughts in mind, it is easy to understand why some teachers believe it wise to withhold judgment until after a composition has been fully assimilated. It is not unusual for a person to become uninterested in a composition which he liked at first and to grow more fond of one which did not interest him when he first heard it. In this connection, first impressions are not always lasting, nor does familiarity breed contempt. On the contrary, we tend to like music with which we are familiar.

Attention Span

The attention span of the child is much shorter than that of the adult. Even the attention of the experienced adult listener may wander. The sight of a person, an object, or a noise, however slight, may momentarily distract attention. Since the attention span of the child is short, compositions selected for hearing should not be long. As the child matures, longer selections from suites and movements from symphonies may be presented.

The Listening Period

Opinions differ as to the time for the listening activity. Some teachers prefer to set aside one or more music periods each week for listening. Others like to spread the activity throughout the day—quiet listening immediately following recess, or animated music when the children have grown weary of other activities. Still other teachers prefer to intersperse the listening activity among other music activities. Regardless of the teacher's preference, the availability of player equipment is often the determining factor.

A final suggestion which has proved to be rewarding and a time-saving device for teachers is the use of file cards in connection with each record. This is an excellent means of accumulating information for himself and for possible use in the classroom. The following may serve as a guide for the enterprising teacher.

Name of composition	Record no. or album
Song book	Page
Composer	Nationality
Information about composer	
Place in history	
Mood	
Type or form of composition	
Special features such as solo or group of instruments	
Correlation with other subjects	
Literature	
History	
Art	
Motivation for listening	

It is further suggested that students keep a list of their favorite compositions and be allowed to play them from time to time.

Teachers in Action

Miss Clark, second grade: "Children, I'm going to tell you a story about a tailor and a bear, and then I'll play music which tells the same story. Pay close attention to the story so that you can follow it when you hear the music.

"The tailor's shop was on the second floor. He was a happy man and often whistled as he worked. One day while he was making a suit of clothes, a bear who had broken away from his master suddenly appeared in the tailor's shop. Although the tailor was frightened, he remembered that bears like music so he tuned his fiddle. The bear came closer. The tailor hurriedly tuned his fiddle again and began to play dance music for the bear. This pleased Mr. Bear and with his big feet he began to dance. Right in the middle of this dance, the owner of the bear entered the shop, took the bear by his halter and tried to pull him away. This made the bear angry for he was having fun dancing, so he and his master had a big quarrel. Much against his will, the bear was led away, and the tailor returned happily to his work.

"Now, we will hear this same story as told by music. The name of the piece is "Of a Tailor and a Bear" by MacDowell. I'll tell you what is happening as the music is played."

Miss Brown does not agree with this approach. She believes that Miss Clark has stifled imagination and creativity by telling the story and giving the title. She maintains that this technique definitely controls response (see chapter 3). Miss Brown believes that the children should be completely free to express themselves as they choose. Since there is no *correct* response, creative expression is the important thing. For example, the bear in the MacDowell story could be a lion or any large animal, and the tailor could be a cobbler or any artisan. After all, Miss Brown argues, music expresses mood and not concrete ideas. She presents "Of a Tailor and a Bear" as follows:

"Children, we are going to hear some very exciting music. After we have listened to the music, we will make up a play about it, letting the music tell us what to do. You may act as the music makes you feel."

Without further comment, the children listen to the music and make up their own stories. With complete abandon and without inhibitions of any sort, each child dramatizes the music in his own way. (See "Creative Response," chapter 3.) Some of the children dance like fairies; others move their arms and hands in expressions of delight and joy. During the conflict, two boys play that they are mad bulls having a fight. Another boy imagines himself as David, peaceably herding sheep when along comes a lion; like David, he struggles with and kills the lion.

Miss Hall disagrees with each of these presentations. She agrees with Miss Brown's criticism of Miss Clark's approach, but believes that Miss Brown's approach gives little or no guidance and thus does not encourage growth. Although she does not desire to stifle creative efforts, Miss Hall believes that complete expression of feeling and abandonment of all control are not in the interest of citizenship development. She combines the ideas of Miss Clark and Miss Brown and the result is *controlled creativity*.

"Children, we are going to hear a very delightful piece of music. Let's see how many things we can hear in the music."

After hearing the music, Miss Hall asks what they heard and writes the words on the chalkboard. Some heard happy music or saw fairies; others heard a lion, an elephant, a fiddle, or a fight. The record is played again with the same purpose in mind. Some of the children gain new ideas, which Miss Hall writes on the board.

"I want to compliment you on having heard so many things in the music. The composer—the man who wrote the music—made this music tell a story. The jig-saw pieces of the story are the things you heard and are written on the board. Now let's put the pieces together: 'Once upon a time, there was a man who made clothes, a tailor. . . .

"Can anyone guess the name of this piece? That is very close, Henry, for its exact title is 'Of a Tailor and a Bear.' Edward MacDowell, an American who loved children, wrote the music. Would you like to hear more of his music?

"Tomorrow you may dramatize or act out the story if you like. Which of you would like to be the tailor, the bear?"

Miss Hall's presentation is a "middle of the road" approach which many teachers prefer. This, too, is listening to music creatively. Although there are controls, they are so mild as not to hamper the imagination, for creativity and imagination had full sway during the first two hearings. The over-all and lasting impression which the children gain from such listening and dramatization is in keeping with the composer's intention and the title. Their interpretation is basically the same as that of the conductor of the orchestra.

Knowing that this piece had been a favorite of the children while they were in the second grade, Miss Smith, a third grade teacher, plays it a number of times as the children follow the notation (S. *Music Now and Long Ago*, p. 108).

Richard, who was doing practice teaching in the third grade, used Skilton's "War Dance" (Cheyenne) (Victor Indian Album), in connection with a unit on American Indians. He introduced the music as follows:

"Boys and girls, we are learning many interesting things about Indians. They, like us, enjoy singing and dancing. How many of you have heard Indians sing or seen them dance? Here is a beautiful picture of Indians singing and dancing which you may look at as the music is played."

After the playing of the record, Richard asks, "How many of you can show me the rhythm of the tom-tom?"

The drums are distributed, and after hearing a brief passage of the music again, the children begin to play. The entire class joins in the rhythm of *one*, two, three, four; *one*, two, three, four. Some are clapping as others pat their feet. Richard, who has seen a pow-wow, moves his feet in characteristic Indian step patterns. Some of the children join with him.

When the recording is repeated on another day, the children again freely join the rhythmic activities. Richard calls special attention to the brief melody by asking the class to sing it. He explains that the Indian melodies are usually very short and that they are chanted over and over as dancers perform. After another hearing, Richard tells the class that a real Indian taught this melody to Mr. Skilton, who arranged it so that many people could play it on instruments. When the children are thoroughly familiar with the music, Richard leads the class in a discussion of what they think the Indians are doing and then reveals the title of the piece.

Phyllis, a fourth grade student teacher, used "Rusty in Orchestraville" (Capitol DC-115) and "Peter and the Wolf" (RCA Victor DM-566). After one hearing, Phyllis pointed to pictures of each instrument or group of instruments as they were heard in the music. Later she let the children identify the instruments as they listened. On another day, she invited a trumpet player, a violinist, and a clarinetist to demonstrate their instruments for the class.

During the study of Independence Day by a sixth grade, Harvey, with the aid of the regular teacher, prepared a bulletin board display of historic pictures related to the occasion. All during the study, Harvey interspersed recordings of American patriotic songs (Victor Patriotic Album). Harvey gave bits of information about each song, but for the most part let the children read about them. He found good material in *Stories of Our American Patriotic Songs* by Lyon. The study came to a climax with Harvey's effective reading of a stanza from Scott's *Lay of the Last Minstrel*, "Breathes there a man with soul so dead who never to himself hath said, 'This is my own, my native land. . . .'"

For Further Development

1. Discuss the presentations of Misses Clark, Brown, and Hall and Phyllis, Richard, and Harvey. Indicate the strong and weak points of each.

2. Make a list of ways to arrest and hold the attention throughout the playing of a composition.

3. Analyze your listening habits. What do you listen for? Do you enjoy or appreciate music?

4. Class committees select one of the following projects for class demonstration and report:

a) Select three recordings for the third grade. Plan each presentation carefully, your purpose being to gain active listening.

b) Select three recordings of program music. Plan each presentation so that creative listening is possible.

c) Make a list of recordings for use in connection with a unit on the Colonial period. Indicate various means of creating interest or setting the mood for listening to the music of this period. See chapter 9.

d) Make a list of recordings for use in connection with a unit on Pioneer days. See chapters 12 and 13.

e) Make a list of recordings illustrating our patriotism, independence, humor. See chapters 11, 12, and 13.

f) Make a list of recordings relating to occupations. See list of recordings in chapters 11, 12, 13, and 14.

g) Arrange for a listening period to hear some of the recordings listed below. Make a list of those you desire for your record collection.

Recordings

RCA Victor Record Library for Elementary Schools. The library contains six albums (one for each grade) for listening. Notes for the teacher are included in each album.

"Our Singing World" series, Ginn and Company

"Together We Sing" series, Follett Publishing Company

"Music for Living" series, Silver Burdett Company

Composer's Story and Music (See catalogues of Vox, Period, and Columbia.)

Children's Record Guild and Young People's Records, The Greystone Corp., 100 Sixth Ave., New York 13, New York. Many records on a wide variety of subjects especially designed for children.

Film strips for the following are available (Consult your local or state film library): The Sleeping Beauty, William Tell, A Midsummer Night's Dream, The Swan Lake, The Bartered Bride, Scheherazade, Peter and the Wolf, Hansel and Gretel, The Nutcracker Suite, Peer Gynt, The Firebird, The Sorcerer's Apprentice.

The following Victor recordings are listed as suggestions for the type of material available for the various grades. The teacher should feel free to use them at any level when needed.

First Grade

LM-1752 March Militaire (Schubert), March of the Little Lead Soldiers (Pierne), and Funeral March of a Marionette (Gounod), played by Boston Pops Orchestra.

CAE-251 Humoresque (Dvorak), The Rosary (Nevin), The Swan (Saint-Saens), and Liebesleid (Kreisler), played by William Primrose, violinist with orchestra.

ERA-26 The Music Box (Liadoff), Pop Goes the Weasel, Turkey in the Straw, Pavanne (Gould), The Toy Trumpet (Scott), played by Boston Pops Orchestra.

CAL-142 Waltz in A-Flat (Brahms), Cradle Songs (Brahms), At Dawning (Cadman), Waltz (Tchaikovsky), played by Festival Concert Orchestra.

LM-1166 Ave Maria (Schubert), Folk Dance (Beethoven), Hebrew Melody (Achron), The Bumblebee (Rimsky-Korsakoff), played by Jascha Heifetz, violinist.

LPM-3120 Dixie (Emmett), Listen to the Mocking Bird, played by Cities Service Band of America.

CAE-141 Song of the Volga Boatmen, The Skater's Waltz (Waldteufel), Song of India (Rimsky-Korsakoff), played by Festival Concert Orchestra.

CAL-153 Barcarolle (Offenbach), Humoresque, Solitude (Tchaikovsky), Trumpet Prelude (Purcell), played by Star Symphony Orchestra.

Second Grade

ERA-29 Thais Meditation (Massenet), Träumerei (Schumann), and Minuet in G (Beethoven).

CAL-100 Carnival of the Animals (Saint-Saens).

LCT-1050 Adagio (Bach), Moment Musical (Schubert), Songs Without Words (Mendelssohn), Träumerei (Schumann), Evening Star (Wagner), Melody in F (Rubinstein), The Swan (Saint-Saens), Songs My Mother Taught Me (Dvorak), Flight of the Bumblebee (Rimsky-Korsakoff), Intermezzo (Granados), played by Pablo Casals, cellist.

CAL-142 Cradle Song, Waltz in A-Flat (Brahms), Perpetuum Mobile (Strauss), Cuckoo Clock (Castillo), Coronation March (Meyerbeer), Lohengrin, Prelude to Act 3 (Wagner), Sheep and Goat Walkin' to the Pasture (Guion), Hora Staccato (Dinicu), Chanson Triste, Polonaise (Tchaikovsky), and Drink to Me Only with Thine Eyes, played by Festival Concert Orchestra.

LM-69 Sousa Marches including El Capitan, High School Cadets, The Thunderer, Semper Fidelis, Washington Post, Stars and Stripes Forever, played by Boston Pops Orchestra.

CAL-121 Andante Cantabile (Tchaikovsky), Waltz (Tchaikovsky), The Last Spring (Grieg), played by Minneapolis Symphony Orchestra.

EPA-606 Guadalcanal March (Rodgers), Invercargill, Battle Hymn of the Republic, Pitter-Pat Parade, played by Cities Service Band of America.

LRM-7042 Chicken Reel, Fiddle Faddle (Anderson), played by Boston Pops Orchestra.

ERA-56 The Bells of Saint Mary's (Adams), Onward Christian Soldiers (Sullivan), The Lord's Prayer (Malotte), Holy, Holy, Holy (Dykes), sung by Robert Shaw Chorale.

THIRD GRADE

LM-1809 The Blue Danube and Tales from the Vienna Woods (Strauss), Orchestra.

LM-1800 Sweet and Low (Barnby), In the Gloaming (Harrison), None but the Lonely Heart (Tchaikovsky), The Rosary (Nevin), Through the Years (Youmans), Ave Maria (Schubert), All Thro' the Night (Welsh), Lullaby (Brahms), and Songs for Male Chorus (Schubert), sung by Robert Shaw Chorale.

LM-1238 Country Gardens, Shepherd's Hey, Molly on the Shore, Mock Morris, Early one Morning, Handel in the Stand, Irish Tune from Country Derry, Berceuse (Sibelius), Valse Triste (Sibelius), The Sleigh Ride (Mozart), Preludes 4 and 24 (Chopin), played by Percy Grainger, pianist, and Stokowski Orchestra.

ERA-53 Minuet in G (Paderewski), Prelude in C-Sharp Minor (Rachmaninoff), Allegro Appassionato (Saint-Saens), played by Jose Iturbi, pianist.

LM-8 Nutcracker Suite (Tchaikovsky), played by Philadelphia Symphony.

LBC-1028 Pomp and Circumstance March (Elgar), Finlandia (Sibelius), played by Royal Festival Orchestra.

LM-1910 Liebestraum (Liszt), Candle Light Waltz (Mason), Liebesleid, Liebesfreud, Caprice Viennois (Kreisler), Waltzes (Gounod), Espana Waltz, Tres Jolie Waltz (Waldteufel), Kammenoi-Ostrow (Rubinstein), Moonlight Sonata (1st Movement) (Beethoven), played by Boston Pops Orchestra.

CAL-192 To a Water Lily, To a Wild Rose (MacDowell), Prelude and Fugue in E-Flat (Bach), Largo (Handel), Pomp and Circumstance March (Elgar), Fest March (Wagner), played by Chicago Symphony Orchestra.

Fourth Grade

LM-1701 Amahl and the Night Visitors (Menotti).

ERA-32 Clair De Lune (Debussy), Liebestraum (Liszt), and Polonaise in A-Flat (Chopin), played by Jose Iturbi, pianist.

LM-1165 Invitation to the Dance (Weber), Dance of the Toy Pipes (Tchaikovsky), Russian Sailor's Dance (Glière), Polka (Smetana), Minuet (Boccherini), Brasileira (Milhaud), Hornpipe (Handel), Minute Waltz (Chopin), Gavotte (Gluck), La Danza (Liszt), played by First Piano Quartet.

LRM-7005 Finlandia (Sibelius), Espana Rapsodie (Chabrier), played by Boston Pops Orchestra.

LM-1004 Grand Canyon Suite (Grofé), played by Toscanini NBC Symphony.

LM-1093 Irish Suite includes The Irish Washerwoman, The Minstrel Boy, The Rakes of Mallow, The Wearing of the Green, The Last Rose of Summer, The Girl I Left Behind, played by Boston Pops Orchestra.

LM-7002 Peer Gynt Suite (Grieg), played by Boston Pops Orchestra.

LM-1803 Peter and the Wolf (Prokofieff), played by Boston Pops Orchestra.

LM-1872 Papillon, Shepherd Boy, March of the Dwarfs, Spring Dance, Berceuse, Albumblatt (Grieg), played by Artur Rubinstein, pianist.

LRM-7054 William Tell Overture and Semiramide Overture (Rossini), played by Toscanini and NBC Symphony Orchestra.

Fifth Grade

LP-87 Fantaisie-Impromptu in C-Sharp Minor, Waltz in D-Flat, Waltz in C-Sharp Minor, and Etude in C Minor (Chopin), played by Jose Iturbi, pianist.

LM-1798 Overtures of The Mikado, The Pirates of Penzance, H.M.S. Pinafore, Iolanthe, The Yeoman of the Guard (Gilbert and Sullivan), played by Boston Pops Orchestra.

LM-9017 Hungarian Dances Nos. 1-6 (Brahms), The Moldau (Smetana), Husitska Overture (Dvorak), played by Boston Pops Orchestra.

LM-84 Chopin favorites including Fantaisie-Impromptu in C-Sharp Minor, Nocturne in E-Flat, Etude in E, Waltz in C-Sharp Minor, Prelude in D-Flat, Three Ecossaises, Etude in G-Flat, played by First Piano Quartet.

LM-1118 The Sorcerer's Apprentice (Dukas), Dance Macabre (Saint-Saens), played by Toscanini and NBC Symphony.

LM-1774 Aurora's Wedding (Act III from The Sleeping Beauty by Tchaikovsky), played by Leopold Stokowski and his Symphony Orchestra.

LM-9005 Ballet Music from Faust, Waltzes (Gounod), Waltzes (R. Strauss), Ballet Music (Goldmark), Dance of the Hours (Ponchielli), Dance of the Camopristi (Wolf), Dance of the Buffoons (Rimsky-Korsakoff), played by Boston Pops Orchestra.

LM-1134 Capriccio Italien, 1812 Overture (Tchaikovsky), played by Boston Pops Orchestra.

LM-1069 Music from Carmen includes Prelude, Argonaise, Intermezzo, Dragoons of Alcala, Nocturne, Bullfight, Habanera, Changing the Guard, March of the Smugglers, Minuet, and Farancole (from L'Arlesienne Suite) and Gypsy Dance, played by New York Symphony Orchestra.

Sixth Grade

LM-6033 Rhapsody in Blue (Gershwin), played by Morton Gould, pianist with orchestra.

LRM-7002 Hungarian Rhapsody Nos. 1 and 2 (Liszt) and Hungarian Dances Nos. 2 and 3 (Brahms), played by Boston Pops Orchestra.

LM-162 Latin America includes The Continental, La Cumparsita, Carioca, Brazil, Jalousie, Malaguena, La Paloma, Ritual Fire Dance, played by Boston Pops Orchestra.

LM-1012 Mother Goose Suite and Bolero (Ravel), played by Boston Symphony Orchestra.

LM-1180 Til Eulenspiegel's Merry Pranks and Death and Transfiguration (R. Strauss), played by RCA Victor Orchestra.

LM-7009 Water Music Suite (Handel), played by Chicago Symphony Orchestra.

CAL-198 Polka (Stostakovich), Ritual Fire Dance (Falla), Dance Macabre (Saint-Saens), played by Luboshutz and Nemenoff, duo-pianists.

CAL-269 Kipling Songs includes On the Road to Mandalay (Speaks), Danny Deever (Damrosch), Gunga Din (Spross), Fuzzy Wuzzy (Speaks), Boats (McCall), sung by Norman Cordon, bass.

LRM-7035 Overture (Orpheus in Hades by Offenbach), Poet and Peasant Overture (Suppe), Moto Perpetuo (Paganini), Hora Staccato (Dinicu), played by Boston Pops Orchestra.

CHAPTER 5

Eyes to See

What about Reading?

Man had been making music for centuries before he developed a system of notation. In fact, it was not until around the tenth century A.D. that a system of symbols which could indicate rhythm as well as pitch began to emerge. Guido d'Arezzo was one of the originators of this system. Among the accomplishments of the Guidoian era are the invention of the staff and clefs, and the establishment of universal systems of pitch names, using letters and Latin syllables. Modern notation is an ingenious system which gives both specific and general information as to the composer's intent. For example, although pitches are indicated exactly, deeper meanings or feelings can be shown only in a general way. For the real message, the performer relies upon his own musicianship and sensitivity. These can only be acquired through experience in music. Symbols can only form a basis for interpretation. If we do not understand this limitation, we may become confused in our initial approach to music reading. It is well to remember that symbols came as a result of music and not the other way around.

Reading music is a complex skill extensively involving the ear and eye in translating abstract music symbols into pitch and time concepts. Although the road to mastery is long, it can be most interesting, stimulating, and rewarding for both teacher and pupil.

In the interest of clarity, it seems advisable to note that the term "music reading" means different things to different people. To some it means reading *at sight,* which term in itself is confusing. For example, does sight reading mean singing at sight, where the ear is the guide, or reading a piano score, where the ear is not necessarily involved? Does it mean reading a hymn tune or an operatic aria—a clarinet part for a simple march or for a symphony? Or does it mean reading music on two or more staves, where multiple rhythms and melodies are encountered, such as in a Liszt piano etude or an orchestral score for a Beethoven symphony? Certainly, sight-reading a single melodic line, unencumbered by additional melodies and rhythms, is not as complex as reading a full orchestral score. However we define it, reading music at sight is a highly complex skill, and great time and effort are required to develop proficiency. Consequently, we are not concerned with music sight-reading as such in the elementary grades.

We are, however, concerned with music reading. Since reading implies understanding, we are also concerned with simple elements of form. Webster defines reading as the ability to "take in the sense of, as of language, by interpreting the characters with which it is expressed." This clearly defines music reading at any level of difficulty. It all boils down to understanding the musical score. Defined in terms of the elementary school child, music reading is a developmental process of discovering the meaning of the symbols which represent music. The child is going through a similar process in language reading. There is no implication that one should be able to execute any rhythmic or tonal pattern with one sweep of the eye.

Why Teach Music Reading?

The reasons for teaching music reading may be summarized as follows:

1. *To further musical development and understanding.* Without the aid of the eye, all music learning must come by way of the ear. This retards musical growth.

2. *To make possible extensive exploration of music.* The ability
to read music enables us to enjoy more music, for we can assimi-
late a piece quickly and efficiently.

3. *To insure values that carry over into adulthood.* Skillful reading can provide a means of relaxation through pleasant do-it-
yourself activities. A leader or member of a church choir, civic
club, barber-shop group, or community chorus will find greater
enjoyment if he can read music easily and confidently.

How to Teach Music Reading

Following the path in man's development, we remember that
music was first learned by ear—the rote method. Man did not
begin with *do,* G, key signatures, and half, quarter, and eighth
notes. He began with music as a means of expression. From
experience came the need for symbols. Similarly, we first understand symbols through music and not the other way around. To
attempt an explanation of symbols without relating them to
music is to defeat, or at least to delay, the whole reading process.
Music cannot be explained except in terms of itself, for verbal
explanations are almost useless unless one has first experienced
music. To place music reading first is the opposite of what Lowell
Mason meant by "teaching the thing before the sign." Properly
taught, music reading may well be called *applied music,* for it is
not something separate or apart from music itself. This is why
group instruction in music in the schools should begin with
learning by ear. The ear is arrested by idiomatic expressions of
tone and time in music.

During the period of learning by ear, the teacher uses hand
levels to indicate the up and down movement of the melody. This
helps to give the child a visual concept of relative pitches. In
a sense, the child is reading music when he follows and imitates
the hand movement of the instructor. To be sure, there is a lack
of accuracy about such reading, but neither was there accuracy in
the ancient Greek and early Medieval symbols of music. They
merely indicated rising and falling inflections for the voice;
rhythm was governed by the words.

Also important for the reading program are rhythmic activities. As has already been noted, rhythms are first learned by listening. The symbols for tone lengths are introduced gradually, as they are associated with such familiar activities as walking, running, and skipping. Establishing a feeling for, and response to, various rhythmic patterns is highly important.

Wide experience in responding to tonal and rhythmic groups is the necessary background for music reading. This does not mean that they should be discontinued when formal reading activities are begun; on the contrary, they should continue and, if possible, be intensified. The initial and subsequent responses to tone and time should never be considered merely "things to do" or "busy-ness." They are meaningful activities directly related to, and contributing to, the reading of music. Again it must be pointed out that wide experience in responding to tonal and rhythmic groups, prior to the introduction of symbols, parallels the pattern of learning language.

Constant emphasis on "the thing before the sign" seems necessary in view of the fact that it is so easy for a teacher, especially an inexperienced one, to revert to his own approach to music reading: translating symbols into musical concepts. The child learns by the reverse process: translating tone and time concepts into symbols. Abstract symbols have meaning for the mature reader; they mean nothing at all to the inexperienced child. Also, the theoretical aspects or rudiments of music which are of importance to the teacher are not necessarily applicable to the child's present needs, and should be introduced only when necessary for the child's further development.

When music books are first placed in the hands of the child, his eyes are first employed in reading music. Since this is the child's first experience in seeing a musical score, he should be oriented and led to make important observations. The first of these has to do with the staff—the lines and spaces on which the notes are placed. Quarter and eighth notes are now identified and are associated with the rhythmic activities of walking and running. The high and low placements of notes on the staff are associated with hand levels representing relative pitches. Attention is called to the fact that the words for each line and verse appear under the staff and notes. At this stage of advancement, the observations are of a general nature, for the transition from ear to eye must be a gradual one.

The songs are still taught by rote, and the child is gradually led to make general observations about the notation: for example, here the melody and notes seem to walk up the lines and spaces, and here they run down; here there is a skip up or down, and the melody then turns in the opposite direction; one portion of the song looks like another part. Since these portions look alike, do they sound exactly the same, or is one part higher or lower than the other? Special attention must be directed toward the notes themselves. Since the children are in the process of learning to read language, they are naturally inclined to focus on the words. Although this is an additional aid in learning the song by rote, it does not contribute to music reading. Music reading involves a wider focal area than does language reading. From the very outset the child should be encouraged to look at both the words and the notes.

Questions may arise which demand specific answers. For example, if a child who has been taking piano lessons asks a question concerning the clef, key, or time signature, compliment the child, answer the question as briefly as possible, and move on to the business at hand. Most of the children are not yet ready to understand detailed explanations of such matters, but such general observations as suggested above orient the visual aspects of music reading.

Specific procedures are quite another matter, and on these there is a wide diversity of opinion. Some teachers are quite certain that Latin syllables are the correct approach to reading music; others are just as certain about letters or scale numbers. In fairness to these different approaches, it must be pointed out that good results have been obtained with each. In fact, *good teachers get results regardless of any so-called method.* The question is: does the approach result in the greatest comprehension for all the children? This is a matter for each individual teacher to decide. The decision should not be influenced by the way the teacher was taught. It should be made only after comparing the attainments of each approach in the elementary classroom. The

teacher who critically examines each approach—even each statement he makes—according to whether the children understand it
is on the road to a successful teaching career. It is not the author's
intention to dictate the best approach, for this would only fan
the fire of pointless argument. The purpose here is to present the
strong and weak points in each approach, leaving the decisions
to the judgment of the individual teacher.

The trend toward the instrumental approach is gaining mo-
mentum. Melody instruments, resonator bells, electric organs,
electronic pianos, and regular pianos are available and are more
plentiful today than in the past. For this reason, the use of
instruments, particularly of the keyboard type, is emphasized in
these pages. The reader is asked to consider carefully the instrumental approach in the light of its practicality and the avenues
for learning and understanding which it opens.

The Latin Syllables

As has been stated, Latin syllables were introduced by Guido
d'Arezzo around the tenth century. The large number of chant
melodies used in the church of the time was rapidly increasing,
and Guido's system was intended to be a memory aid for church
singers. It has been used continuously since Guido's time and is
popular in the American school today.

In using the system of syllables, we associate relative sounds
with syllable names. The name of the syllable helps to recall the
sound. Therefore, there is no point in learning the syllable name
unless it is associated with the sound. The syllables, as applied
to the moveable *do* system, are illustrated below.

The syllables for chromatic tones are shown below, in the key of E.

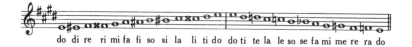

do di re ri mi fa fi so si la li ti do do ti te la le so se fa mi me re ra do

During the first grade, the syllables are usually learned by rote as an added stanza or as part of the text of a song. When books are given to the children, short tonal groups are identified by syllables, which the children sing. (See G. *Singing On Our Way* pp. 7, 8, 9, 11.) Later the children are taught to locate *do* from the key signature and to observe that *do, mi, so,* and *ti* are always placed alike, either on lines or spaces, depending upon the location of *do.* These locations may be observed in the illustration on page 106. As the children develop a feeling for the relative sound existing between the tones of a key, a neutral syllable such as *la* or *loo* is substituted for the syllables, and finally words are used.

There are many reasons for using syllables, one being that there is a different syllable name for each chromatic tone. Another reason is that each syllable, in itself, is euphonious. Finally, syllables help establish a feeling for the key. For example, E may be the keytone of E major or minor, the leading tone in F major or minor, or the third tone of the C scale. But as *ti* it is the leading tone of the scale of F.

On the unfavorable side of the ledger is the unfamiliarity of these syllables as terms. Children are not particularly interested in learning what they regard as meaningless nonsense syllables. They are useless in explaining intervals. Furthermore, their use makes it unnecessary for the student to understand the key signature, so that understanding of the musical score is limited. In some methods of instruction the staff is not even used. Instead, hand signs are used to represent the syllables, or a chart such as the following is employed.

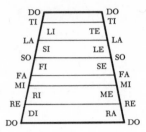

If syllables are employed, they should always be used in connection with the staff. Even when associated with staff notation, they may prove confusing because the same general staff picture can call forth different syllables as shown below.

Scale Numbers

The principle of scale numbers is the same as that of syllables: in both systems sounds are associated with a name. In this case, numbers are substituted for syllables. In their favor is their familiarity, their value in explaining the general classification of intervals, and their applicability to harmony.

On the other hand, numbers are not conducive to good vocal habits, and chromatics cannot be explained by their use. If the principle behind the employment of numbers is that sounds are associated with numbers, then the whole principle is defeated by such a contradiction as this:

If the student can sing the pitches represented by 3, 6, and 7, he does not need numbers or other crutches.

In the use of either syllables or numbers, emphasis is placed upon the recognition of tonal groups. This corresponds to a similar principle used in the recognition of words. Children are taught to recognize certain combinations of letters as words; in music they are taught to recognize groups of notes such as the following:

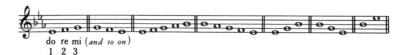

do re mi (*and so on*)
1 2 3

Letter Names

Many teachers believe that letter names are more practical than either syllables or numbers because they may be applied to both the staff and instruments. Although this is true, it is not the whole truth. For instance, in the illustration on page 108 it is impossible to sing the words "F-sharp"; one must sing "F" but think F-sharp. If the child can do this, he need not be bored by singing letter names. One of the chief objections to the use of letters is that all of them, with the exceptions of F and A, have the vowel sound of E, the most closed of the vowel sounds. Their use is conducive to vocal tension.

On her first day as an instructor, a student teacher observed the regular teacher drilling a fifth grade group on the staff letter names. The teacher pointed to various lines and spaces and the children responded by *saying* the letter names. This drill was of less value than the use of charts such as that shown on page 108. The children had no idea what sounds were represented or how these were related to the keyboard.

Another teacher was observed drilling the children on key signatures: "two sharps is the key of D, three flats is the key of E-flat." The children had no idea which degrees of the staff were affected or what the relationship was to singing or playing music.

The information which these two teachers were trying to convey is important but should not be presented as a separate body of knowledge. There is an element of truth in the statement "knowledge doesn't keep any better than fish." All rudiments of music must be applied if they are to have meaning for the children.

Instruments

We now come to the subject of instruments. Especially important are keyboard instruments such as the piano. More and more teachers are coming to believe that the piano is the basic instrument for all music learning. By playing himself, the student can gain broad concepts and a wide range of meaningful experiences in music. He will encounter meter, rhythm, and combinations of rhythms, as well as harmonies and their relation to melody and rhythm. Many teachers believe that use of the piano can illuminate the total concept of a musical composition, that is, the musical score.

Furthermore, they consider using the piano the only sensible approach to understanding such specific elements of notation as steps, half-steps, scales, flats, sharps, the key signature, and chords. Then, too, they consider the piano valuable from the standpoint of the ear. Ear training is the alpha and omega of all music learning and yet the greatest weakness in group instruction in music is probably in this area. This weakness is due to the difficulty of causing syllables and numbers to have real and accurate meaning for the children. By playing as well as singing tonal and rhythmic groups, the child becomes more vividly aware of music notation and its meaning. In ear training, frequent recall over a long period is important, and more repetitions are possible when the student is able to play than when we rely upon group singing.

As stated above, the ability to hear harmonies is best developed through keyboard experiences. Singers and instrumentalists who are not pianists encounter greater difficulty in hearing harmonies than do pianists. For example, the clarinetist hears the harmonic background of the music he plays in the band, but he sees only his part and may have little conception of the chords he is hearing. The pianist sees as well as hears the chords.

The first question that arises in considering the keyboard instrumental approach is whether enough instruments are available. A few fortunate schools have several pianos in the music room. Others have only one piano or a portable reed organ. Even though a school has only one piano available, it can afford multiple sets of melody bells or resonator bells. These are especially useful at the first grade level.

The second question which arises concerns the technical aspects of playing the instrument. In other words, is it possible to teach a child to play the piano in group instruction? The answer to this question is that this has been done, and is being done, both with children and adults. However, this is usually impractical because of a lack of pianos and because other phases of the music program would be neglected. What, then, is the aim of the keyboard approach? It is to teach children to *play short tonal groups as an aid to hearing and as a means of understanding the musical score.*

The same short passages which are taught vocally by syllables or numbers may be played, and with no greater effort. For example, many songs end with *mi, re, do* (3, 2, 1). It is a simple matter to teach a child to play such a pattern by ear; he merely needs to imitate the teacher. Since the child is not, at first, reading from the staff, the key, sharps, and flats are not a problem. After a few experiences, the teacher explains that in moving from 3 to 2 and 2 to 1 he skips a key on the piano. With this information, and with a minimum of guidance, the child may *play the passage beginning on any key of the piano.* When the child has developed confidence in such explorations of the keyboard, the letter names of the piano keys and corresponding staff positions may be gradually introduced. This may be done very simply by playing the above passage (3, 2, 1) in the keys of C, F, and G.

In the same manner, other scale passages found in songs may be re-enforced by playing them on the piano or melody bells. For example, the melodic passages 1, 2, 3, 4, 5 and 5, 4, 3, 2, 1 of the scale are found in many songs. These, as well as other new tonal

patterns, should be introduced by ear, this being followed by
playing by the student. For example, the pattern 1, 2, 3, 4, 5
may be introduced in the key of G or C. The child is then led
to discover that in playing he skipped a key between each two
adjacent scale numbers except 3 and 4. He must do the same
thing in playing the passage starting on any key on the piano.
Starting on F, he discovers the need for a black key (3 to 4, A to
B-flat). In like manner, the child is led to discover the scale from
song material found in the various song series.[1]

By this keyboard approach, the child discovers the whole-step
and the half-step, the interval pattern of the scale, sharps and
flats, the key signature, and the reason and necessity for these.
At the same time, staff notation is gradually taking on real meaning for him, as he learns to apply portions of it in a very practical
way. By playing simple passages and singing them while they
are played by others, *he is eventually able to sing them without
dependence upon the piano or upon the group.*

We should not overlook another advantage of the instrumental
approach. It enables one to hear and understand chords more
easily. For example, having played the passage 1, 2, 3, 4, 5, the
child may play 1, 3, 5, both successively (as a melody) and simultaneously (as a chord). When he has learned this one chord he
has, in a sense, learned three: the I chord in C (C E G) is also
the IV chord in G and the V chord in F. The I chord in F (F A C)
is also the IV chord in C and the V chord in B-flat. The I chord
in G (GBD) is also the IV chord in D and the V chord in C.
The children may be taught to chord to many of the songs found
in the various song series and will have as much fun doing it as
learning "Chopsticks."

How can the child be taught chord progression—that is, how
to move the fingers from one chord to another? This, too, is done
by imitating the teacher. Actually, the finger movement is very
simple, and can be established as a habit when the child is young.
For example, in changing from a I to a V chord in *any key*, the
fingering is the same as shown by the following in the key of C.

---

[1] The idea presented here is carried out in detail in the companion to this
book: Raymond Elliott, *Learning Music* (Columbus: Charles E. Merrill Books,
Inc., 1960), chaps. 1-5.

How does the child know when to change chords? He doesn't! This, too, is introduced by ear. The teacher holds up one, four, or five fingers to represent the I, IV, and V chords. Or the Roman numerals (after they have been introduced) may be written on the chalkboard and pointed to as needed. To assure active participation, all children not actually chording at instruments should either finger the chords on their desks, on cardboard or dummy keyboards, or imitate the instructor in indicating the chord changes. When a child is able to anticipate the chord change, he may take the teacher's place, indicating chords to the class. When their ears are guiding the chord changes for most of the children, no indication of chords is necessary.

Chords for many songs are indicated in the Silver Burdett and the Follett song series. The children may follow chords indicated in the book as soon as they can chord several songs by ear in two or three keys—that is, as soon as finger habits have been established.

Although chording has been discussed here in connection with the piano keyboard, it is not limited to the piano. Three children may play the chords on one set of melody or resonator bells. The teacher simply shows each child where to move for each chord change and then indicates the change of harmony as he does with the piano. The autoharp and other chording instruments also should be used.

The use of chording is highly recommended, whether or not the instrumental approach is used. For example, playing chords as children are reading an unfamiliar song, or endeavoring to hear a difficult passage, is a distinct aid. Furthermore, sounding chords on the accented beat of a measure is an excellent means of maintaining the tempo, and it gives the children support and confidence. Hearing the harmony is an aid in hearing the melody. In fact, most so-called music reading in later years will be done with an accompaniment—in glee clubs in junior and senior high schools, in community clubs or chorus, and in church choirs.

Charts which may be used in connection with the instrumental approach are invaluable aids. The teacher may make these himself using window blinds. For example, it is easy to make a chart showing the relation between the keys, or the holes or valves on an instrument, and the lines and spaces of the staff. The one below is suggested for use with the piano, song bells, or resonator bells.

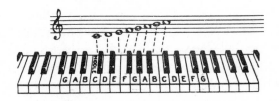

Contributory Reading Activities

Although they are usually given subordinate status in the music reading program, the following activities are highly recommended as directly contributing to good reading and to developing an understanding of the music score.

a) After teaching a song by rote and stressing its tonal and rhythmic patterns, play a vocal recording of it as the children follow the notation. They should clap the rhythm of the melody as they follow the printed page. If there is an instrumental recording, it too should be played as the children clap to the themes as given in the song or written on the chalkboard. A good example is "Come, Let's Be Merry" (G. *Singing and Rhyming*, p. 18) and the instrumental version recorded by Victor in Rhythm Album Six.

b) Children may follow the notation of songs which are not being learned. The teacher may sing these or recordings may be used. Repeated hearings are important. In one hearing the rhythm patterns may be stressed and in another the tonal groups. For example, the teacher may call attention to scale passages or skips, to parts which are alike in rhythm or melody, to sequential patterns, or to contrasting passages. Any song which is not being learned may be used, but especially recommended are such songs as "He Shall Feed His Flock" (S. *Music Near and Far*, p. 56) and "Jesu, Joy of Man's Desiring" (G. *Singing Together*, p. 98).

c) In all rhythmic activities, whether or not they are done in connection with a song, the piano, or a recording, the children should first become acquainted with the music by ear. The rhythm patterns should be written on the board and the children should follow the teacher's pointer as they clap the patterns. The children may then walk, run, or skip to the music.

d) In listening activities, themes should be reproduced or written on the chalkboard. Some of the themes are given in the song series, and others may be found in record albums or music appreciation books. One teacher has made a five-by-eight card file of themes to be used in rhythmic and listening activities in the fifth grade. She uses these themes as a supplementary aid to reading music.

By following such suggestions as those offered above, all music activities may be made to contribute appreciably to the reading program and to a better understanding of the musical score. Music reading is thus being learned at all times. A place in each lesson plan should be reserved for this sort of reading activity, so that *music reading is not an isolated study, but an integral part of the entire music program.*

Regardless of the approach used, a response to tonal and rhythmic groups should be developed first by ear, then by sight. The steps in developing music reading may be summed up as follows:

1. We *hear*, then sing and clap the rhythm.
2. We *hear* and *see*, then sing and clap the rhythm.
3. We *hear*, *see*, sing, and clap simultaneously.

Reading Part Songs

Reading or singing two or more parts can present perplexing problems for both teacher and student, or it can be the most interesting and rewarding of the music activities. The idea that the child's problem in singing in parts is due to weakness in reading is somewhat erroneous; many children and adults who cannot read music can sing harmony parts. The problem is rather one of hearing. How can the child who has had no aural experiences other than the unison, suddenly be expected to hear and sing his part against another? It must be remembered that training the ear requires time, just as developing any skill does. Exposing the ear to harmonic backgrounds should be a part of any program from the very outset.

What musical background is essential for success in part singing? The general answers to this question are:

a) The ability to sing many simple songs with confidence.

b) The ability to respond to various rhythm patterns.

c) An elementary understanding of the notation representing tone and time.

d) *Wide experience in hearing harmonies played on the piano, song bells, and/or other chording instruments during the singing and reading activities.*

Most song series introduce part singing in the fourth grade. The introductory songs usually contain short cadential passages in parallel thirds or sixths. However, this should not be the child's first experience in hearing more than one part. The following suggestions will provide the necessary background in aural experience. They describe this background more specifically than the four general answers given above.

a) As soon as second grade children are sure of a song, the teacher may sing or play a part a third or sixth higher or lower than the melody. This works especially well on the last three or four notes of the final cadence. When the children discover what has been going on, the teacher may play the two parts for them. Furthermore, the parts may be played by the children on the piano, song bells, or melody instruments such as the song flute.

The children may learn such passages by imitating the teacher. It is important to become accustomed to hearing the total effect produced by the combined tones. Examples of the type of cadences referred to may be found in G. *Singing Every Day*, pages 40*a*, 63, 64*b*, 65, 77, and 79.

b) Try singing descant figures against well known rounds which are taught by rote. Excellent examples may be found in *Our First Songs to Sing with Descants* by Beatrice Krone, published by Neil A. Kjos, Chicago. When the children are familiar with the melody, the descant may be taught by the teacher who sings or plays it as the children sing the melody. The children may then be taught to play the descant figure on the piano, song bells, or melody instrument. Later a few children may sing the descant while the rest of the class sings the round melody. The tempo may be established by singing or playing the descant figure twice prior to the entrance of the melody. Piano accompaniment and chords for the autoharp are provided with the Krone descants referred to above. This activity is recommended for third graders.

c) Occasional use of two-part rounds in the third grade is also recommended. Since the conflict of words is a disturbing and confusing factor for the beginner, it is suggested that the first experiences involve the piano or some other melody instrument playing the second entrance of the round as the class sings. This should be soft enough that the children are not disturbed by the "competition" and yet loud enough for them to discover that something interesting is happening. The initial participation of the children may be humming or singing with *loo* as they follow the piano on the second entrance. Finally, the words may be sung by the teacher and by divisions of the class.

After such general and specific experiences as those suggested above, the children are usually ready for song material found in the fourth grade books of the various series. It is recommended that initial experiences be limited to parallel thirds only or parallel sixths only. The former is usually easier for the beginner. Skips wider than the third are difficult at this stage. A difficult skip for the beginner is found in G. *Singing Together*, page 51. In the first measure, the lower voice skips to a tone a half-step higher than the one just sung by the upper voice. Such skips are not wrong, but they are not recommended until students have had considerable experience in singing parts. Songs where the lower part remains stationary are recommended to help those singing the lower part get started. A good example is G. *Singing Together,* page 7.

One problem in part singing is the difficulty of *hearing* two or more parts. Playing one part to "see how it goes" or learning each part separately is not the answer. When additional hearings are necessary, both parts should be played. If the children have difficulty in hearing a particular passage, it is perfectly all right to play both parts and emphasize the difficult one. This may be done as the children sing. Using chording instruments on part songs is also highly recommended. Another valuable aid is playing recordings of part songs.

Various types of part songs are classified below.

1. *One part remaining stationary as another voice moves.* This simple type of song is excellent for the beginner.

   G. Singing Together, pp. 19*b*, 54*r*
   S. Music Near and Far, p. 166*r*
   S. Music in Our Country, p. 66
   F. Music Across Our Country, p. 49

2. *Parallel thirds, with no skips larger than the third.* As suggested elsewhere, this type of voice movement is appropriate for the beginner.

   G. Singing Every Day, pp. 40*ar*, 63, 65
   G. Singing Together, pp. 25*r*, 68*r*, 176
   F. Music Through the Year, p. 16
   F. Voices of the World, p. 141
   S. Music Near and Far, pp. 45, 142
   S. Music in Our Country, p. 161

3. *A simple melody which moves mostly scale-wise, against another voice.*

   F. Music Across Our Country, p. 46*r*
   F. Voices of America, p. 30
   S. Music Near and Far, pp. 106*b*, 115, 138

4. *Songs in which thirds and sixths predominate but other intervals occur.* These are more difficult and should be used only after the children have had considerable experience in part singing.

F. Music Through the Year, pp. 14r, 84b, 89r
F. Voices of America, pp. 26a, 26b, 27, 35, 45, 83r, 90, 112r, 126, 159, 184
S. Music Near and Far, pp. 36br, 95r, 102, 122, 124br, 128
S. Music in Our Country, pp. 7r, 10, 19, 22, 41r, 69r, 72, 109r
S. Music in Our Country, pp. 126, 130, 136, 145, 148r, 150, 151, 152, 164, 168b, 176, 186, 196, 198r, 211
G. Singing Together, pp. 10a, 12b, 13, 24ar, 45r, 46r, 51, 60b, 77r, 79, 88a, 94ar, 95, 113, 147b, 148, 157r, 183r

5. *Songs using imitation—one voice imitates another.* These songs are called *canons*. They differ from rounds in that the melody does not have to be repeated. Listening to the recording while following the voice parts is very helpful in learning such songs. They are to be introduced in the manner suggested for rounds. Playing the instrumental parts given with some of the songs is highly recommended.

F. Music Through the Year, pp. 36, 111r, 112r
F. Voices of America, pp. 22r, 23r, 64r, 11r, 186
S. Music in Our Country, pp. 60, 78
G. Singing Every Day, p. 176r

6. *Three-part songs.* The parts are not to be taught separately. If the children become discouraged, it may be that the selections are too difficult or that the children have insufficient experience in two parts. If additional hearings are necessary, the parts should be played simultaneously. Playing the chords on the piano or some other chording instrument is recommended, as is listening to recordings.

S. Music in Our Country, pp. 6, 134r
S. Music Around the World, pp. 2, 6, 8, 10, 17r, 26r, 45, 58, 95, 96, 98, 167, 201r
G. Singing Together, pp. 188, 192r
G. Singing in Harmony, pp. 41r, 52r, 73r, 93, 104r, 105r, 114r, 152, 154, 176

Form in Music

Greater comprehension in reading music is possible through an understanding of form in music. Basic structure in musical form is exemplified by the folk song. When writing in larger forms, composers merely extend or enlarge upon the fundamental elements of form as found in the simple melodies of the untrained artisan. The general outline or framework of a musical structure, whether small or large, is basically simple.

Let us begin with the fact that music *makes sense.* Try to recall a group of unrelated tones in an unrhythmical setting. Most people find this difficult, for tone and time must be put together in a logical order if music is to *make sense.* How this is accomplished by the composer is a technical matter with which we are not concerned. In support of the claim that musical structure is simple, let us examine three well known melodies and observe certain principles of form which are found in both folk and art music. Such observations can measurably contribute to speed in reading and comprehending.

Skip to My Lou

Traditional Singing Game

This easy-to-remember melody is built from a single motive consisting of two tones, C and A-flat, which are found in the first measure. The idea is repeated in the second measure, reversing the direction of the skip of a third (from C up to E-flat, instead of down to A-flat). Variety is added by decreasing note lengths on the first beat (sixteenths instead of an eighth) and increasing note length on the second beat (quarter note instead of eighths). The third and fourth measures are a repetition of the first two, beginning on a lower pitch. Such repetition of a musical idea at a higher or lower pitch is called a *melodic sequence.*

The fifth and sixth measures are an *exact repetition* of measures one and two. The seventh measure begins, like the third, on B-flat, but moves along the scale instead of skipping, then turns toward the keytone, A-flat. The rhythm continues the characteristic pattern established earlier. Beginning at measure nine, the entire melody is repeated, but given variety by slight rhythmic changes.

The repetition of this simple two-tone motive constitutes a larger idea, four measures long, which is called a *phrase.* The first phrase (measures 1-4), known as the *antecedent* phrase, ends at the end of the fourth measure on a tone of the dominant seventh chord, giving a feeling of incompleteness. A second phrase (measures 5-8), called the *consequent* phrase, ends at the end of the eighth measure on a tone of the tonic chord, producing a harmonic feeling of repose. The two phrases together constitute a *period,* which is analogous to a compound sentence. When the first part of the consequent phrase is an exact repetition of the first part of the antecedent, as in this example, the period is said to be in *parallel construction.* When the consequent phrase is different from the antecedent, the period is in *contrasting construction.* Regardless of its construction, the period may be designated by the letter A.

The period may be extended to form a double period. When this is the case, the two periods bear the same relationship to each other as do the antecedent and consequent phrases of the single period. A good example of this is in "Prayer of Thanksgiving."

Prayer of Thanksgiving

Dutch

It will be observed that the second phrase (see phrase line) ends on the dominant chord, that the third phrase is different from the first, and that the fourth phrase brings the melody to a complete close by ending on the tonic. This, then, is a double period in contrasting construction.

Another example of an entire tune constructed from a small idea or motive is found in "When Love is Kind."

When Love Is Kind

Old Irish Melody

This entire melody is built out of the melodic and rhythmic idea announced in the first two measures. In measures three and five the interval from C is expanded (C to F; C to G; C to A), and the original idea is continued at a higher pitch after each expansion. Such expansion is known as *augmentation*. Beginning at measure nine, the skip from C is extended to the octave and the melody continues by sequence. At measures eleven and thirteen, the interval from C is contracted. Such contraction is known as *melodic diminution.*

These three melodies show how music is put together with melodic and rhythmic logic and therefore makes sense. The principles of structure found in these melodies are highly important for they also are used in the larger forms of music. They may be summarized as follows:

1. A musical composition is developed by an imaginative treatment of a germinal idea or ideas. The idea may be repeated at any pitch, or may be inverted—that is, it may move in the opposite direction. The intervals may be enlarged by augmentation or contracted by diminution. Tones may be made longer or shorter. Such treatment is not limited to the melody, but applies to all voices and/or instruments in the composition. However or whenever these devices are used, *unity* through repetition is the result.

2. A second principle is *contrast.* We have already seen that the second phrase of a period or the third phrase of a double period may be in contrast to the first phrase. The composer uses contrasts to achieve variety and to hold interest. He may change the key from major to minor and vice versa, or he may write an entirely different melody—as in the following:

Swedish Folk Song

This is an example of *binary* or two-part form. Although the second half of the melody differs melodically and rhythmically from the first, the two seem related in style. The contrasting second portion may be designated by the letter B. Although the binary form is not used extensively as such, the idea of contrasting melodies and harmonies is widely used. The principle of contrast is extensively employed in the *ternary* or three-part form, a simple example of which follows:

From Symphony No. 9 Beethoven

The contrasting idea is found at B. This form—*statement, digression,* and *restatement*—is used extensively in the larger works of music on a much greater scale.

Concluding the discussion on the general structure of music, it must be stressed that no set formulas can be applied to the various types of composition, for artists cannot be confined to any sort of strait-jacket expression. Any formula must be considered as a general outline from which a composer may work, but to which he is not necessarily bound. In listening to music, it is not necessary for the layman to identify the principles set forth here by name. He should know what to listen for rather than what to call it.

Teachers in Action

The following examples are actual cases demonstrating various approaches to teaching music reading. The reader is asked to judge for himself which will have more meaning for children.

Miss Hawkins, a regular second grade teacher, began playing a simple melody on the resonator bells just after the children came into the room from recess.

Child: "What are you playing?"

Miss Hawkins: "A song I know. Do you like it? . . . What does the music tell you to do? . . . All right, you may walk as I play."

This child and several other children began to walk to the steady beat of the tune. Without comment, Miss Hawkins played the same melody using eighth notes. Some of the children began to run, but others continued to walk. Miss Hawkins switched back to walking music and then again to running music. This time, all the children responded by running. Without saying a word, the teacher had caused the children to listen and respond.

A child who had been watching Miss Hawkins: "Could I play?"

Miss Hawkins: "I believe you could. Place your hand on mine and we'll play it together first."

Other children gathered around to observe and soon the child was playing the melody in quarter notes. Miss Hawkins began walking to the music and a few children followed. Then Miss Hawkins began to run and presently one of the children told the girl playing the bells to make the music run. At first she faltered, but Miss Hawkins instructed her to strike each key twice and to go faster. Soon she was trying to surprise Miss Hawkins and the children by changing from running to walking music.

The next day, Miss Hawkins had the children find "Running and Walking" (G. *Singing on Our Way*, p. 17). They observed the walking and running notes and made hand-level pictures of the melody. While they were doing this, Miss Hawkins began to play the melody on the resonator bells. Instantly the class recognized it as the melody they had played and sung the day before. The children sang it with numbers and several learned to play the four-toned melody.

Miss Goddard, who preferred the Latin syllables, introduced "The Dairy Maids" (F. *Music Round the Town*, p. 22). After locating the position of *do, mi,* and *so,* the children attempted to sing the melody by syllables. Miss Goddard made the following observations:

1. The children became extremely preoccupied with notes. Because of this, all sense of rhythm was lost, and the song seemed to have neither melody nor rhythm.

2. Sometimes the correct pitch was sung, but with the wrong syllable. At other times, the correct syllable was used, but on the wrong pitch.

3. Some of the children were able to sing the scale passages correctly without regard for syllables.

Miss Goddard concluded that the children needed to establish a stronger association between the syllable names and the relative sounds. Knowing that staff notation was a deterrent, she wrote the syllables on the chalkboard and for several days drilled the children by pointing to the syllables as the children sang. With interest at a low ebb, Miss Goddard pointed to the syllables representing the melody of "The Dairy Maids," and the children did surprisingly well in following the tune. When they attempted to sing the melody from the book, however, the original problems were evident.

Being a conscientious teacher and desiring to find the solution to these problems, Miss Goddard found an approach entirely new to her in the "Message to Teachers" on page 130 of *Music Round the Town* (F). She concluded that her children were not ready to use syllables on the first attempt at singing a song. Realizing that syllables, like all music notation, came about as a result of musical experience, Miss Goddard began to teach the song by rote and then to use syllables on short, familiar tonal patterns. Interest increased and the children became more proficient in applying the syllables to staff notation. The teaching and learning process had been reversed and the results were far more rewarding.

Miss Flowers, a regular second grade teacher, selected "This Old Man" (S. *Music in Our Town*, p. 109). The song was taught by rote and the children played the rhythmic nick-nacks to the various verses. Miss Flowers played the chords as the children sang. Then one day, Miss Flowers played the last three notes of the song. The children observed that this sounded like "rolling home" and found the passage in the song. As time went on, Miss Flowers used the passage in the following ways:

1. She numbered the fingers of the right hand from thumb (number 1) to little finger (number 5), and the children played on their desks and sang the passage by number, beginning on number three (3, 2, 1). Attention was called to the fact that both the words and the music seemed to take the old man home—like home base in baseball.

2. When finger habits were established, the children learned to play the passage on dummy keyboards by imitating Miss Flowers. Finally, they played it on the piano and melody bells, using the letter names A, G, and F. Miss Flowers helped the children locate the corresponding staff letter names by using a chart similar to the one shown in the example on page 114.

3. Miss Flowers explained that a half-step on the piano was played by one key and the next (white or black) and that a whole-step left one unemployed key (white or black) between the two played. The children observed the whole-steps between 3 and 2 and 2 and 1. With this knowledge, the *children could play the passage when found in a song no matter what the key.*

4. The melodic passage was played beginning on B (B, A, G) by observing the whole-steps. The children learned the name of the new piano key (B) and the corresponding staff letter name and sang the letter names.

5. The passage was also played beginning on E (E, D, C). The names of the new keys were learned along with the corresponding staff letter names.

Through this one simple passage, the children became oriented to the keyboard (piano or melody bells), and learned the letter names of white keys and corresponding staff names. Having heard the passage many times, the children knew the sound of 3, 2, 1 of the scale. They listened for the passage in all new songs.

In like manner, Miss Flowers introduced other scale passages found in songs. One of these was 1, 2, 3, 4, 5, which is found in "This Old Man." The children learned about the half-step between 3 and 4 and the whole-steps between all other pairs of tones. When played in the key of F ("This Old Man"), the half-step between 3 and 4 necessitated a black key on 4. In explaining this, Miss Flowers directed attention to the song and the sign on the line B. This was a flat, and it meant that B should be played a half-step lower. Thus, it was a simple matter to explain the B-flat in the key signature. The children listened for this passage in new songs and played it, using their knowledge of steps and half-steps.

In addition to discovering 3, 2, 1; 1, 2, 3; 1, 2, 3, 4, 5; and 5, 4, 3, 2, 1, in many songs, the children found other combinations of these scale numbers. The 1, 3, 5 melodic passage was sounded simultaneously and named the tonic chord. The children played this chord on the piano, melody bells, and autoharp, as Miss Flowers suggested, using it to accompany "This Old Man" and a number of other songs.

In similar manner, other melodic passages and chords were lifted from song content and emphasized. Since new material came from songs being learned and since it was applied immediately to other familiar songs, the interest of the children remained high. Miss Flowers was surprised that the children learned to play "Happy River" so quickly (G. *Singing on Our Way*, p. 104*ar*).

For Further Development

1. Discuss the presentations of Misses Hawkins, Goddard, and Flowers. Indicate the strong and weak points of each.

2. Discuss the use of syllables, numbers, and instruments as approaches to reading. Which of these seem most logical and practical?

3. Make a list of recordings (vocal and instrumental) which may be used to contribute to the reading activity. Indicate the source of the notation. See the recorded material listed in each of the chapters of Part Two.

4. Class committees select one of the following for class demonstration:

a) Select six recorded part songs (one from each of the classifications given in this chapter) and play them as the class follows the notation in the book.

b) Select three recordings of national dances from chapter 9. Present and play them as if the class were a third grade group. Can you identify the form of these selections?

c) Select three recordings of national dances from chapter 9. Present and play them as if the class were a fifth grade group. Relate to social studies. Can you identify the form of these selections?

d) Select three second grade songs. Identify the phrases with letters and indicate the form.

e) Select three fourth grade songs. Identify the phrases with letters and indicate the form.

Recordings

a) Songs which the children may follow as the records are played.

G. Singing on Our Way, p. 83*r*, 154 (Victor Rhythm Band Album).

G. Singing and Rhyming, p. 18*ar* (or Victor Rhythm Album Six).

G. Singing Every Day, p. 54 (Victor Listening Album Four), 88*r*, 116*br*.

G. Singing Together, pp. 74*r*, 97*r*, 98*r*, 104*r*, 106*r*, 131*r*, 160*r*, 197*r*, 197*r*-212*r*.

G. Singing In Harmony, pp. 73*r*, 108*r*, 121*r*, 127*r*, 134 (Victor Christmas Album), 135 (Victor Christmas Album), 142*br*.

S. Music Near and Far, pp. 34*r*, 36*br*, 56*r*, 166*r*, 18 and 41 (Victor Listening Album Four.)

S. Music in Our Country, pp. 41*r*, 134*r*.

S. Music Around the World, pp. 22*r*, 26*r*, 34*br*, 44*r*, 46*r*, 101*r*, 118*r*, 165*r*, 181*r*.

F. Music Through the Year, pp. 19*r*, 20*r*, 21*r*, 36*r*, 89*r*, 111*r*, 112*r*.

F. Music Across Our Country, pp. 46*r*, 56*r*, 60*r*, 115*r*.

F. Voices of America, pp. 22*r*, 23*r*, 36*r*, 64*r*, 83*r*, 111*r*, 122*r*.

b) *Notation (instrumental) which children may follow while listening to the recording.*

G. Singing Every Day, pp. 72*r*, 84*r*, 89*r*, (or Victor Listening Album Four), 90*r*.

G. Singing Together, p. 106*r*.

G. Singing in Harmony, pp. 124*r*, 130*r*, 212-237 (Peer Gynt Suite, Victor LM-7002).

S. Music Now and Long Ago, p. 108 (Victor Listening Album Two).

S. Music Near and Far, pp. 65 (Victor Listening Album Two), 146 (Victor LM-69).

S. Music in Our Country, pp. 9 (Grand Canyon Suite, Victor LM-1004), 161 (Victor, CAE-240), 15 (Clair de Lune, Victor ERA-32).

S. Music Around the World, pp. 112 (Rhapsody in Blue, Victor LM-6033), 187 (Victor Rhythm Album Six).

F. Music Through the Year, pp. 41 (Dance Macabre, Victor ERA-15), 60-61 (Nutcracker Suite, Victor WRY-9000), 150 (Victor LM-69).

F. Voices of America, pp. 183 (Victor Listening Album Four).

F. Voices of the World, p. 54 (Peer Gynt Suite, Victor LM-7002).

Songs

a) *Songs in which the tonic and dominant harmonies are employed.*

Put Your Little Foot	G. Singing Together, p. 31*r*
Skip to My Lou	G. Singing and Rhyming, p. 44 S. Music in Our Town, p. 59 S. Music Through the Day, p. 68
Hot Cross Buns	G. Singing on Our Way, p. 45*ar*
Paw-Paw Patch	G. Singing Every Day, p. 51*r* F. Music Through the Year, p. 15*r* S. Music Through the Day, p. 14

Here We Go Round
   the Mulberry Bush   G. The First Grade Book, p. 49

Luby Loo   G. The First Grade Book, p. 50r

b) *Songs in which the tonic, subdominant, and dominant chords are
employed.*

Twinkle, Twinkle, Little Star	G. Singing on Our Way, p. 106a
	S. Music Through the Day, p. 20a
	F. Music 'Round the Clock, p. 4
On Top of Old Smoky	S. Music Around the World, p. 57
Old McDonald Had a Farm	G. Singing and Rhyming, p. 136r
Old Folks at Home	G. Singing Together, p. 70
	F. Music Through the Year, p. 136r
Brahms's Lullaby	G. Singing Together, p. 77r
	S. Music in Our Country, p. 168
	G. Singing on Our Way, p. 83
Silent Night[2]	S. Music in Our Country, p. 211
	F. Music Round the Town, p. 85

---

[2] For an extensive list of songs employing various chords see Raymond Elliott,
Learning Music (Columbus: Charles E. Merrill Books, Inc., 1960).

CHAPTER 6

Minds to Create

What about Creativity?

Because of his power to reason, man is by far the most creative of earth's creatures. Man's accomplishments in all areas of human endeavor are proof of his creative nature.

In the creative process man begins with things already in existence. The physicist begins with matter, the biologist with cells, the chemist with the composition and transformation of matter. The initial step in creativity, then, is one of discovery. Having made the discovery, man's curiosity leads him to experiment and thus accumulate knowledge. He applies imagination to this knowledge, tests with reason, and then the creation comes into being.

The extent and quality of man's creative powers depend upon his discoveries, observations, experiences, reasoning capacity, and imagination. Continuous expansion in these areas through the ages has vastly enlarged man's power to create and thus keeps our copyright and patent offices far behind. Because of a child's limitations, his creative efforts, like man's early attempts, will be relatively crude and elementary. However simple, creativity is just as essential for a child's development as it has been for the march of civilization.

With these thoughts in mind, it is evident that the creative activity is not confined to music. Its application in music, however, has the same possibilities in any subject—freshness, originality, newness, uniqueness, ingenuity, and individual inspiration. Music is an especially creative art, for imagination is a quality equally essential to the composer, to those who re-create his work (performers), and to the ultimate beneficiary—the listener and "appreciator."

Why Teach Creativity?

The answers to this question may be summed up as follows:

1. Man is by nature creative; Americans are particularly productive.[1]

2. Creativity is the basis for progress in all human development. It is essential for individual growth.

3. Self-expression[2] is an absolute necessity, and creative expression is an excellent means of developing a well-rounded, well adjusted individual. For this reason schools should provide many avenues for it. Activities in music afford ample opportunities for such expression.

4. Teaching creatively helps the instructor to avoid an archaic presentation of subject matter and consequently to hold the student's interest. It makes otherwise dry facts, figures, and dates take on living significance.

5. Creative activities in music promote the understanding and appreciation of music.

In conclusion, it should be pointed out that the creative process is at work when the child immerses himself so completely in an activity that it becomes uniquely his own.

How to Teach Creatively

As may be evident from the foregoing, *the focal point of creativeness in the classroom is an alert and imaginative teacher.* Like

---

[1] See "American Characteristics," chapter 11.

[2] See "Need for Self-Expression," chapter 1.

a radio station, he transmits stimulating wave signals of curiosity, inspiration, and imagination. He radiates confidence, encouragement, and respect for the individual. He creates interest by questions, class discussions, pictures, illustrations, and places the children in the center of situations at hand. As an illustration of this type of teaching, witness the following actual occurrence in a high school English class.

The class complained about "stupid" theme topics. As an example, one student mentioned *A Winter Day*. The teacher replied, "Oh, that's a very interesting topic, but like other subjects, we must use our imagination. For example, let's imagine that it is the most severe day of winter. What do you see, hear, feel, taste, and smell?"

The students listed the following which they saw in their minds' eyes: hungry birds outside the window, barren trees laden with ice, snow on distant hills, a pond where boys and girl were skating (one fell down), a car stuck in a snow drift, cars moving cautiously, steaming radiators, boots, scarves, overcoats, furs. At this point, the teacher stopped to say that the list of what we could see was governed only by what we had seen in the past and could recall. She suggested that the class make a similar list for each of the other senses mentioned above. After completion of the list, she explained, the only problem of writing the theme would be one of mechanics.

A sixth grade choir was singing a prayer song for the PTA. During rehearsals, the teacher had led the children to imagine quietness, humbleness, and sincerity. The result was an expression of simple beauty. However, because of the many distractions contingent on performance the spirit of prayer was lost. As the children began to sing, the teacher merely folded her hands in a reverent manner, and the feeling of prayer was regained.

From these illustrations, it may be concluded that the creative teacher does not hesitate to suggest or to give guidance. However, he attaches great importance to the manner in which guidance is given. The creative teacher senses when to give and when to withhold aid. He has no pedagogical formulas, for these would destroy his own initiative and individuality. The music teacher mentioned above had not anticipated the dilemma which arose. She merely assumed the spirit of prayer and put herself in a prayerful mood; the movement of her hands was almost automatic.

The creative teacher does not withhold constructive criticism or directions which inspire the children to greater effort. His judgment in these matters is not based upon adult standards but on child potential. Realizing that the only difference between the instructor and the student is one of acquired knowledge, skill, and experience, the teacher shares these with the students on the level of their understanding. Although the child is free to think and speak, the teacher realizes that he is the bridge between the child and maturity. The teacher is, therefore, a constant but pleasant challenge, his purpose being to develop potentials. By sharing his richer background with them, he gradually opens new avenues for creativity on the part of the children. The teacher's job is to supply a rich and wide variety of experiences. In doing this, he does not drive; he leads—leads the children to *discover*. He does not dictate; he inspires—inspires the children in initiative.

The teacher who is not creative has become embedded in the ruts of his own pedagogical formulas. His is a teacher-centered classroom. His thoughts and methods are self-centered; he does not project or radiate toward the children. He drills on the memorization of key signature, time signatures, and the relative value of notes. He does not understand that these can best be taught in connection with the music itself. He tells the children about music, forgetting that it is more important for them to experience it. He shows them how they should respond to the rhythm. He does nothing to awaken imagination or inspire creativity.

When such a teacher senses a lack of response to his teaching, he should re-examine his technique. The chances are good that he, and not the students, is at fault. The wife of a great music teacher related to the writer how her husband took himself to task after each rehearsal. The assumption was that any apathy or lack of spontaneity on the part of the group was his fault. After each rehearsal he would ask, "What did I do wrong? Why was the response not greater?" It is no wonder that he is considered one of America's greatest teachers.

Creative Activities in Music

Creativity in the teacher, rather than elaborate and expensive equipment, is indispensable for creative music activities. However, basic equipment is important. The essentials include song books, a good record player, a well-chosen collection of records, rhythm instruments, song or resonator bells or other melody instruments, and a piano if at all possible.

One of the first references to creativity in these pages was in connection with the defective singer, chapter 2. One suggestion given there had to do with the teacher's repetition of melodic bits which the defective singer might originate. A second suggestion concerned the singing of a melody to statements made by the children, and a third dealt with melodic and rhythmic names for each child. Of course, the child's ability to create melodic passages will grow as he acquires experience in responding to tone and time. The first attempt at a longer passage should involve adding a phrase to a given melody. Two excellent examples for the beginner may be found in G. *Singing and Rhyming*, pages 20 and 21. In these examples, the words guide the response, which will usually be a repetition of the melody. Other ready-made phrases of this type may be found on pages 32, 82, 115, 131, and 157 of G. *Singing and Rhyming*.

These beginning attempts, as well as other worthy creations, should be written on the chalkboard, and used as a means of developing awareness of notation for various rhythmic patterns. Even if writing the tune is impossible for the teacher, the children should have the creative experience of making up their own melodies.

Writing an additional stanza to a song is another stimulating creative activity. The established poetic meter and rhyme serve as excellent guides. After some experience with additional stanzas, the children may try writing poems for their own songs. The words may be written on the chalkboard. When rhythm and melody have been established, the notation should be written above the words and the children led to discover the meter through the accent.

The purpose of such creations is not musical perfection or the development of composers, but rather the observations that come as a result of creating. If the child has grown through creative expression, the process has been successful.

The rhythm instruments provide another creative medium.[3] Discriminative listening, selection of the proper instruments to adequately express the character of the music, observation of like and unlike phrases, awareness of change in rhythm and tempo, and consciousness of dynamics are highly valuable. Properly presented, all of these lead to creative thinking, imaginative interpretation, and the development of musical taste. The rhythm instruments may also be a valuable means of developing awareness of the notation of rhythm patterns.

Paralleling these creative efforts should be many opportunities for free expression of feeling. The children may be encouraged to add a new step to a dance, add new action to a singing game, or dramatize a song or an instrumental piece, either of program or of pure music.

A twofold creative activity, and one of the most satisfying for both teacher and pupil, is art work combined with listening. Students at all levels have shown remarkable insight in such activities.

Another stimulating and creative activity is the development of an assembly program by the class. A fifth grade class originated the plot, words, music, and costumes for a ten-minute musical skit. Such class activities are highly valuable provided they are not done at the expense of other class work. A sixth grade teacher interested her class in selecting stanzas of traditional Christmas carols which told the complete story of the Nativity, reaching a climactic close with "Joy to the World." The program was done in appropriate homemade costumes for Mary, Joseph, the Christ Child (doll in stable with flashlight halo), and the angelic choir. Appropriate stage lighting enhanced the beauty of the costumes and scenery. The program met with such community approval that it was repeated annually.

In another school the fourth, fifth, and sixth grades presented a program during National Music Week. This program consisted of folk songs from the countries considered in social studies. In characteristic costume, a representative of each country gave a resumé

---

[3] See "Rhythm Instruments," chapter 3.

of the customs of the people and a brief explanation of each song. The script was selected in a contest in language study. The songs were sung by a chorus composed of members from the various classes and directed by the best conductor from each of the three grades. A seventh grade girl played the piano accompaniment, two students played autoharps, and other students danced to three of the songs. Still others, especially those who had difficulty singing the two-part songs, had charge of lighting, staging, and curtain. The program continued with the singing of a group of American folk songs, and closed with the audience and the students singing the "Star Spangled Banner."

Correlation with Social Studies

The person who teaches music creatively will keep in mind areas other than music which are designed for child development—particularly social studies. The outline below is given as a guide for music specialists, who will generally be less familiar with the social studies than will regular elementary teachers. Details of these studies vary in different parts of the country, so the outline must remain general. The over-all aim is to introduce the child to the world about him. In the lower elementary grades, the study begins with the child's immediate environment and gradually expands to embrace the neighborhood, the community, and, in the upper grades, the distant regions of the world. (Since the topical indexes of the various music series are so complete, it seems inadvisable to list song material here.)

GENERAL OUTLINE FOR LOWER ELEMENTARY GRADES

Where We Live
    Home
    School
    Community
How We Live
    Safety
    Food
    Clothing
    Shelter

The World About Us
    Plants
    Animals
    Seasons
    Nature (sun, moon, stars, etc.)
    Weather

Transportation

Communication

People Who Supply Our Needs
    Farmer
    Dairyman
    Grocer
    * Baker
People Who Serve Us
    Policeman
    Fireman
    Postman
    Newsman
    Doctor

Special Occasions
    Birthday
    Halloween
    Thanksgiving
    Christmas
    Valentine's Day
    Easter

With the immediate environment as a background, studies in the upper elementary grades expand to embrace history, civics, geography, and current affairs. The over-all purpose is to introduce the child to the people of the world—their manner of life, occupations, and problems. There is constant emphasis on the contributions of other people in other times and places, especially within our own nation. Music materials for these areas are listed throughout Part Two of this book.

GENERAL OUTLINE FOR SOCIAL STUDIES IN THE UPPER ELEMENTARY GRADES[4]

The United States

Geography
    States
    Principal cities
    Rivers
    Oceans
    Canals
    Mountains
    Plains
    Deserts
    Climate
History
    Colonial days
    Indians
    Independence
    Westward movement
    Life in various areas
National Heroes
Special Occasions

Industries and Occupations
    Fishing
    Farming
    Ranching
    Mining
    Lumber
    Oil
Transportation and Communication
    Exploration trails
    Pony Express
    Railroads
    Rivers
    Telegraph
    Airlines
Patriotism
Immediate Neighbors
    Canada
    Mexico

---

[4] See "National Characteristics," chapter 9.

OTHER NATIONS

South America
> Argentina, Bolivia, Brazil, Chile, Colombia, Peru, Uruguay, Paraguay, Ecuador, the Guianas

Western Europe
> The United Kingdom (England, Scotland, Wales, Northern Ireland), Ireland (Eire), Holland (The Netherlands), Belgium, Luxembourg, Germany, France

Central Europe
> Poland, Czechoslovakia, Switzerland, Austria, Hungary, Romania, Bulgaria, Yugoslavia

Scandinavian Europe
> Norway, Sweden, Finland, Denmark, Greenland, Iceland

Southern Europe (Bordering the Mediterranean)
> Italy, Greece, Albania, Spain, Portugal

Russia

Africa

Southwestern Asia
> Turkey, Syria, Lebanon, Israel, Jordan, Saudi Arabia, Iraq, Iran, Afghanistan

Southern and Eastern Asia
> China, Pakistan, India, Japan, Siam (Thailand), Indochina, Malaya, Tibet, Manchuria, Formosa, Burma, Indonesia, Philippine Islands

Australia and the Pacific Islands
> Australia, New Zealand, Hawaii

Correlation with Literature

Another area which may be readily related to music is that of poetry and literature. Since a bibliography for both students and teachers is included with units of study established by school systems, no books are listed here.

The following suggestions indicate possibilities for correlation between literature and music. All selections listed may be found in *Story and Verse for Children*, edited by Mariam Blanton Huber, the revised edition, published by the Macmillan Company, New York, 1955. The general subject is indicated in parentheses. These poems and stories may be used in connection with songs or instrumental music.

FIRST GRADE

Mother Goose Rhymes (Mother Goose songs)
Birthdays—Marchette Chute (Birthday songs)
Time to Rise—R. L. Stevenson (morning)
The Swing—R. L. Stevenson (swings or nature)

Bed in Summer—R. L. Stevenson (seasons)
Thanksgiving Day—Lydia Child (S. *Music Through the Day*, p. 113; G. *Singing on Our Way*, p. 74—Thanksgiving)
A Visit from St. Nicholas—Clement Moore (Christmas)
Who Has Seen the Wind—Christina Rossetti (wind and nature)
The Wind—R. L. Stevenson (wind and nature)
Rain—R. L. Stevenson (rain and weather)
Clouds—Author Unknown (clouds)
All Things Bright and Beautiful—Cecil Alexander (nature)
Three Little Kittens—Eliza Lee Follen (G. *The First Grade Book*, p. 80—Pets)
The Gingerbread Boy (G. *The First Grade Book*, p. 199r)

SECOND GRADE

The Land of Counterpane—R. L. Stevenson (toys)
Hallowe'en—Harry Behn (Halloween)
Boats Sail on the River—Christina Rossetti (clouds)
Little Star—Jane Taylor (G. *Singing on Our Way*, p. 106; S. *Music Through the Day*, p. 20—nature)
The Frost Pane—David McCord (summer or winter)
The Three Billy Goats Gruff (G. *Singing on Our Way*, p. 167r)
Lazy Jack (G. *Singing on Our Way*, p. 51r—animals)

THIRD GRADE

Nancy Hanks—Rosemary and Stephen V. Benét (Lincoln)
As Joseph Was A-Walking—Old Carol (Christmas)
Hiawatha's Childhood—Henry W. Longfellow (Indian)
Three Kings Came Riding—Henry W. Longfellow (Christmas)

FOURTH GRADE

The Year's at the Spring—Robert Browning (spring)
April—Sara Teasdale (spring)
The Garden Year—Sara Coleridge (seasons)
The Sea Shell—Amy Lowell (sea)
Those Who Go Forth Before Daylight—Carl Sandburg (occupations)
Buffalo Bill—Ingri and Edgar d'Arlaine (Westward movement)
Valley Forge and Victory—Jeanette Eaton (Washington)
The Covered Wagon—Emma Brock (Westward movement)

FIFTH GRADE

Children of the Wind—Carl Sandburg (birds or nature)
Fog—Carl Sandburg (S. *Music Around the World*, p. 44—Fall)
Paul Revere's Ride—Henry W. Longfellow (Paul Revere or national heroes)
Hansel and Gretel—Ludwig Grimm (G. *Singing Together*, p. 193r;—Tales and legends)

SIXTH GRADE

Something Told the Wild Geese—Rachel Field (G. *Singing in Harmony,* p. 192r—
> Fall)

I Hear America Singing—Walt Whitman (occupations)

The Village Blacksmith—Henry W. Longfellow (S. *Music Near and Far,* p. 32—
> occupations)

Git Along, Little Dogies—Author Unknown (F. *Voices of America,* p. 151r—
> occupations)

Columbus—Joaquin Miller (Columbus or national heroes)

Another excellent source is *One Thousand Poems for Children,* edited by Elizabeth H. Sechrist, published by Macrae Smith Company, Philadelphia, Pennsylvania, 1946. The poems in this book fall into the following classifications: For the Nursery, Cradle Songs, Riddles and Finger Plays, From Morning to Night, Fairies and All, Creatures Great and Small, The Great Outdoors, Poems of Praise, Poems that Sing, Stories in Verse, Poems of Patriotism, Poems for Fun, Poems for Holidays, Poems and History, Songs of the Seasons, Nature in Poetry, The Animal Kingdom, Humorous Verse, Holiday Poetry, Poems of Reverence, and Old Favorites.

Guide to Musical Activities

Just as the music specialist may be somewhat hazy concerning social studies, the regular elementary teacher may have difficulty in formulating an over-all view of music activities at the various grade levels. Although any outline must be general and flexible, it is hoped that the following will serve as a guide.

FIRST GRADE

A. Singing
> Vocal orientation
> Aiding the child to "carry a tune"
> All songs taught by rote
> Wide choice of songs about home, school, friends, pets, nature, safety

B. Rhythm
> Rhythmic orientation
> Aiding the child to respond to music by use of large muscles in walking, running, galloping, skipping, dramatization, and singing games

C. Listening

    Aural orientation

    Wide experience in listening actively to familiar and unfamiliar music to sense its message through mood

    Because of limited attention span, selections should not be too long. Listening to high and low, fast and slow passages

D. Instrumental

    Introduction to rhythm instruments

    Gradual introduction of individual rhythm instruments for use in songs

E. Reading

    No music reading as such. However, ear-training in rote learning and use of hand levels for pitch are initial steps in reading.

F. Creative

    Child singing his own melody

    Individual freedom in responding to rhythm

    Discriminative listening in connection with rhythm instruments

SECOND GRADE

A. Singing

    Continuation of vocal orientation

    Learning many songs by rote

    Improving tone quality through imitation

B. Rhythm

    Wide experience in responding to rhythm as in first grade with increasing emphasis on singing games and creative rhythmic activities

C. Listening

    Wide experience in listening to comparatively long selections and observing like and unlike phrases

    Listening to determine mood

    Listening to solos on familiar instruments

    Listening for high and low, fast and slow, loud and soft passages

D. Instrumental

    Continued use of rhythm instruments on familiar songs and instrumental pieces

    Identifying familiar instruments by sight and sound

E. Reading

    General observations of notation of rhythm—walking or quarter notes, running or eighth notes, notation for skipping and galloping rhythms

    General observation of notation of pitch—high and low gradually leading to playing short tonal patterns such as 3, 2, 1, and singing such passages in unfamiliar songs without dependence upon the instrument

    Gradual discovery of keyboard and staff letter names

F. Creative

    Child singing his own melody or musical name

    Individual freedom in response to rhythm

    Greater freedom in choice of instruments to accompany songs

THIRD GRADE

A. Singing

    Continuation of vocal orientation

    Learning many songs by rote

    Improving tone quality through imitation and feeling for mood

    Singing descants to familiar melodies

B. Rhythm

    Wide experience in responding to rhythmic patterns, with increasing emphasis on singing games and creative rhythmic activities

C. Listening

    Wide experience in listening to somewhat longer instrumental selections, observing like and unlike passages

    Listening to solos on less familiar instruments

    Listening to brass, woodwind, and string choirs of orchestra

    Listening to selections from suites

    Listening to determine mood

D. Instrumental

    Continued use of rhythm instruments

    Identify less familiar instruments by sight and sound

    Identify brass, woodwind, and string choirs of orchestra by sight and sound

    Playing tonic and dominant chords on piano, melody bells, and autoharp

E. Reading

    Detailed observation of notation of pitches and rhythms

    Introduction to various time signatures

    Continuation of discovery of keyboard and staff letter names

    Playing longer tonal patterns, such as 1, 2, 3, 4, 5, and scale songs and singing these passages in unfamiliar songs without dependence upon the keyboard

    Following notation of familiar music as recordings are heard

F. Creative

    Child singing and clapping his musical name or combination of names

    Individual freedom in response to rhythm

    Increased freedom in choice of instruments to accompany songs

    Creating an additional phrase for a song

    Creating an additional stanza for a song

    Creating new steps or movements in rhythmic activities

FOURTH GRADE

A. Singing

    Learning more difficult songs by rote

    Improving tone quality through imitation and interpretation of mood

    Singing two-part rounds

B. Rhythm

    Continuation of all rhythmic activities

    Responding to more complicated rhythmic patterns

    Learning simple folk dances

C. Listening

    Listen to larger works of music such as complete suites

    Listening to effects produced by combining various instruments and choirs of instruments

    Listening for contrasts in tempo, harmony, and dynamics

D. Instrumental

    Continued use of rhythm instruments and possible correlation with notation

    Emphasis on playing melody and chording instruments

    Use of I, IV, and V chords on familiar songs

E. Reading

    Detailed observation of notation of various relative note lengths and more involved rhythms

    Explanation of time signatures

    Playing many tonal patterns and learning to sing these in unfamiliar songs without dependence upon the instrument

    Playing and singing short passages in thirds and sixths

    Following notation of unfamiliar songs as recordings are heard

F. Creative

    Interpretative response to rhythm and mood

    Creating additional phrases to songs and perhaps adding thirds on the final cadence

    Creating additional stanza to familiar songs

    Creating new steps and movements to folk dances

    Deciding on instruments to accompany songs and dances

FIFTH GRADE

A. Singing

    Learning many songs by note and rote

    Singing songs with descants

    Singing three-part rounds

B. Rhythm

    Continuation of all rhythmic activities

    Responding to more complicated rhythms—dots, sixteenth notes, and triplets

    Learning additional folk dances

C. Listening

    Continuing to listen to larger forms of music such as suites and movements from symphonies

    Listening to effects produced by combining various instruments and choirs of instruments

    Listening to contrasts in tempo, harmony, dynamics, and style

D. Instrumental

    Emphasis on playing melody and chording instruments

    Use of I, IV, V_7 chords on familiar and unfamiliar songs

    Chording to folk dance selections

E. Reading

Further exploration of notation of various tone lengths—dots, sixteenths, triplets

Further exploration of time signatures

Playing and singing many familiar and unfamiliar tonal patterns

Playing and singing thirds and sixths as found in two-part songs

Following notation of selections as recordings are heard

F. Creative

Interpretative response to rhythms and moods

Creating a two-phrase song

Creating words for song and deciding on rhythm and melody

Creating new steps and movements to folk dances

SIXTH GRADE

A. Singing

Learning many songs by note and rote

Singing songs with descants

Singing three-part rounds

Singing a few three-part songs, especially those in which rhythmic and tonal patterns are repeated

B. Rhythm

Continuation of various rhythmic activities with special emphasis on folk dances

Responding to more complicated rhythms

Learning additional folk dances

C. Listening

Continuing to listen to larger forms such as suites, symphonic poems, and movements of symphonies

Listening to selections from operas and oratorios

Listening to combinations of instruments and voices

D. Instrumental

Emphasis on playing melody and chording instruments

Use of II and VI chords in chording experiences

Chording to folk dance selections

E. Reading

Continuation of emphasis on time signature and accurate response to tone lengths

Playing and singing many familiar and unfamiliar tonal patterns

Playing and singing two-part songs

Following notation of selections as recordings are heard

F. Creative

Interpretative response to rhythm

Creating two-phrase songs

Creating words for songs and deciding on rhythm and melody

Originating ideas for assembly or other programs

Visual Aids

In addition to the suggestions above, the following visual aids can measurably enhance teaching in any area.

1. *American Heritage,* the magazine of history, 551 Fifth Avenue, New York 17, New York. Each issue (six issues per year) contains approximately thirty pictures in color and seventy in black and white. Such pictures are excellent for use in connection with American history at any level and are particularly appropriate in introducing their country to the children. A limited number of tear sheets of pictures are available from the publisher. *American Heritage* has also published three illustrated books—*Great Historic Places* (1957), *The Revolution* (1958), and *The Pioneer Spirit* (1959).

2. Prints and slides are highly recommended and may be obtained from the following:

University Prints, 15 Brattle Street, Cambridge 38, Massachusetts. Over 550 fine arts subjects are available as slides or prints. All prints are 5½ x 8. Write for catalogue and free samples.

Dr. Konrad Prockmann, 2378 Soper Avenue, Baldwin, Long Island, New York. Colored slides.

Perry Pictures, Department 1, Malden, Massachusetts.

Metropolitan Museum of Art, 5th Avenue and 82nd Street, New York.

Museum of Modern Art, 11 West 53rd Street, New York.

National Art Gallery, Washington 25, D. C.

3. Films and tapes are available on a wide variety of subjects including music. Consult local and state film libraries for catalogues.

4. Picture and news magazines such as *Life, Look, Saturday Evening Post,* etc., contain art and social studies material in color. One elementary teacher has made a file of these articles and pictures, with categories covering such elementary fields as animals, holidays, the West, ranching, and farming.

For Further Development

1. Various class committees select one of the following for class reports:

a) Select song and recorded material for a program on occupations in the United States during the period following the Civil War. Include folk dances. See chapter 13.

b) Select song and recorded material to be correlated with social studies of the fifth grade. Include folk dances, national anthems, and music by representative composers. See chapter 9.

c) Select song and recorded material to be correlated with social studies of the sixth grade. Include folk dances, national anthems, and music by representative composers. See chapter 9.

d) Select songs and recorded material to be correlated with children's literature, grades one, two, and three. Use any one of the song series.

e) Select song and recorded material to be correlated with children's literature, grades four, five, and six. Use any one of the song series.

2. Arrange for a listening period to hear representative music of recorded material listed in chapter 14. Make a list of your favorites.

CHAPTER 7

Hands to Play

What about Instruments?

Unlike the voice, instruments are man-made and are mechanical devices for making music. For centuries, they have been a means by which man has expressed himself. Wherever we find man singing, we find him playing instruments. This is as it should be, for each of these complements the other. The discussion in this chapter includes rhythm and social instruments as well as standard instruments of the band and orchestra.

Because of their mechanical nature, some of the instruments are particularly valuable as aids in learning to sing. This is especially true of the keyboard type, such as the piano. When the keys of the piano are pressed down, definite pitches are produced—absolute and relative. For this reason, this type of instrument is basic for developing the accurate hearing necessary for singing and for playing other instruments. Furthermore, keyboard instruments are valuable in explaining such fundamentals of music as steps, half-steps, sharps, flats, and so on.

Other instruments sound less definite to the untrained ear. For example, the tones of brass instruments are produced by the vibration of the player's lips in a mouthpiece and by the manipulation of valves. The sounds of reed instruments are produced by the vibration of a single or a double reed and the manipulation of keys. On string instruments such as the violin, tones are produced by the vibration of strings and by the placement of fingers on a finger board. The pitch on all such instruments may vary depending upon the ear and the motor skill of the performer.

Since the elementary school provides opportunities for exploration in many areas, the child should be introduced to, and have ample opportunity to become familiar with, all media for musical expression. The teacher should guard against prejudicing the child toward either vocal or instrumental music. The tendency to overstress the area of the teacher's specialization is a serious weakness at the grade school level. The teacher should remember that some children like to sing, while others prefer to play instruments.

Why Teach Playing of Instruments?

There is an element of truth in statements which imply a worthy use of leisure time, such as "The boy who blows the horn is not the boy who blows the safe; the girl who plays the piano is not the girl who picks your pocket; the child who draws the bow is not the child who draws the gun."

Many benefits may be derived from a good program of instrumental instruction.

1. Playing an instrument causes a child to become aware of staff notation. When singing, he may be following others, or guessing. When playing an instrument, he is on his own and must be definite in his judgment.

2. Playing in a musical organization helps develop a sense of belonging to the school and to the community. Young people who participate in parades, athletic events, and concerts are making a contribution to life in their community. They are discovering the rewards of group cooperation for the achievement of a collective goal.

3. Playing an instrument and participating in musical organizations add social status to the individual.

4. Playing an instrument is a means of self-expression.

5. Playing an instrument is a means of relaxation when the day's work is done. Many teachers and other professional people find it particularly rewarding.

6. An opportunity can usually be found (or made) to use these skills in adult life by playing in community musical organizations.

How to Teach Instruments

Instrumental activity at the grade school level includes actual participation, as well as learning about instruments through listening activities.

The question of *how* to teach the playing of instruments immediately suggests the question of *when* to begin the instruction. Concerning the latter, there are two very important considerations:

1. *The visual development of the child.* The ability of the average child to focus has not fully developed when he enters school. Adding further to this problem is that reading music involves a wide visual sweep compared to the linear movement in reading language. In reading music, the eyes must move horizontally, vertically, and at many angles, while observing many details along the way.

2. *The coordination of both large and small muscles.* The motor dexterity involved in manipulating keys and valves, tongue and lips, when playing an instrument demands the coordination of small muscles. In general, the large muscles of the legs and arms are the first to develop and to be brought under control. For this reason, the first physical response to rhythm involves the large muscles of the legs, and the first instruments introduced are the rhythm instruments which employ the large muscles of the arms. The involvement of smaller muscles must come gradually as the child develops control in their use.

Parents often ask elementary teachers at what age their child should begin piano lessons. This is a difficult question to answer, for individual differences, interest, and the two points mentioned above must be considered. Taking all of these into account, together with the need for mental discipline, one music instructor started his two children on dancing lessons during the first year of school and began piano lessons during the second year. The children developed a good sense of, and response to, rhythm while their ability to focus and to control small muscles was developing. This teacher believes that the children's achievements in piano at the end of the first year equaled those of others who had studied the instrument for as long as two years. However, children who manifest a strong interest in, and aptitude for, any instrument should have the opportunity to study regardless of their age.

Some schools are fortunate in being able to offer group instruction in piano. The third grade seems to be the favorite level to begin such instruction. The suggestions in chapters 5 and 8 concerning keyboard experiences during the second grade provide an excellent background for class piano instruction.

Instrumental classes for the standard band and orchestra instruments are often begun during the fifth and sixth grades. The keyboard activities suggested throughout these pages provide an ideal background for such instruction. However, some teachers prefer that instrument classes be initiated at the junior high school level, and that the stress during grade school years be on singing, keyboard experiences, rhythm instruments, and melody and chording instruments. They believe that grade school is a place for wide exploration in all areas of music and that instrumental classes narrow the field of activity. Furthermore, they fear that the grade school will become a recruiting ground for junior high school bands and orchestras.

Rhythm Instruments

Regardless of these differences in opinion, most teachers agree that rhythm instruments are ideal for the beginner. These include such instruments as those listed below. Many of these are similar to the standard instruments used in band and orchestra.

Such instruments should not be confused with toys, nor should they be considered as pre-orchestra or pre-band instruments. They are real instruments which the child can now manipulate with his large muscles and which make a definite contribution to the child's musical growth. Although playing in a band or orchestra may later result from such activity, this is not its primary purpose.

Although the first experiences with rhythm instruments are not associated with conventional musical notation, various rudimentary symbols for their use are printed in the song series. These are helpful to the teacher. Two different types of symbols employed are:

1. Woodblocks (or any instrument):

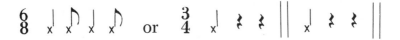

2. Triangles △ , sticks ✕ , blocks ☐
Various rhythm instruments are shown below. The number suggested for a class of average size is given in parentheses.

Rhythm Instruments[1]

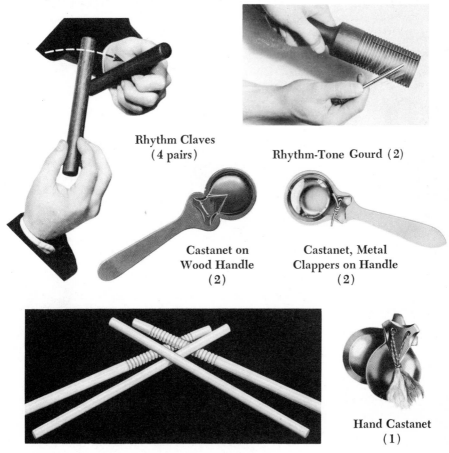

Rhythm Claves
(4 pairs)

Rhythm-Tone Gourd (2)

Castanet on
Wood Handle
(2)

Castanet, Metal
Clappers on Handle
(2)

Hand Castanet
(1)

Rhythm Sticks (8-10 pairs)

[1] Courtesy of Conn Corporation, 1101 E. Beardsley Ave., Elkhart, Indiana. A
Handbook for Rhythm Band is available from the Conn Company.

Rhythm Instruments[1]

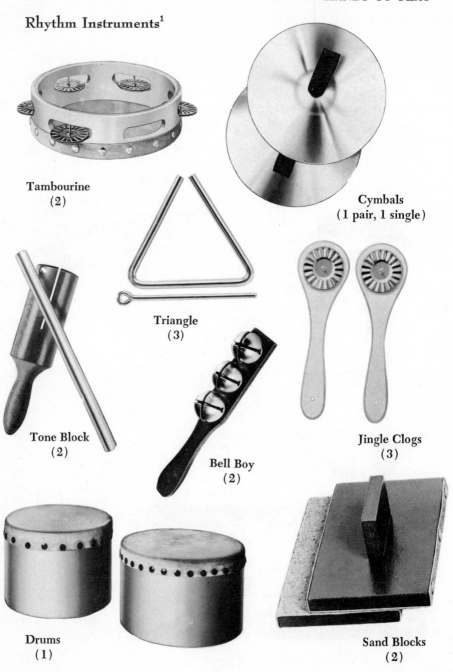

Tambourine
(2)

Cymbals
(1 pair, 1 single)

Triangle
(3)

Tone Block
(2)

Bell Boy
(2)

Jingle Clogs
(3)

Drums
(1)

Sand Blocks
(2)

[1] Courtesy of Conn Corporation, 1101 E. Beardsley Ave., Elkhart, Indiana. A *Handbook for Rhythm Band* is available from the Conn Company.

Melody Instruments

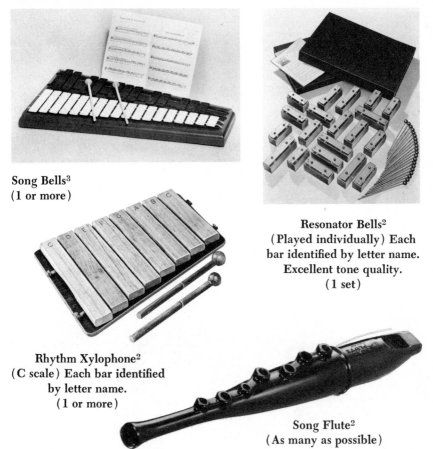

Song Bells[3]
(1 or more)

Resonator Bells[2]
(Played individually) Each
bar identified by letter name.
Excellent tone quality.
(1 set)

Rhythm Xylophone[2]
(C scale) Each bar identified
by letter name.
(1 or more)

Song Flute[2]
(As many as possible)

The xylophone, resonator bells, and song bells are of the keyboard type, and may be used for playing the melody or for chording. Each is played by striking a bar with a mallet.

The Song Flute and other instruments like it—the Tonette, Melody Flute, Flutophone, Symphonett—are built in C and are played by covering and uncovering holes. To play the C scale, cover all holes and raise one finger at a time beginning with the finger nearest the bell of the instrument. The tone has a flute-like quality. An instruction book is available for such instruments.

---

[2] *Ibid.* A tuned resonator bell instructor is available from the Conn Company.
[3] Courtesy of Walberg and Auge, Worcester, Massachusetts. The Song Bells pictured here is #1121.

Recorder[4]

The recorder is an old instrument for which a great deal of music was composed by the masters. There are soprano, alto, tenor, and bass recorders. The soprano recorder (pictured above) is probably the most practical for grade school use. It is played in the same manner as the Song Flute.

Chording Instruments

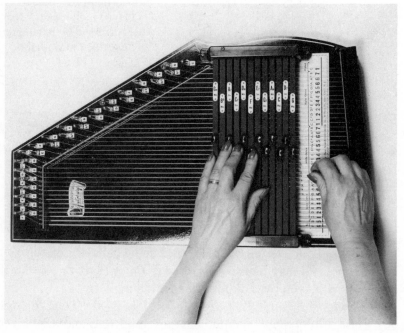

Autoharp[5]   Model #73   12 Chords

---

[4] The Weiss German-made recorder is pictured above through the courtesy of David Wexler and Company, 823 South Wabash Avenue, Chicago 5, Illinois.

[5] Courtesy of Oscar Schmidt-International, Inc., Jersey City, New Jersey. An instruction book is available from Oscar Schmidt-International.

The autoharp is one of the most popular chording instruments. It is played by pressing down on the button of the desired chord and strumming the strings with a pick. One may strum on either side of the chord bars. The chords are indicated on the bars. This instrument is very easy to play, and the tone quality is good. It is valuable in aiding the child to hear chord changes. Many adults find it a rewarding instrument for relaxation.

The Ukulele[6]

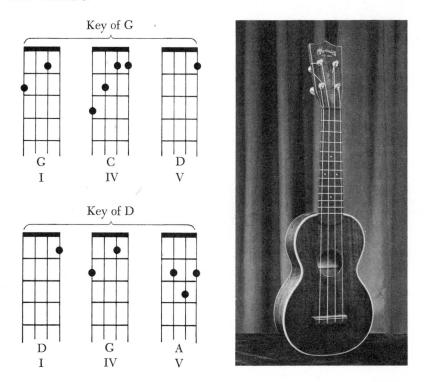

The strings of the ukulele are tuned to A, D, F♯, and B on the piano or on a chromatic pitch pipe. Tonic, subdominant, and dominant chords are shown above in the keys of G and D. The instrument is played by pressing the strings on the frets indicated and strumming the string with a pick or with the fingers.

---

[6] Courtesy of C. F. Martin and Company, Nazareth, Pennsylvania.

The Guitar[7]

The strings of the guitar (left to right) are tuned to E, A, D, G, B, and E. Tonic, subdominant, and dominant chords for the keys of G and C are indicated above. The instrument is played by pressing the strings on the frets indicated and strumming the strings with a pick or with the fingers. Because of its large neck, the guitar is generally not used until the sixth grade.

Other Melodic and Chording Instruments

As mentioned in chapter 5, there is now available a wide choice of instruments of the keyboard type which are valuable for instruction in the grade school. A number of these are miniature, portable

---

[7] Courtesy of Gibson Inc., Kalamazoo, Michigan.

electric organs. A volume control is available with each instrument. Most of these instruments are equipped with accordion-
sized keys although a few are available with regular piano-sized
keys. Some of these organs are equipped with plastic reeds,
whereas others have steel reeds. The ones pictured below have
steel reeds. As will be observed, a number of the instruments pictured here are chord organs; that is, chords may be played by
merely pressing a button. As on the autoharp, the chords are identified by letter names. The chord organ is particularly recommended for teachers who have had limited keyboard experience.
Such instruments may be used both as a melody and as a chording
instrument. The teacher or a student may play the melody while
others play the chords. The cost of such instruments is very
modest, so that at least one is a possibility for each school. Since
specifications and prices are subject to change, it is recommended
that the teachers consult a local dealer or the firms listed in foot-
notes for detailed information.

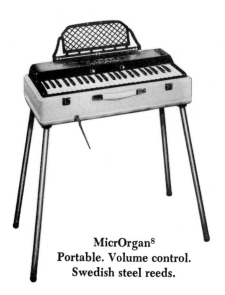

MicrOrgan[8]
Portable. Volume control.
Swedish steel reeds.

Gretsch Organ[9]
Portable. Volume control.
Swedish steel reeds.

[8] Courtesy of Chicago Musical Instrument Company, 7373 North Cicero Ave.,
Chicago 46, Illinois.
[9] Courtesy of Gamble Hinged Music Company, Inc., 312-14 South Wabash
Avenue, Chicago 4, Illinois.

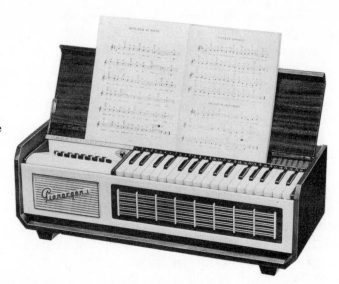

Pianorgan[10]
Table Model. Portable
Chord Organ. Full-
size piano keys.
Swedish steel reeds.

Pianorgan.[11]
Portable Chord Organ.
Full-size piano keys.
Swedish steel reeds.

---

[10] Courtesy of Gamble Hinged Music Company, Inc., 312-14 South Wabash
Ave., Chicago 4, Illinois.
[11] *Ibid.* Other models available.

Wurlitzer Chord Organ.[12]
A real two-manual spinet organ
with one octave of pedals.

Wurlitzer Electronic Piano.[13]
Portable. Volume control.
Earphone attachment. Multi-
piano monitor system available
for class piano instruction.

---

[12] Courtesy of The Wurlitzer Company, DeKalb, Illinois.
[13] *Ibid.*

The Melodica[14]

The melodica is a recently developed instrument which has very worthwhile possibilities in the elementary school. It is a wind instrument with a piano type keyboard, and may be used as a melody or as a chording instrument. It is pitched at 440, and it is in tune. The tone quality is good. It is an excellent, inexpensive instrument for explaining the fundamentals of music. It has a two-octave range.

Instruments of the Band and Orchestra

Whether or not instruction on the standard instruments of the orchestra and band begins at the grade school level, the instruments should be emphasized as a part of the exploration program. This may be done by identifying the instruments by sight and sound. Recordings which feature the various instruments alone or in combinations are listed at the close of this chapter. Individual giant size pictures of the instruments, or wall charts of the

---

14 Courtesy of M. Hohner, Inc., 351 Fourth Avenue, New York 10, New York.

brass and woodwind families, may be purchased at very reasonable prices from the Conn Company. Beautiful charts showing the instruments of the orchestra may be purchased from J. W. Pepper and Sons, Inc., 1423 Vine Street, Philadelphia 2, Pennsylvania. Also available from the same firm is a handbook which gives an analysis of each instrument and lists illustrative recordings. As a review, and as a reference for elementary teachers, the various instruments are shown below.

Brass Instruments[15]

Trumpet

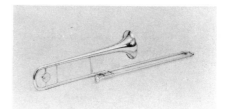

Trombone

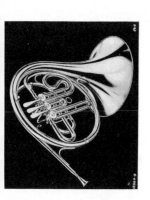

French Horn

Bass Horn

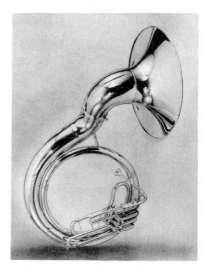

Sousaphone

---

[15] Courtesy of Conn Corporation, Elkhart, Indiana.

Woodwind Instruments[16]

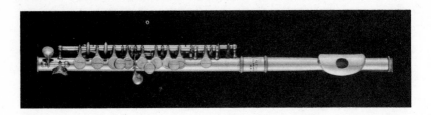

Piccolo

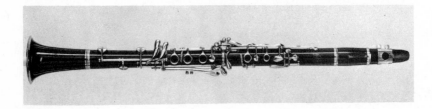

Clarinet

Flute

English Horn
(Oboe similar in appearance)

---

[16] Courtesy Conn Corporation, Elkhart, Indiana.

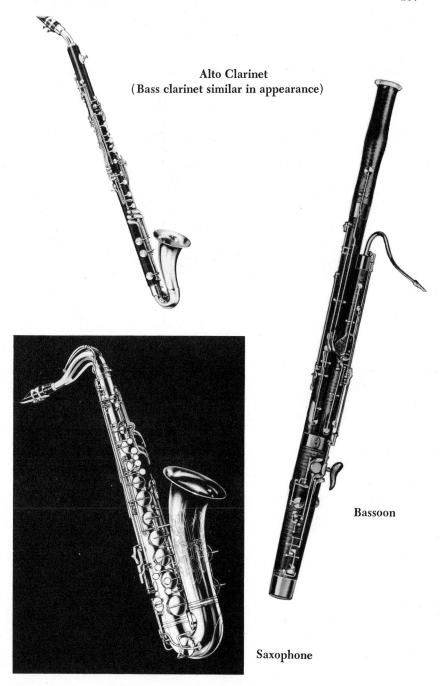

Alto Clarinet
(Bass clarinet similar in appearance)

Bassoon

Saxophone

String Instruments

Violin[17]

Viola[17]

Violoncello[18]

String Bass[18]

---

[17] Courtesy of Fawick Strings, Inc., 5885 Lorain Avenue, Cleveland, Ohio. Instruments by Thomas L. Fawick.

[18] Courtesy of Kay Musical Instrument Company, 1640 Walnut Street, Chicago, Illinois.

Percussion Instruments

The percussion instruments include the bass drum, snare drum, tympani, chimes, triangle, bell lyra, and cymbals. Other percussion instruments are often introduced for special effects.

For Further Development

1. Have a ukulele or guitar player demonstrate his instrument's use in chording.

2. Learn to play the autoharp, chording to as many songs as time will permit.

3. If one of the chording instruments of the keyboard type is not available, visit a local music dealer for a demonstration.

4. Arrange for a listening period. As you listen to instrumental recordings, try to identify the instruments by sound.

Recordings

Victor E-104. This album contains carefully selected examples of string, woodwind, brass, and percussion instruments. The harp and celeste are included.

Victor Basic Record Library for Elementary Schools. The listening and rhythm albums contain many fine examples featuring instruments.

Folkways FT 3602. The Orchestra and Its Instruments. Solos, duets, trios, quartets, with various combinations of instruments, showing how each instrument plays its part in the total sound of the orchestra. Commentary and accompanying notes.

Many of the recordings listed throughout these pages feature various instruments such as:

Strings: The Flight of the Bumblebee (Rimsky-Korsakov) and The Swan (Saint-Saens)

Woodwinds: Chinese Dance from the Nutcracker Suite (Tchaikovsky) and Morning from the Peer Gynt Suite (Grieg)

Brass: March from the Nutcracker Suite (Tchaikovsky) and Peter and the Wolf (Prokofieff)

Percussion: Cloudburst from the Grand Canyon Suite (Grofe) and Trepak from the Nutcracker Suite (Tchaikovsky)

CHAPTER 8

Comprehensive Teaching

What about Theory of Music?

One of the elementary teacher's most perplexing problems concerns the presentation of the rudiments or theoretical aspects of music. The teacher must remember that through years of practice the system of music notation has become familiar to him, but it is new to the student. For this reason, *the instruction should be spread over a long period of time, and each phase should be applied immediately.* Equally important is the explanation itself, for the teacher is often inclined to present each phase of music theory just as it was presented to him at the college level. Since such an adult approach assumes a musical background, it is inappropriate and confusing to the inexperienced child. Other

171

important factors are child readiness and interest. As an over-all guide to the teaching of music theory, the following suggestions are offered:

1. See to it that experience precedes explanation.
2. Apply each principle as soon as it has been explained.
3. Follow a logical order of presentation.
4. Use terms carefully.

Before considering various approaches to the subject, a word of clarification seems advisable. Webster defines "theory" as "the general or abstract principles of any body of facts; pure, as distinguished from *applied,* science or art; as the theory of music." He places theory in general in the realm of the speculative and goes on to state that theory is opposed to practice, sometimes to fact. There is, of course, nothing amiss with Webster's definition, but rather with the long-standing use of the term *theory* as it applies to music. Actually, the term is a misnomer. The term *theory* as it applies to music is not opposed to practice but complementary to it. The relation between theory and practice in music corresponds to the relation between *science* and *art.* Webster defines "science" as "systematized knowledge," "art" as "knowledge made efficient by skill." Thus, the theory of music is the knowledge of music systematized, while the music that we play and hear—the practice of music—is that systematized knowledge made efficient by the skill of the performer.

In other words, music is not one thing and its theory another. When we really teach music, we are involved with its so-called theoretical aspects each step of the way. Music is what we hear, but behind the auditory experience is that systematized knowledge applied to the skill of the performer. In the teaching of music our eventual aim is to make the message of music meaningful through this system and to develop the necessary skills for bringing the sum of the science and art of music to full fruition. With this thought in mind, the so-called theory of music *should never be presented as a separate and unapplied body of knowledge.*

When should instruction in theory begin? The answer may be found in another question: "When should instruction concerning the staff, clefs, letter names, time signature, and note lengths begin?" The logical answer is that these specifics should be introduced when the child is ready, when they can be applied, and when they are needed for further development. All of this we say that we know but when should the tonic chord, for example, be introduced? The answer is, "When the child is playing one." Shall we inform the child that it is a major chord? The answer may be found in another question: "Does it have another name?"

Another question concerns the introduction to ear training. The answer is that all phases of musical growth except motor skill are dependent upon the ear. Ear training is the alpha and omega of music instruction. It is begun with the first song learned by rote.

Why Teach the Rudiments

The rudiments of music are taught in order to give the child an understanding of the symbols used in the musical score. It is unfortunate when children have little or no understanding of notation after having been exposed to music for a period of six years.

How to Teach Rudiments

The teaching of the rudiments of music will be approached differently, of course, depending on whether one uses syllables, numbers, or instruments in teaching notation. Those who use syllables or numbers will be limited, for the most part, to a practical treatment of the staff and its relationship to keyboard instruments. For example, some teachers who use either syllables or numbers limit the instruction to finding the line or space location of *do* (1) from the key signature and to locating the other tones of the scale from the key tone. Other teachers include the staff letter names so that the key may be identified by letter name. Still others include the placement and memorization of the sharps and flats in the key signature.

Those who use the instrumental approach, however, find it necessary to explain many of the specifics in far greater detail. Since this approach is more involved, we have given it the greatest emphasis in the following presentations. Those who use syllables or numbers may employ any suggestions in the material presented that seem to have practical application within their own method. A suggestion will not have practical application within their own method if it requires the child to memorize information that is not applied to the actual performance of music.

Suggestions relative to the instrumental approach are not to be construed as arbitrary, but rather as general guides. There are many attractive ways to introduce specifics so that they have meaning for the child, and the teacher is urged to use his own imagination in this matter. It is necessary, however, that a logical order be followed. Again it must be emphasized that the material presented should be spread over a long period of time and that other music activities should not be slighted. The reader is asked to examine each of the following presentations in the light of the four points listed at the beginning of this chapter.

Teachers in Action

Miss Johnson devotes a portion in the middle of each music period to the rudiments of music. She begins and ends each period with regular singing, rhythm, or listening activities. In the sessions on rudiments, the children are drilled on staff letter names, the placement of sharps and flats in key signatures, the names of the keys, scales, time signatures, and note values. Miss Johnson is convinced that knowledge of these fundamentals is prerequisite to understanding the message of music. She is determined that in this way her pupils will know something about music. Being a music enthusiast herself, she is disturbed when only a small minority of the class is even mildly interested. She attributes this to the parents' lack of interest and the pupils' lack of talent. These apparent deficiencies confirm her contention that only the talented few do anything with music. With these talented ones in mind, Miss Johnson believes that her emphasis on the rudiments of music is justified. The general disinterest and unruliness of the class are attributed to the fact that this is a spoiled generation. These children simply need discipline—mental discipline. So when the children begin to wiggle, Miss Johnson gives them a test on the key signatures or assigns them the task of writing ten measures in $\frac{4}{4}$, using different note lengths in each measure.

Mr. Jones, the principal, knows little or nothing about music and is therefore at a disadvantage in discussing the matter with Miss Johnson. He does know, however, that these children are not as enthusiastic about music as are children in other city schools. Miss Johnson considers this comparison unjust because of the difference in the economic and cultural status of the constituents of the schools. Mr. Jones requests the superintendent to assign Miss Johnson to a more cultured area of the city. The other principals, however, are reluctant to approve such an exchange. Stung by injured pride, Miss Johnson allows her artistic temperament to overcome her usual cultured dignity, for her musical ability, as she sees it, has been questioned. After all, did she not graduate with honors from a very reputable university? Has she not been organist and choir director at the same church for the past twenty years? Is she not the standard-bearer in the local music club, and the most popular organist for weddings and funerals? Mr. Jones does not question her musicianship but only her salesmanship. Since he cannot gracefully change the situation, he resigns himself to his swivel chair, twiddles his thumbs in rhythmic acquiescence, and silently prays for Miss Johnson's retirement.

In great contrast to the above approach, Miss Bates seldom mentions any specifics of music. Her purpose is to interest and develop all children through participation in various music activities. She believes that those who have great interest and are talented should be studying music privately. Since only a small minority of the children seem interested in learning something about music, little time is devoted to the specifics and to music reading. As a result, her children participate in rhythm activities and songs with great abandon. They are enthusiastic about music, for it brings complete relaxation and enjoyment.

Some of Miss Bates's colleagues complain that the music period is a time of fun and play. Since no assignments are made and nothing has to be learned, it is only natural that the children love the period. Miss Bates's critics argue that this play attitude must give way to the work attitude encouraged in other subjects. Schools are designed as institutions of learning and learning should result from each subject that is taught. Since Miss Bates must of necessity teach largely by rote, and since the children are not required to think or reason, her colleagues maintain that the children are not developing mentally. They believe that Miss Bates misses many opportunities for child development by her approach. Joining in the chorus of criticism are some of the music teachers, who feel that Miss Bates brings discredit to music by treating it as a fad or frill. They believe that such instruction has no real educational value save in its social and recreational implications. They maintain that the school board is perfectly justified in frowning upon music, *as Miss Bates teaches it,* in the interest of economy.

Miss Elson disagrees with both Miss Johnson and Miss Bates, believing that both approaches are extreme. In the case of Miss Johnson, knowledge is never applied and is therefore of no value or interest to the children. In the case of Miss Bates, the children learn nothing to apply. Being well educated and possessing broad cultural concepts, Miss Elson believes that music is related to the gamut of man's experience and that it should be employed as a means for learning in general. To her, music is not an isolated subject, for it is interwoven with the history and development of man. This approach implies work, but Miss Elson believes that even the work associated with learning can be an enjoyable experience—that there is satisfaction in self-nurture. To her, learning can be as pleasant as gathering roses if one knows how to avoid the thorns.

Miss Elson uses the instrumental approach. Realizing that symbols grew out of musical experiences, she invariably presents "the thing before the sign." Immediate application is always made, so comprehension is possible. By learning to play simple melodies, the children gain additional opportunities for hearing tonal patterns which they will encounter over and over in youthful and adult musical experiences.

Playing a Tune

The second grade children are entering the classroom after recess. Miss Elson is seated at the piano playing "Hot Cross Buns" (G. *Singing on Our Way*, p. 45), which the children have learned by rote. Several children gather around the piano and begin to sing. Soon the entire class joins in the song. As the song ends, Mary remarks, "I wish I could play the piano like you, Miss Elson."

Miss Elson is both sensitive and responsive to such remarks, for they indicate interest and readiness. She recognizes an opportune time to begin keyboard experiences. So she says, "Mary, you and each of your classmates can learn to play the piano, and it is as much fun as singing. Each of you can learn to play "Hot Cross Buns!" Place the tips of your fingers of your right hand on the desk and begin by pressing down on the middle finger. Your middle finger is number three and your thumb is number one. Which finger is number two? We only need to use these three fingers to play "Hot Cross Buns."

Miss Elson places the third finger of her right hand on B and slowly plays and sings the melody as the children imitate the fingering. She plays on a dummy keyboard[1] which is hung at the front of the room. When the children have established finger habits, Mary is invited to play the melody on the piano. Miss Elson plays the dummy keyboard, as Mary and the remainder of the class imitate her. In time, each child has an opportunity to play the dummy keyboard, the piano, and the melody bells.

"You will notice, boys and girls, that the black keys on the keyboard are in groups of twos and threes. We began our melody on the white key to the right of three black keys. The name of this key is B, the next is A, and the last one we played is G—B, A, G.

---

[1] O. Boschan, Practice Piano Keyboard, Bergenfield, New Jersey.

Let's play the melody again, singing the letter names of the keys instead of the words. Now let's sing the melody with the numbers 3, 2, 1. You will notice that when we move from 3 to 2 we skip a key—a black one. The same thing happens when we move from 2 to 1.

"How many of you can find another B, A, G on the piano? I wonder how many B's we can find?"

The children play B, A, G at various places on the piano and Miss Elson explains high and low sounds—higher sounds are to the right and lower sounds to the left. Miss Elson asks two children to play "Hot Cross Buns," one playing high and the other playing low.

Miss Elson uses numbers to identify scale tones, and not primarily as relative pitch names. In other words, she stresses the letter names as applied to the keyboard and the staff. For similar reasons she does not use Latin syllable names. She believes that the letter names may be learned in the same length of time that it takes to learn the nonsense syllables. The letter names are familiar and have meaning to the children when applied to the keyboard and staff.

The Staff

Miss Elson begins by singing "Running and Walking" (G. *Singing on Our Way*, p. 17), a song which the children have learned by rote and to which they have walked and run in rhythm activities.

"Children, have you ever wondered how we learn to sing and play? It is done much as we learn to talk and read. In learning to read, we first listen to the sound of words and then speak them; later we learn how these sounds are written by using letters. In much the same way, we learn to sing and play. First, we listen to the sounds and then sing and play them; later we learn how the sounds are written. Today we are going to see how music is written. If you will open your books to page seventeen, you will see how 'Running and Walking' is written. What is the first thing you notice, Johnny? Yes, lines. Let's count and number these lines, beginning on the bottom line. Now let's count and number the spaces between the lines, beginning in the bottom space. All together the lines and spaces are called the *staff*. This is like all the people in one family having the name of Smith, Brown, or Jones. Just as each member of a family has his own given name, such as John or Frank, so each line and space of the staff has a given name. Before long we will learn the name of each line and space. Right now we want to remember that all together the lines and spaces are called the staff." Miss Elson prints the word "staff" on the chalkboard.

"What else do you notice about the song 'Running and Walking'? Yes, the funny-looking things on the lines and in the spaces. These are called *notes*. The notes above the words *left, right* are walking, or *quarter*, notes. We walk to such notes. Notice how they are made." Miss Elson draws a note on the chalkboard, "powders its face," and adds a stem.

"The notes above the word *running* are running, or *eighth*, notes. We run to such notes." Miss Elson draws one on the chalkboard and asks how it differs from a walking, or quarter, note. "The open-faced notes at the end of the line are half notes. They are the ones on which we stop or hold.[2]

"What else do you notice about the notes? Yes, James, some are placed higher on the staff than others. In fact, the high and low places for notes on the staff remind us of the hand movements we have been using. Let's sing the song again, letting the notes tell us when to move our hand up and down."

When the song has been sung, accompanied by appropriate hand motions, Miss Elson says, "So you see, boys and girls, that music is written on five lines and spaces called the staff. The notes tell us to sing high or low, fast or slow. From now on, we will look for quarter, eighth, and half notes to learn whether the music goes fast or slow. As time goes on, we will learn many more interesting things about the staff and notes.

---

[2] Although the terms *half, quarter,* and *eighth note* have no real meaning for the children at this stage of development, Miss Elson believes it wise to use correct terms as soon as possible. Our understanding of a word—the word *mother,* for example—grows in time through constant use and association.

"Since you can already play 'Hot Cross Buns,' don't you think it would be fun to write the music on the staff? You can help me do this. As I told you before, each line and space has its own name just as you and I have names. These are letter names, and are the same as the keys on the piano. Let's play 'Hot Cross Buns' again, beginning as we did before on the white key to the right of three black keys. Sing the letter names B, A, G as you play. Since we know the names of three keys on the piano, let's find these same names on the staff. The name of the third line of the staff is B, so we will write a note on it. The note tells us to play B on the piano. Since A is the next key below B on the piano, where will A be on the staff? Second space is correct. And G? Second line is right." As Miss Elson writes the note heads on these staff degrees, the children notice that the notes do not have a line joined to them as the notes in the book do. She adds this line and explains that it is called a *stem*. "What kind of notes are these? Do they tell us to walk, run, or stop? Yes, the first two notes tell us to walk, so they are . . . ? Right, quarter notes. The third note tells us to stop, so it is a half note. Now let's sing and play these three notes. I'll point to each note on the staff as you play and sing B, A, G."

By listening to the next three tones of the song and comparing them with the first three, the children decide that they sound the same and therefore should be written in the same manner. Henry writes these notes on the chalkboard. When the children progress to the next passage in "Hot Cross Buns," some of them continue playing the melody. Through questions and by repeating the passage, Miss Elson leads them to discover that these are running, or eighth, notes. She writes them on the chalkboard and the children sing and play the entire melody, using the letter names.

In answer to a question about the "funny-looking thing" which the teacher had drawn at the beginning of the staff, Miss Elson explains that this is an old way of making the letter G. Since this letter G curls around the second line of the staff, it names that line G.

On another day, Miss Elson teaches the children to play "Hot Cross Buns" beginning on A. Since A and G are already familiar, the children have only to learn the new letter F on the piano and on the staff. In teaching the melody at this new position, Miss Elson merely instructs the children to begin on A and reminds them to skip a key between 3 and 2 and between 2 and 1. The melody is written on the chalkboard and played and sung by letter names as before.

On still another day, Miss Elson asks the children to play "Hot Cross Buns," beginning on the white key to the right of two black keys. They are reminded to skip a key as they move from 3 to 2 and from 2 to 1. In the manner described above the children learn the location of E, D, and middle C on the piano keyboard and on the staff. The melody is written on the chalkboard, played, and sung as before.

Thus, the children have learned C, D, E, F, G, A, and B on the piano and the staff. Miss Elson reminds them of this and writes the notes on the chalkboard as the children play and sing them. When they have played B, Miss Elson explains that they are again at C on the piano and on the staff—that these letters are repeated over and over on the keyboard and the staff. With this information available, Miss Elson leads the children to discover the letter names of the remaining lines and spaces of the staff.

Although "Hot Cross Buns" has been repeated a number of times, the experience has not been boring, for the children have been making new discoveries with each repetition. Because of these repetitions, 3, 2, 1 and 1, 2, 3 of the scale have been aurally established. The children are instructed to listen for these sounds in all new songs. Miss Elson introduces several new songs which contain these tonal patterns. She has found good examples in the following:

G. Singing on Our Way, pp. 7, 8, 9, 13, and 14
S. Music in Our Town, pp. 3, 7ab, 8, 11, 16, 19, and 24
F. Music Round the Town, pp. 5, 14, 21, 22, 26, 28, and 30

After learning these songs by rote and discovering the familiar scale tones, the children played 3, 2, 1 as written in each song. They knew the beginning note in each case, and Miss Elson merely reminded them to skip a key between the notes. The children were surprised when they discovered that "Mary Had a Little Lamb" was built, with one exception, out of 3, 2, 1 and 1, 2, 3 like "Hot Cross Buns."

As a review, and employed as a keyboard game, Miss Elson devised cards. The notes B, A, G; A, G, F; and E, D, C were written on different cards. On another card were the notes representing the C scale. Still another card pictured the notes C (third space), D, E, F, and G. Each child chose a card and placed it on the dummy keyboard or piano so that staff notes appeared directly above the corresponding keys. Each played the passage as three children of his choice sang. New cards were provided as the children learned new melodic passages. By using these cards, the teacher was aware of the progress being made by each child. With only three children singing at a time, she could follow each child in developing the ability to "carry a tune" and to match tones.

After learning "The Happy River" (G. *Singing on Our Way*, p. 104*ar*), by rote and singing it by scale numbers, a few of the children were able to play the song by ear. Miss Elson led the students to rediscover the letter names, and the melody was played on piano, melody bells, and dummy keyboard. The children discovered the half-step between 3 and 4 after it was explained that a *half-step was from any key on the piano to the next key above or below, white or black. A whole-step occurred when there was a key between two keys.* Miss Elson illustrated these two points on the keyboard and called special attention to the whole-step between 4 and 5.

After these experiences with "The Happy River," the children listened to find 1, 2, 3, 4, 5 and 5, 4, 3, 2, 1 in new songs being learned. Miss Elson found good examples in the following:

G. Singing on Our Way, pp. 7, 18*r*, 19*r*, 20, 27*b*, 30*b*, 40*b*, and 156*ar*
S. Music in Our Town, pp. 19, 31, 54, 109, 113*r*
F. Music Round the Town, pp. 23*r*, 26*r*, 46*r*, 54*r*, 84*r*, 122*r*

The children discovered that it was necessary to play a black key on 4 in the key of F in order to make the half-step between

3 and 4. The term B-flat was unnecessary at this point, for the children were simply being oriented to the keyboard and to melodic passages. Such specifics as sharps, flats, and key signatures will be introduced only when needed for further development. At the present, they would only clutter the road.

Through singing and playing experiences, the children eventually discovered the whole scale. They observed the half-steps between 3 and 4 and 7 and 8, and the whole-steps between all other adjacent pairs of tones. Miss Elson found scale songs in the following:

G. Singing on Our Way, pp. 22b, 29r, 40a, 41, and 50r
S. Music in Our Town, pp. 39r, 60, and 94
F. Music Round the Town, pp. 65 and 93 (song bell interludes)

The children easily played the scales in these songs by observing the steps and half-steps.

The children also learned to play tonic chord skips by singing songs from:

G. Singing on Our Way, p. 30a
S. Music in Our Town, p. 12r
F. Music Round the Town, 34r

Many examples of skips between 1, 3, and 5 were discovered in new songs being learned and Miss Elson encouraged the children to sing them with and without the aid of the piano. Next, they played these tones simultaneously and Miss Elson introduced the term tonic chord—1, 3, 5.

The skips between 1, 3, and 5 gave rise to a new series of cards for the keyboard game. These contained scale passages combined with skips between members of the tonic chord. They were selected from songs which had been learned by rote.

The F clef was explained when it was needed to play the left-hand part in such songs as "Mary Had a Little Lamb" and "Ride Away" (G. Singing on Our Way, pp. 14 and 133b respectively). The F clef, Miss Elson explained, was an old way of making the letter F, and she showed that when placed on the fourth line, it names that line F—the first F below middle C. The remaining

lines and spaces of the bass staff were named with the first seven
letters of the alphabet. Miss Elson explained that music written
with G as a clef was called *treble*, meaning high, and that music
written with F as a clef was called *bass,* meaning low. At this
point, the teacher revealed a chart which she had prepared on a
white window shade. This was placed at a prominent place in the
room where it remained for several weeks.

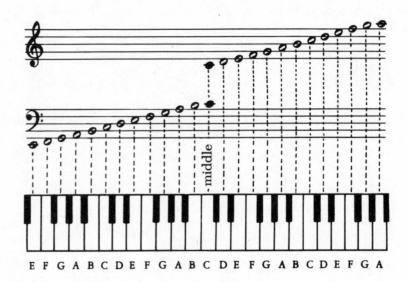

The repetition of the letters A, B, C, D, E, F, and G was explained, as well as octaves. As one child pointed to various letters
on the two staves of the chart, the children located the correct
keys on the piano.

Sharps, Flats, and the Key Signature

Miss Elson asked the children to sing the familiar song "Hippety
Hop" (G. *Singing on Our Way,* p. 20). They played the familiar
passage 1, 2, 3, 4, 5 of the first two measures starting on F. They
recalled the half-step between 3 and 4 and the black key which
was necessary on 4 to make the melody sound right. Miss Elson

called the black key a *flat* and explained that the lines and spaces may also be used to name black keys on the piano. "This is done," she explained, "by placing an additional sign on the line or space." She wrote the first two measures of "Hippety Hop" on the chalkboard and placed a flat before the note on B. "This is a flat and means to play the next key to the left of B—the key one half-step lower than B." Books were opened to page 20 and the children were asked to find a flat. They found one on B. "The flat is placed at the beginning of the song, and we must remember to play each B one half-step lower than B. B-flat makes the half-step between 3 and 4 which we have already been playing."

Miss Elson continued, explaining that signs such as flats at the beginning of a song are known as the key signature or the sign of a key. She asked each child to write his name and explained that this was his signature or sign—that no two people sign their names exactly the same.

"The key signature is the sign of a key and tells us which key the music is in—which scale it fits. In order to know the name of the key, we must find the line or space on which the scale begins." Miss Elson again referred to "Hippety Hop" and asked the children to play 4, 3, 2, 1 (B-flat, A, G, F). "F is 1. F is therefore the name of the scale or key.

"When two or more flats are found in the key signature, 1 may be found in the same manner; the flat farthest to the right is 4 of the scale." Miss Elson also pointed out that the flat to the immediate left of the last one is the name of the key. The children found the keys of all songs being learned.

After teaching "The Clown" (S. *Music in Our Town*, p. 94) by rote, Miss Elson played the last four measures. The children recognized the passage as a scale and noticed that two black keys were used. The notes of the passage were written on the chalkboard—without sharps. Miss Elson played the notes as written and the children realized that the melody was different. She then placed a sharp before each C and F and explained that these sharps tell us to play the keys to the right (a half-step higher) of C and F. After demonstrating, she played the scale passage using a C-sharp and an F-sharp. A few of the children played the scale on the piano, melody bells, and dummy keyboard.

The Time Signature

All during the first grade, the children had responded to music through rhythms of walking, running, galloping, and skipping. The music told them what to do. At times they had said "left, right" as they walked or "one, two, three, four" as they played soldier. In the second grade, with many such experiences as a background, the children were ready to understand to some degree the meaning of the time signature.

Since Miss Elson had interested the children in observing many things about the musical score, she often got questions about the "numbers" at the beginning of songs. Once, when the question was asked, Miss Elson answered, "You will remember that we have often counted 'one, two' or 'one, two, three, four' as we marched like soldiers to the music. Well, two over four tells us to count 'one, two' as we walk to quarter notes—remember we walk to quarter notes. Four over four tells us to count 'one, two, three, four' as we walk to quarter notes."

All during the first grade, Miss Elson had been very careful to establish the feeling for the relative time values of notes. With this as a background, she merely reminded the children that when we run to music we go twice as fast as when walking—that we take two running steps to one walking step. "In running to music," she explained, "our feet say 'one and two and' instead of just 'one, two' and they go twice as fast."

These were the initial explanations. They were given in connection with a song being learned. When the rhythmic feeling became established and the children were ready to begin reading, the process was reversed. That is, the children first walked and ran, clapped and counted, to find what the music told them to do.

Three-quarter time was explained as swinging music that said "one, two, three." It was like skating, and counting "one, two, three" as each foot took its turn.

"Six-over-eight time," Miss Elson explained, "is galloping music to which we count 'one, two, three, four, five, six.' When the music goes too fast to count six, we lazily count 'one, two' and let the other counts go galloping by. We often find skipping music in six-over-eight time."

An explanation of relative time values such as the whole, quarter, eighth, and sixteenth was not attempted until the children had learned to divide the whole into parts in number study. In the explanation, Miss Elson referred to the divisions of the whole note and not to a specified number of beats for each. That is, she did not associate four counts with the whole note and two with the half. The lower digit of the time signature was explained as telling us what kind of note—quarter, eighth, or half —to give a count.

Miss Elson explained the measure bar as follows: "The little line drawn across the lines of the staff is called a *bar*. It tells us when to count *one*. When I conduct, I draw bars for you as my hand comes down on count *one*."

Chording

After the children had had wide experience in playing the tonic chord as explained earier in this chapter, Miss Elson introduced the dominant chord as follows: "Play the tones of the tonic chord (C, E, G—1, 3, 5) together. Now move the third finger down a whole-step to D and the thumb down a half-step to B. The little finger, like 'this little piggy,' stays home on G. The last chord we played is the *dominant* or five chord. You will notice that we played G, B, and D but not in that order. We just played the D and B nearest at hand."

Miss Elson wrote C and G on the chalkboard. The children played each chord as their teacher indicated by pointing. Occasionally Miss Elson indicated the tonic chord by holding up one finger and the dominant chord by displaying five fingers. When the children became proficient in fingering the chord change, Miss Elson began to sing "Put Your Little Foot" (G. *Singing Together*, p. 31r). She indicated the chord change as suggested above. The children also played these chords on the melody bells (one child on each chord tone) and on the autoharp.

Miss Elson's first aim in chording at the keyboard was to establish finger habits. Having done this, the children were soon able to play chords in any key.

The second aim was to establish an aural feeling for the chord changes suggested by a melody. At first, Miss Elson indicated the chord change, but gradually left the decision to the children. At times she let students who were good at hearing chord changes direct the performers by indicating the changes with one and five fingers.

For keys other than C–G, for example—Miss Elson wrote G and D on the chalkboard. With a few reminders, but depending mostly on finger habits, the children were soon playing the I and V chords in G and in other keys.

Rhythmic chording was introduced with the familiar "Put Your Little Foot." Two children were seated at the piano. The child on the left played C in the bass on count *one* while the child on the right played the C chord on counts *two* and *three*. At a signal from the teacher, the rhythm was repeated for the G chord. Miss Elson indicated the rhythm for the bass with her left hand and the rhythm for the treble with the right. Chord changes were indicated with the fingers. After starting the children with an "um-pa-pa" rhythm, the teacher began to sing the melody "Put Your Little Foot."

For the subdominant chord, Miss Elson built a chord on the fourth (IV) tone of the scale—F, A, C in the key of C. She explained that the tones were not always played in that order. "In going from the I to the IV chord we usually move the fingers the shortest distance possible. In the key of C, for example, the thumb remains on C, the middle finger moves up a half-step to F, and the little finger moves up a whole-step to A."

When finger habits had been established between the I and IV chords, the teacher explained that "very often the IV chord is followed by the V chord. This is played by moving each of the fingers down to a tone of the dominant chord. Notice that the middle finger moves farther than the others."

On another day, Miss Elson explained that they might play F instead of D in the dominant chord (key of C). This is known as the dominant seventh chord (V_7). The children played the I and V_7 chord on familiar songs. Still later, the children learned to go from IV to V_7 by keeping the third finger stationary and moving the thumb and little fingers down to the familiar tones of the dominant. When a question was asked concerning the little 7 by V (V_7), Miss Elson built a four tone chord on the fifth tone of the scale and counted up seven staff degrees from the *root* to locate the upper tone of the chord. As time went on, the children played the I, IV, and V_7 chords on several of the songs listed at the close of this chapter.

Major and Minor Modes

After presenting a song in the minor key and listening to comments by the children, Miss Elson explained that most of our music is written in either the major or minor *mode*. "Mode," she explained, "means style or manner and has to do with the way the steps and half-steps are arranged in the scale. As you know, the major scale has a whole-step between each of its tones from 1 to 8—except between 3 and 4, and 7 and 8, where there are half-steps. The whole-steps and half-steps come at different places in the minor scale than they do in the major scale, and this makes the scales sound much different. The easiest way to discover this difference is to play first one scale and then the other. Let's play the familiar C scale. Now play the same scale, but with 3 and 6 a half-step lower. This is the minor scale, on which music in the minor mode is based. In playing chords in the minor mode, we continue to lower the third and sixth of the scale." Miss Elson also explained that a minor scale is named after the tone on which it begins and that the third tone of the minor scale tells us the key signature.

As the need arose, Miss Elson explained other matters relating to the two modes. "Sometimes both the major and minor modes are found in the same song—C major and C minor, or C minor and C major.

"Equally interesting is that a minor scale is often found to begin three half-steps below a given major, such as C major and A minor. The sharp or natural often found on the seventh tone of the minor scale is necessary to make a half-step between 7 and 8."

Statements to Avoid

Examples of the type of statement to avoid are:

A flat lowers a note a line or space.

A sharp raises a note a line or space.

Sharps and flats are the black keys.

The G clef is so named because it is placed on the second line, which is G.

Play the black (or white) note on the piano.

A measure is the space between two measure bars.

The time signature tells us the number of notes in a measure.

A whole note gets four beats; the half note gets two, and the quarter, one.

For Further Development

1. Discuss the presentations of Misses Johnson, Bates, and Elson in the light of the four suggestions made at the beginning of this chapter.

2. Using the outline for the various grades given in chapter 6, make a list of the specifics which may be introduced at each grade level.

3. Write your plan for the introduction of each specific. Make sure that the order is logical, that terms are comprehensible, and that the material can be applied.

4. Arrange for a listening period to hear the music of the Romantic period. See chapters 12 and 13. Make a list of your favorite recordings, those which you would like for your record library.

PART 2 Materials

CHAPTER 9

Prologue—With a Song in His Heart

For ages past, people have been making music. Whether in the savage tribe or in a modern civilized group, music has been present on every important occasion in the lives of people—love, marriage, worship, war, death. The peoples of ancient Sumer, Egypt, Babylon, Assyria, Greece, and Rome created music and song, danced, and played musical instruments. Although our written symbols for preserving music did not begin to take form until around the tenth century A.D., music was already comparatively well developed by 5000 B.C. Long before man could read or write, he was pouring out his expressions of joy and sorrow, his deepest feeling and longings, in song. Of course, these were not written down at the time but passed on from one generation to another by ear. The development of language and written symbols only intensified man's musical expression so that the higher the intellectual or cultural level, the greater the musical development.

Music has always been so intimate a part of man, so expressive of his thoughts, customs, and feelings, that it must be considered an important revelation of his character and nature. What is man like? Why does he behave as he does? The answers to these and other questions may be found, in part, in his music.

Self-Portrait in Song

One of the greatest of man's self-portraits is the *folk song.* Here is his own account of his nature and behavior. Folk songs probably can best be described in the words of Abraham Lincoln as songs "of the people, by the people, and for the people." They were not composed by professional musicians and were not written down at the time of their creation. In fact, many of them are the result of communal effort, with succeeding generations adapting or making alterations. Their natural, easy, spontaneous, unsophisticated expression of thought and feeling, their straight-forward manner, honesty, and sincerity, are completely refreshing in an environment of the parvenu and sycophant whose extraneous attitudes are complicated by the pseudo expressions of "arty" art. Folk songs, like the Bible, do not disguise the character and deeds of man, but picture him as he really is—at his worst and at his best.

Music is not something that has been imposed upon the people; it has grown up with them as part of their daily living and as an expression of their deepest feelings. Just as there are differences in geography, climate, politics, racial characteristics, language, and philosophy, so there are differences in musical instruments, dances, and songs. To really know man, then, one must not only know his history but must also make a study of what he has said and how he has said it. Since man so vividly reveals his nature and character in song, we may consider this medium as a group interview. With this in mind, we should not consider a song as an end in itself, but rather as a means to an end—the understanding of a people at a particular time and place in history. The object is not only to learn a song but also to know its creator and understand his message in the light of his time. To interpret any musical composition outside its historical setting is to miss its most significant message. It is for this reason that the study of music is so fascinating, leading one to a consideration of all areas of the humanities. Therefore, the presentation in these pages follows a chronological order, so that the reader may correlate song material with the history and literature of various periods, thus gaining a deep insight into people.

In examining the relationship between music and other areas of human endeavor, consider the following questions:

Could one fully appreciate Beethoven's *Eroica* ("Heroic") *Symphony* without knowing that Napoleon was the hero to whom the composition was dedicated, and that the dedication was renounced when Napoleon declared himself Emperor? Would not one miss the real message if he did not understand the conditions which molded Napoleon and Beethoven?

Would not one miss the whole point in "The Two Grenadiers" if he did not understand the love and loyalty inspired in his soldiers by Napoleon? It is important that in this song two Germans, Heine and Schumann, expressed the patriotism of France, even to the extent of employing the "Marseillaise" at the climax of the song.

This treatise is not a history of man or of his music. It is a panoramic view, and at best it can only help to quicken an interest that may eventually lead the student to discover his counterpart in the musical expressions of his fellow human beings and to grow in his understanding and appreciation of man.

In later chapters, the musical activities and characteristics of different historical periods will be sketched and then illustrated by means of selected songs and recordings. First, however, the musical characteristics of the various nationalities will be briefly described.

National Characteristics

Listed below are the musical characteristics of various nationalities as expressed in both song and dance. Because of their use in school, their tie-in with social studies, and as an aid to the teacher in extending his musical horizons, a number of types of instrumental compositions are included as illustrations. These have been based on, or developed from, traditional dances of various nations. Like folk songs, dances of the people embody the basic elements of musical form and have played a prominent part in the development of the larger forms of music. In each, one may expect to hear a statement of the main theme (first melody) followed by a digression (second melody). The original theme will usually be stated again in the closing portion of the composition (simple ternary form). Occasionally, there may be more than two themes.

North and South America

CANADA. The music of Canada definitely shows European influence. Approximately one-third of the people are French-Canadian, and in certain areas French is the language in everyday use.

F. Voices of America, p. 170r
S. Music in Our Country, p. 20
F. Voices of the World, p. 12

MEXICO. Mexican music is influenced by the Spanish and Aztec cultures. The rhythm is invigorating and the melodies are haunting.

S. Music Around the World, p. 61
F. Voices of the World, p. 164
G. Singing in Harmony, p. 7
S. Music Near and Far, p. 170r
Capitol T-10205 Clauson in Mexico

SOUTH AMERICA. The folk music of South American countries shows a strong Spanish influence. Many of the old Spanish tunes, particularly dance tunes, may be heard in Mexico, Cuba, and even in lower California. The music is characterized by engaging and irresistible rhythms and by sweet, haunting melodies. There are many dances, such as the tango (Argentina) and the habanera (Cuba). The marimba comes from Guatemala, Mexico's neighbor on the south. Maracas and castanets are characteristic rhythm instruments.

Argentina
F. Music Through the Year, p. 117r
S. Music Near and Far, pp. 50r, 52ar
Brazil
F. Music Round the Town, p. 24r
S. Music in Our Country, p. 156r
S. Music Around the World, p. 216r

Chile
G. Singing in Harmony, pp. 81r, 169r
S. Music Near and Far, p. 173r
S. Music Around the World, pp. 165r, 178r
F. Voices of the World, p. 170
Venezuela
F. Voices of the World, p. 176
Equador
F. Music Round the World, p. 31r
F. Voices of the World, p. 174
Records:
Capitol T-10089 Music of Peru
Capitol T-10088 Music of Bolivia
Capitol T-10053 Argentine Tangos
Capitol T-10115 Music of Paraguay
Capitol T-10134 Brazilian Guitar

Western Europe

ENGLAND. Shakespeare's many references to music as well as its known importance in court affairs during the reign of Queen Elizabeth indicate that music had been a definite part of the daily lives of people prior to this period. The Gregorian chant, brought to Britain by St. Augustine in A.D. 597, contributed to a formal structure; the Normans provided a romantic flavor; Italian and French instruments gave variety; Puritan psalms interposed a gloomy touch; and the Cavaliers' drinking songs added a dashing gaiety. As we shall see, English music exerted a strong influence in young America.

Hey or Hay. This was an English country dance. Although associated with the May Day festivals, it is not a morris dance. It is believed that its derivation is from the French *haie* (hedge), in which the dancers stood in two rows representing hedges. The rhythm is joyous and invigorating.

Gigue or Jig. This is an old English dance which derived its name from the early fiddle. The tempo is lively. It is the final dance in suites. It is usually in two parts, each of which is repeated. It is very often in $\frac{6}{8}$ meter.

Galliard. This merry old dance, though at first considered vulgar, was popular in Elizabethan England.

Hornpipe. This is another of the old English dances. It is very spirited and energetic. There are usually two sections, each of which is repeated.

F. Music Round the Town, pp. 101, 107
F. Voices of the World, p. 21
G. Singing in Harmony, p. 50
S. Music Around the World, p. 222r
S. Music Near and Far, p. 160
Victor 41-6174 English Dance
Victor 41-6181 Maypole Dance
Victor 41-6175 Ribbon Dance

SCOTLAND. The music of Scotland is interesting because of its unusual rhythm and melody, indicating the influence of the national instrument, the bagpipe. Because of the restricted range of this instrument, many Scotch tunes are based upon the pentatonic or five-tone scale. The words of some of their more familiar songs were written by Robert Burns.

Reel. The origin of this spirited dance is obscure. Today it is associated with the Scotch and Irish. It is a dance of the people.

F. Music Around the World, pp. 8, 66
F. Voices of America, pp. 144, 146
G. Singing in Harmony, p. 29
F. Music Through the Year, p. 68
Victor 41-6179 Highland Fling
Capitol T-10081 Scottish Pipes

IRELAND. The music of Ireland, like that of Scotland and Wales, is very old. According to Hecatorus, an Egyptian historian, Irish harpers and singers were already active by 500 B.C. Even before St. Patrick came to Ireland in A.D. 432, music was used in the Irish worship service and a system of musical notation was in existence. Harp contests date back to the sixth century and were held in Tara's Hall. Irish songs combine joy and sorrow. The jig is the most characteristic popular dance. In addition to harps and fiddle, the Irish also use bagpipes.

S. Music in Our Country, p. 38
F. Voices of the World, p. 38
F. Voices of America, p. 133
Capitol T-10028 My Ireland

WALES. The Welsh bards were among the first storytellers. They were very popular and exerted a tremendous musical influence during the twelfth century. The Welsh love to sing and are known for their song festivals and contests which date back to the seventh century.

    S. Music Around the World, p. 17*r*
    S. Music Near and Far, p. 169
    G. Singing in Harmony, p. 90
    F. Music Across Our Country, pp. 115*r*, 150
    F. Voices of the World, p. 18
    G. Singing Everyday, p. 102

HOLLAND, BELGIUM, LUXEMBURG. Since the language of these countries includes French, Dutch, and Flemish, it is to be expected that the music should reflect these influences. The Dutch are partial to the sea and show a strong liking for sailor songs and dances. They also love the psalms and old hymn tunes of the Dutch Reform Church. A collection of these was in the Ainsworth Psalter which the Dutch brought to America on the Mayflower.

    S. Music Now and Long Ago, pp. 29, 92*b*
    S. Music Near and Far, p. 162
    F. Music Across Our Country, p. 109
    F. Music 'Round the Clock, p. 82*r*.
    F. Music Round the Town, p. 34*r*
    G. Singing in Harmony, p. 143
    Victor 41-6176 Chimes of Dunkirk

GERMANY. The Germans have always manifested a strong interest in music. They love to sing and dance. Their legends and heroic deeds were sung by the Minnesinger and Meistersinger. Martin Luther made many religious adaptations of German secular tunes for use in the Lutheran worship service. One of the immortal Lutheran hymns is "A Mighty Fortress is Our God."

Waltz. This is an important dance of Austria and Germany which, like the minuet, has sustained its popularity through the ages. It often consists of a series of dances which may be of different lengths. Excellent examples are those by Strauss and Chopin. *Valse* is the French word for waltz. The characteristic $\frac{3}{4}$ rhythm is easily recognized.

Allemande. This is an old German dance. Its form is often irregular but is usually in two parts each of which is repeated. It
was used in the early suites. It is in a flowing quadruple rhythm.

Schottische. This is a dance resembling the polka and sometimes
called the German polka.

Galop. The galop is a dance of German origin and is very
spirited. It may contain an introduction, two trios and a coda.

F. Music Through the Year, pp. 156, 169
F. Music Round the Town, p. 74r
G. Singing in Harmony, p. 23
S. Music Near and Far, pp. 3, 145
F. Voices of the World, p. 86
Victor 41-6177 Bummel Schottische
Victor 41-6179 Kinderpolka
Capitol T-10149 Bielefelder Kindechor (Children's Choir of Bielefeld)

AUSTRIA. The music of Austria is similar to that of Germany.
The waltz, which originated in Austria, is a favorite dance of
both Austria and Germany.

S. Music Near and Far, p. 68
F. Voices of the World, p. 90
S. Music Around the World, p. 14r
Capitol T-10154 Austrian Folk Music

FRANCE. Charlemagne's directive that the Gregorian chant
should be taught in the schools exerted a strong Christian influence on French song. The influence of the troubadours is also
present. Many French songs are very old and deeply emotional.
French songs may be heard in Louisiana and in other French
settlements in the United States and Canada.

Minuet, Menuet or Menuetto. This is an old French dance
which was used in the early suites and reached its highest
development with Haydn, Mozart, and Beethoven. It has remained popular through the centuries. Originally, it was a stately
dance used at royal courts and aristocratic balls. When it was
introduced into the suite, sonata, and symphony, however, its
pace was quickened and its character somewhat altered. Haydn,
a practical joker, sometimes used it in a humorous manner and
his student Beethoven went a step further in making a joke of it,

thus transforming the minuet into a *scherzo,* meaning joke. The difference between the minuet and the scherzo is therefore one of tempo and character rather than form. In the larger works, a second contrasting minuet follows the first. This is known as the *trio,* since it was originally written in three-part harmony. The trio is followed by a return to the original section. In other words, A, B (trio), A, as in the march form.

Loure. This is another of the French dances which may be found in some suites. It is performed in a very legato style, since it is a descendent of bagpipe tunes.

Gavotte. This is an old French dance which was used in the suites and remains popular today. It has been described as a "brisk round for as many as will." It has two parts, each of which is repeated.

Courante. This dance is of French and Italian origin, its name being derived from *courir,* to run. It moves at a rapid tempo in triple meter. The dance was used in suites and followed the allemande. It, too, is in two parts, each of which is repeated.

Anglaise. This old dance is believed to have originated in France or England. It is lively and energetic and may be found in some suites.

Rigaudon. This is a gay and lively old French dance which was used during the time of Louis XIII. It became popular in England during the seventeenth century. It is usually in three or four parts.

Bourrée. The origin of this dance is not definitely known. It is usually considered to be French, although some contend that it is Spanish. It is to be found in some suites and is also in two parts, each of which is repeated. It is in a quick and jovial triple meter throughout.

Dance Macabre. This is French for "dance of death." The tradition of this dance, though not the music, goes back to the Middle Ages.

F. Music Round the Town, p. 117
S. Music Near and Far, p. 152
S. Music in Our Country, p. 69r
G. Singing Together, p. 42r
Victor 41-6181 Minuet

Central Europe

POLAND. Unlike some other Slavic races, the Poles are devoted Roman Catholics, and this has tended to give their music a European flavor. The use of instruments has affected the rhythm and melody of their songs. European and Asiatic people have used Poland as their battleground. These three influences have caused Poland's music to differ in some respects from that of other Slavic peoples, although it retains some Slavic characteristics.

Mazurka. This is a national dance of Poland which was known as early as the sixteenth century. The original dance took the character of an improvisation, the dancers originating new steps and figures. Originally it was considered vulgar. Chopin changed the dance to such an extent that its original characteristics are hardly apparent. The mazurka may be in two to four parts. The best examples are found among the fifty-two mazurkas for piano solo by Chopin.

Polonaise. This is probably the most animated and chivalrous of the country dances. It is of Polish origin. Chopin, a true son of Poland with a deep national feeling, developed it to a very high degree and brought to it international fame. Chopin, of course, altered its dance nature as he did that of the waltz and the mazurka. The form usually involves one section following another, with a final return to the first. A trio is sometimes found following the second section.

F. Music Through the Year, p. 35
S. Music in Our Country, p. 208*b*
G. Singing Together, p. 115*r*
Capitol T-10084 Music of Poland

HUNGARY. Hungarian music is characterized by syncopation and great contrast in rhythm, reflecting to some extent the gypsy influence. Then, too, the Hungarians are a quick and temperamental people. Although gypsy music is associated with Hungary, it must be remembered that gypsies simply copy and alter the music of the land they roam. Since they were employed as musicians by the influential Magyars, Hungarian gypsies exerted wide influence.

Czardas. This dance is of Hungarian origin. It consists of two movements, one slow and the other fast. Some of the best examples of this dance are found in certain of Liszt's Hungarian rhapsodies.

F. Music Round the Town, p. 13r
F. Voices of the World, p. 118ab
F. Music Through the Year, p. 161
Victor 41-6182 Hungarian Dance
Capitol T-10085 Music of Hungary

CZECHOSLOVAKIA, BOHEMIA, MORAVIA. Although influenced to some extent by Germany, Austria, Poland, and Hungary, the music of these peoples is Slavic in feeling. All Slavic people are fond of the dance and their songs reflect this influence. The polka which is popular today originated in Bohemia.

Polka. This is a well known "round dance" of Bohemian origin.

S. Music in Our Country, pp. 198r, 180
G. Singing in Harmony, pp. 40r, 41r
F. Voices of the World, p. 108
G. Singing Together, p. 21
F. Voices of America, p. 20r
S. Music in Our Town, p. 108r
S. Music Around the World, p. 85
Victor 41-6182 Czechoslovakian Dance

SWITZERLAND
S. Music Around the World, p. 3
S. Music in Our Country, p. 185
G. Singing Together, p. 20r
F. Voices of the World, p. 75
S. Music Now and Long Ago, p. 50r
S. Music Near and Far, p. 4r
Capitol T-10161 Swiss Mountain Music
Capitol T-10009 Music of the Swiss Alps

Southern Europe (Bordering the Mediterranean)

ITALY. For ages past, singing has been a favorite pastime for Italians. Like other Latin peoples, the Italians are gay, passionate, and fond of excitement. Song is a natural expression of the Italian lover. Since the guitar and mandolin are favorite instruments, the harmonic structure of the Italian song is very simple. Songs from Naples and Venice reflect the influence of the sea.

Tarantella. This is a rapid Italian dance, the tempo of which increases as the dance progresses. Castanets and tambourines are often used as accompaniment and the sections alternate between major and minor keys. It is usually dramatic in character, since it was believed that the dance was a cure for the bite of the tarantula spider.

S. Music in Our Country, p. 164
G. Singing in Harmony, pp. 79, 52r

SPAIN and PORTUGAL. Moorish and gypsy influence are reflected in the life and expression of the Spanish. Many of their songs are based upon dance rhythms and are unusual and of rare beauty. Favorite instruments are the mandolin, tambourine (to accent the beat for the dancers), and castanets (for additional rhythmic effects). The Spanish influence may be observed in South America, in California, and along the borders of the Rio Grande.

The music of Portugal is similar to that of Spain but with less excitement.

Bolero. This is a Spanish dance in triple meter. The monotonous and colorful rhythm of this dance is easily recognized and remembered.

Sarabande. This is a serious and stately dance of Spain. When it first appeared, it was considered somewhat vulgar but in time it became one of the most dignified of the country dances. It is found in suites just before the concluding *gigue.* The sarabande is in slow triple rhythm.

Fandango. This is another national dance of Spain. The first and last parts were usually in minor keys with the *trio* or middle portion in a major key. The accompaniment was usually a guitar and castanets.

F. Music Round the Town, p. 62r
S. Music in Our Country, p. 18
G. Singing Together, p. 151r

Capitol T-10045 Spanish Guitars
Capitol T-10157 Spanish Castanets

GREECE
S. Music Around the World, p. 12r
S. Music Near and Far, p. 62r

Scandinavian Europe

NORWAY. Many of the folk songs of Norway reflect a geographical influence. They are the songs of the forester, herdsman, fisherman, and hunter. The *yodel* is used to call cattle home from the mountains. Other songs are humorous and vigorous, and some are tender and poetic.

F. Music Across Our Country, p. 15r
G. Singing in Harmony, p. 95
G. Singing Together, p. 27r
Victor 41-6173 Norwegian Dance
Capitol T-10069 Songs of the Norwegian Fjords

SWEDEN and DENMARK. Like other Teutons, these people love poetry, music, and dancing, the latter yielding a pantomimic description of the people.

Swedish folk songs are characterized by their happy nature, some of them suggesting the Tyrolean yodel. The national instrument is the lute, which came to Sweden from Italy.

The music of Denmark is similar to that of Sweden, although more strongly marked by German and French influences. The reel, which is similar to the Scotch and Irish reel, is a favorite Danish dance.

F. Voices of America, pp. 107r, 116, 117
F. Voices of the World, p. 50
F. Music Across Our Country, pp. 12r, 67r
F. Music Through the Year, p. 64r
S. Music Through the Day, p. 5r
Victor 41-6169 Danish and Swedish Dances
Victor 41-6170 Swedish Dances
Capitol T-10039 Swedish Polkas and Hambos
Capitol T-10176 Swedish and Norwegian Songs, William Clauson

FINLAND and ICELAND. Owing to the influence of deep forests and numerous lakes, the songs of Finland and Iceland are mystical and melancholy, expressing deep emotion and tenderness. In the warmer climate of the south of these countries, songs are of a brighter character. As in Sweden, there are numerous songs of the herdsman.

The music of Iceland has changed little through the centuries. Even the secular songs are based upon ecclesiastical modes of the early church.

F. Music Across Our Country, p. 13r
S. Music Near and Far, p. 72r

Russia

Since a majority of the Russian people are peasants, there is a wealth of folk song and dance. Because of Russia's vast size and sectionalism, there is great variety in their music. Many songs are sad, and in minor keys, reflecting the oppression of the people, the severe climate, and the toil on the land. However, the minor mode often gives way to the major, producing contrasting emotional effects. Since no instruments are used in the worship service of the Russian Orthodox Church or the Greek Orthodox Church, voices are highly developed, particularly the low male voice. Russian religious music of the past is among the most beautiful in the world. The most popular folk instrument is the *balalaika,* and the favorite peasant dance is the *trepak.*

F. Voices of the World, pp. 119, 122
S. Music Around the World, p. 62
G. Singing in Harmony, p. 38r

Africa

African music is characterized by strong rhythm. Many of their songs, like those of the American Indian, are constructed from a very few tones which are repeated. Some of their songs remind one of our own Negro spirituals in that the leader and the chorus alternate in singing.

S. Music Around the World, p. 112r
S. Music Near and Far, p. 86r
F. Voices of the World, pp. 136, 137, 141
Capitol T-10114 Music of the African Zulus

Southwestern Asia

Much of the music of Southwestern Asia shows the influence of the chant. This is particularly true of Israel. Many of the melodies are in minor keys and very beautiful.

S. Music Near and Far, p. 60br
S. Music Around the World, p. 97
F. Voices of the World, pp. 124, 125, 126, 127, 128
Capitol T-10064 Jewish Music

Southern and Eastern Asia

Since ancient times music has been a definite part of Oriental culture, being used extensively in religious ceremonies and dances. Even so, Oriental peoples have been slow in developing music as a pure art form. Although examples of the eight-tone scale may be found in Oriental music, the pentatonic (five-tone) scale is the favorite. Most strange to the Occidental ear is the division of tones into many parts, which gives an out-of-tune effect. String and wind instruments are used. Drums, bells, gongs, and many other types of percussion instruments are in common use. Instrumental music is more popular than vocal, the singing being of a high, nasal quality.

CHINA
F. Music Through the Year, p. 32r
F. Music Across Our Country, p. 23r
S. Music Around the World, p. 172r
Capitol T-10087 China

INDIA
S. Music Around the World, p. 174br
F. Voices of the World, pp. 144, 145
Capitol T-10090 Modern Motion Picture Music of India

JAPAN
S. Music in Our Country, p. 163r
S. Music Near and Far, p. 141r
F. Voices of the World, p. 150
F. Music Across Our Country, p. 19
Capitol T-10195 Music of Japan

KOREA
F. Voices of the World, p. 153

PHILIPPINES
F. Voices of the World, p. 175
G. Singing in Harmony, p. 83
S. Music Near and Far, p. 13r

JAVA
F. Voices of the World, p. 140

Australia and the Pacific Islands

AUSTRALIA
S. Music Near and Far, p. 53

HAWAII
S. Music in Our Country, p. 152
F. Voices of the World, p. 160
F. Music Across Our Country, p. 29
S. Music Near and Far, p. 111r

Records

Special attention is directed to the following recordings which are recommended for use in connection with certain nationalities mentioned above.

Capitol[1] PBR-8345 (two records—Roger Wagner Chorale) which includes the following pieces. Wales: Men of Harlech; All Through the Night; The Ash Grove. Scotland: Loch Lomond; Flow Gently, Sweet Afton; The Blue Bells of Scotland. England: Greensleeves; Oh, Dear, What Can the Matter Be?; When Love is Kind; Oh, No John; Barbara Allen. Ireland: Cockles and Mussels; The Minstrel Boy. Italy: Santa

---

[1] Capitol Records, Inc., Hollywood and Vine, Hollywood 28, California, is connected with the only world-wide recording network and can supply recordings from any country.

Lucia; La Vera Sorrentina. France: J'ai du bon Tabac; It etait une Bergere; Au clair de la Lune; Frere Jacques; Adieux à la Jeunesse. Spain: Ayer te he Visto; Baile de Gaita. Germany: Du, Du liegst mir im Herzen; Muss i denn, Lebewohl; O Tannenbaum; Die Lorelei. Norway: Jeg lagde mig sa silde. Denmark: Gaaer jig udi Skoven. Sweden: Ack, Varmeland, du skona. Holland: Rosa.

Folkways FD6501 Folk Dances of the World's People. Vol. 1 includes dances from the Balkans and Middle East.

Folkways FD6502 Folk Dances of the World's People (Europe).

Folkways FD6503 Folk Dances of the World's People (Caribbean and South America).

Folkways FD6504 Folk Dances of the World's People (Middle East).

Folkways FS3881 National Anthems: U.S., Belgium, Canada, Czechoslovakia, Great Britain, France, Germany, Israel, Japan, Mexico, Netherlands, Turkey, USSR.

Folkways[2] FS3882 National Anthems: Ireland, Yugoslavia, Greece, Cuba, Philippines, New Zealand, Panama, Brazil, Italy, Australia, Poland.

America, the Melting Pot

To cover adequately the folk songs of any one nation, or even of a racial group within a nation, would require volumes. Because of their value for instruction in the American schoolroom, however, we will present a panorama of songs of American heritage in the chapters which follow. These songs, like Americans, are related to other people of the world. We hope that the student will extend his musical horizons and hence his understanding of other races by a thorough study of these songs.

Americans are the most miscegeneous group of people ever joined in a common cause. In our veins flows blood from all peoples of this globe, and for this reason America has been called the melting pot of the world. We are white, brown, black, yellow, and red with additional variegated shades to soften the contrast. Coming from all corners of the world, we have brought the philosophies, feelings, customs, religions, songs, and dances of our

---

[2] Folkways Records and Service Corp., 117 West 46th Street, New York, N.Y., has a very large collection of authentic folk music.

ancestors with the intent of blending them into what we so proudly call Americanism. Our distinction as a race lies in our heterogeneous qualities, and in this respect we are unlike any other nation.

Moreover, America is the melting pot of the world in the songs she sings, for many songs she holds dear are actually "foreigners" which have been "naturalized." It is interesting to observe changes in music and text in the naturalization process as the songs were adapted to their new world environment or acclimated to local areas. Furthermore, it is interesting to observe the influence on song of climate, geography, political conditions, and racial characteristics.

We will begin our inventory of American songs with a glance at our best known Christmas carols. Although not usually classified as folk songs, the Christmas songs of America certainly belong to the people and, as we shall see, are borrowed for the most part from other peoples of the world. A list of the best known of these songs follows. Information pertaining to each is given as a reference for the teacher.

Christmas Carols

Silent Night (Stille Nacht). This immortal carol has found its way into the heart of all Christendom and has been translated into almost one hundred languages. It was composed on Christmas Eve, 1818, at Oberndorf, Bavaria. Special music was needed for the midnight mass. In desperation the vicar of the church, Joseph Mohr, wrote the verses and Franz Gruber, the church organist, composed the music. Since the organ was broken, a guitar was used as accompaniment.

Oh Come, All Ye Faithful (Adeste Fideles). This great hymn of the ages is, like "Silent Night," a universal favorite throughout Christendom, having been translated into over one hundred tongues. A manuscript by John Wade, dated 1751, contained the melody. The song was used as a processional for Christmas midnight mass in France. It is sometimes sung in America to the words "How Firm a Foundation."

The First Noel. This old folk song carol dates back to the sixteenth century and probably originated in France, although it is also claimed by England. "Noel" is from the Latin word *natalis,* from which we get our word nativity, and has come to refer to the birth of Christ. It will be noted that the first verse refers to the shepherds and that other verses refer to the Three Wisemen who came later to Bethlehem.

Hark! The Herald Angels Sing. Charles and John Wesley were the founders of the Methodist Church. Charles wrote hundreds of religious poems which have been set to hymn tunes. "Hark! The Herald Angels Sing" is one of these and was written in 1739. The melody is from a Mendelssohn cantata which was written in Leipzig in 1840 to commemorate the 400th anniversary of the invention of printing. Some years later Dr. W. H. Cummings, an English organist, adapted the melody to Wesley's poem.

Joy to the World. Isaac Watts, like Charles Wesley, wrote hundreds of hymns which are still in use in Protestant churches. Watts, a minister, was forced to leave the pulpit because of ill health. In 1719, he published a collection of hymns and paraphrases based upon the Psalms. "Joy to the World" is one of the latter and is based on the Ninety-eighth Psalm. The melody we sing to this beautiful text is Lowell Mason's adaptation of Handel's "Antioch."

Away in a Manger. This fifteenth-century German melody is sometimes attributed to Luther and often appears under the title "Luther's Cradle Hymn." There is no evidence, however, that he wrote it, although he may have used it. It is loved by children and adults throughout the world.

God Rest Ye Merry, Gentlemen. Although already a popular Christmas song of merry England, this carol was immortalized in Charles Dickens' *Christmas Carol.* The tune dates back to at least the seventeenth century.

O Little Town of Bethlehem. The words of this favorite American carol were written by Phillips Brooks, rector at Holy Trinity Church, Philadelphia, and later Bishop of Boston. It is said that Brooks got the inspiration for the poem while on a visit to Bethlehem and later wrote the poem for the children of his church. Lewis Redner, organist and Sunday school superintendent at the Philadelphia Church where Brooks was rector, wrote the music. Although Phillips Brooks was one of the greatest pulpit orators of all times, he probably never delivered a message that has lived in the hearts of the people as has "O Little Town of Bethlehem."

Good Christian Men, Rejoice. This old favorite has helped good men to "rejoice with heart, and soul, and voice" through the years. The song as we know it is a paraphrase by John Neale (1819-1866) of "In Dulci Jubilo." Its origins are unknown, but legend has it that Henry Suso, a Dominican priest of the fourteenth century, dreamed of hearing angels singing the carol. John Neale, a retired minister, translated many Latin and Greek hymns into English.

We Three Kings of Orient Are. The words and music of this favorite American carol were written by the Reverend John Hopkins, rector of Christ's Church (Episcopal) at Williamsport, Pennsylvania, in 1857. The words, of course, are based upon legend, for there is no scriptural reference to the number or names of the kings. Christ's royalty is represented by the gift of gold, His divinity by frankincense, and His suffering by myrrh.

The Coventry Carol. A scene in the Corpus Christi pageant sponsored by Queen Margaret of England in 1456 portrays the women of Bethlehem lamenting in song the edict of Herod for the slaughter of their children. While the text and music as we know them were not in the original play, the idea is the same. The text is by Robert Croo, 1534, and the melody originated in 1591, when the pageant was revived.

Lo, How a Rose E'er Blooming. "Lo, how a Rose e'er blooming, From tender stem hath sprung, of Jesse's lineage coming, as men of old have sung." These lines refer to the prophesy concerning the coming of Christ (Isaiah 11:1)—a flower blossoming in spiritual winter. The song is of fifteenth-century German origin and was probably used as a Twelfth Night carol. Michael Praetorious (1571-1621) is the composer, and the carol was first published in Cologne in 1600. This carol is an excellent example of Renaissance rhythmic flow and turns of melody, for it has come down to us almost untouched from its original form.

Angels We Have Heard on High. The Latin version of this old carol is "Gloria in Excelsis Deo," and in England it is known as the "Westminster Carol." It is believed that this angels' hymn goes back to the second century and that it is one of the first hymns of the early Church. The first portion of the melody as we know it is of French origin, while the second part is from a Latin chorale.

Cantique de Noel (O Holy Night). The Christmas season would not seem complete without singing or hearing this favorite. It was written by Adolphe Adam (1803-1856), a well known French composer of comic operas. He also taught composition at the Paris Conservatory. Of his many compositions, "Cantique de Noel" is the most frequently performed.

Good King Wenceslas. The text by Dr. John Mason Neale (see "Good Christian Men, Rejoice") is based upon a dialogue between the King and his page, the concluding verse embodying the very essence of the Christmas spirit. The tune is from a Swedish Lutheran Hymnal, 1582.

O Christmas Tree (O Tannenbaum). The idea of a tree and gifts is from an ancient custom and was not associated with Christmas until the time of Martin Luther. The evergreen is symbolic of the ever-living Christ. In America, the old German tune is also sung to the words "Maryland, My Maryland" (See "Patriotic Songs," chapter 11).

I Saw Three Ships. This fifteenth-century carol shows the influence of the sea. One wonders whether the legendary three ships might have sprung from the legends of the three kings. The three gifts in this case are Mary, Christ, and Joseph (English version).

Beautiful Savior (Crusader's Hymn). Although appropriate for any season of the year, this ancient song is almost invariably heard during the Christmas season. There is no evidence to support the claim that the hymn was sung by the Crusaders during the twelfth century. The words date back to 1677, and the beautiful melody to 1842. Whatever its origin and history, it is a perfect combination of words and music to instill the deepest reverence in the human heart. Although many fine choral arrangements have been made of this song, the one by F. Melius Christiansen of St. Olaf College is the favorite.

I Heard the Bells on Christmas Day. The words, published in 1867, are by Henry Wadsworth Longfellow. His son was seriously wounded during the Civil War; hence the verse "and in despair I bow'd my head: 'There is no peace on earth,' I said. For hate is strong, and mocks the song of peace on earth, good will to men." The music is by a London organist, J. Baptiste Calkin.

It Came Upon the Midnight Clear. The words, first published in 1850, are by the Reverend Edmund H. Sears, a Unitarian minister. The music is by Richard Willis, a Boston composer and son of Nathaniel Willis, who founded the *Youth's Companion.* The song is sung throughout England and has long been an American favorite.

While Shepherds Watched Their Flocks. This carol was published in 1700, by Nahum Tate, a literary associate of John Dryden. Tate was Poet Laureate of England in 1690. There are two musical settings to the poem, the adaptation of the Handel melody probably being the most popular in America.

Deck the Hall. This old Welsh tune was used in Yule celebrations which included the burning of a Yule log, singing, dancing, drinking from the Wassail Bowl, and decorating with holly and ivy. This is a secular carol and gives insight into the customs of the times. The rhythm and words indicate that it, like many other secular carols, was danced.

Records

RCA Victor Library for Elementary Schools—Christmas Album.
Capitol P8353 Joy to the World—Roger Wagner Chorale (includes most of the traditional carols).

CHAPTER 10

The Dream of a Nation

Introduction: Before the Pilgrims

The First American

America was the land of the free and the home of the brave long before white men invaded the continent. It is estimated that over one million Indians occupied the plains, deserts, and forests of America. Here the Iroquois and the Sioux Nations, and the Choctaw, Cherokee, Creek, Seminole, Blackfeet, Comanche, Navaho, Hopi, Zuni, and many other tribes dwelt in their wigwams, log huts, and tepees. With their bows and arrows, their tomahawks and spears, they roamed the forests and plains, killing buffalo, deer, and turkey for food. They also raised small quantities of maize, tobacco, peanuts, and cotton.

The Indians were animists, believing that men, animals, plants, and all other natural objects were inhabited by souls. As a result they worshipped many gods, particularly those of the sun and of maize. They believed that right and justice would ultimately triumph, a basic American philosophy.

Like other peoples, savage or civilized, the Indians employed music in their worship as a medium of communication between man and god. Each tribal group cherished many songs and dances, in which rhythm was a more prominent characteristic than melody. Irregular rhythms were common, and the Indian possessed the unusual ability to sing in one rhythm while beating the tom-tom in another. The songs were well balanced between major and minor keys, and the primitive pentatonic or five-tone scale was employed. Music played an important role in the daily life of the Indians, as it has for all peoples of the earth.

With the Indian's strong interest in music and his frequent use of it in tribal affairs, it might be expected that he would have exerted a tremendous influence on future American music. Such has not been the case. Due to the hostilities growing out of the white man's encroachment on Indian territory, the pride and aloofness of the red man, and the superior attitude evinced by the invader, the influence of Indian music has not been great. But thanks to the tribes which preserved the rituals of their ancestors—rituals which were accompanied by chant, song, and dance—interest in Indian music is increasing. Since the Indian lived in close harmony with nature, many of his songs concern the sun, moon, stars, and other gods which he worshipped. Some of these songs are beautiful and Indian chants and melodies are finding their rightful place as part of the American heritage in the song series for children. In addition, some of the Indian melodies have been used by American composers in larger compositions.

Songs and Recordings

Listed below are Indian songs and recordings of authentic Indian music or music based upon Indian culture.

S. Music in Our Country, pp. 6, 8r, 12, 14, 49r, 73, 191r, 207
S. Music Around the World, pp. 37, 99
S. Music Near and Far, pp. 8r, 9, 71r, 91
S. Music Now and Long Ago, pp. 87r, 88r, 89, 90ar, 90b
F. Music Through the Year, pp. 44r, 164, 165
F. Voices of America, pp. 76, 77, 79, 80r, 81r

F. Music Across Our Country, pp. 31*r*, 32*r*, 33*ar*, 33*br*, 35*r*, 36, 38,
                                84, 85, 132*a*, 132*b*
G. Singing and Rhyming, pp. 49*ar*, 50*a*, 72*a*
G. Singing Every Day, pp. 55*r*, 70*b*, 128*ar*
G. Singing Together, pp. 138, 139

Music of the American Indians (Victor Indian Album): Chant of the
Eagle Dance—Hopi Indian Chanters; Winnebago Love Song, Love
With Tears—Cheyenne; Pueblo Lullaby—Wium; Omaha Ceremonial;
From An Indian Lodge (Woodland Sketches—MacDowell); Love Song
(Suite No. 2 "Indian"–MacDowell); The Sunrise Call—Zuni (arr. Toyer);
Dance Song—Omaha; Butterfly Song—Hopi; Shuffling Feet—Sioux;
Shawnee Indian Hunting Dance (Skilton); War Dance—Cheyenne
(Suite Primeval—Skilton).

Waters of Minnetonka (Lieurance), Victor C 27; Columbia 35986.

Love's Wooing, Victor 20983.

Album of Sioux and Navajo Songs and Dances recorded by Willard
Rhodes. Folkways, 117 W. 46th Street, New York 19, New York.[1]

The European Scene—The Renaissance

During the period of America's exploration, the scene across the
Atlantic was quite different. For several centuries, Europeans had
been going through a change in attitude and viewpoint known in
history as the Renaissance. This transformation reached its peak
during the sixteenth century. To understand the tremendous development in all areas of human endeavor it is necessary to glance
at the changes in viewpoint that had engulfed the European
culture.

The Renaissance (rebirth) was not a revolutionary change from
the so-called dark ages but rather a gradual quickening of interest
and activities in all phases of life—philosophy, art, music, literature, exploration, and science—in contrast to the relatively static
endeavors of the immediate past. It was more comparable to an
adolescent development than to a rebirth—a period marked by a
change from the Scholasticism and church authority of the Middle
Ages to an era of greater skepticism and individualism. The period
might be described as a time when men looked back but moved
forward. The trend was toward expression rather than repression,

---

[1] Folkways and Victor each have albums of Indian music.

and toward an interest in secular or worldly affairs. Religion was loosing its place as the central theme in art, music, and literature. Great stress was being placed upon humanism as evidenced by interest in Greek and Roman classics, freedom, individualism, and the dignity of man. Breaking the shackles of the Middles Ages, the individual was now expressing himself in all areas of human activity. He was discovering himself as well as the world about him.

The collective impact of the development can best be imagined by glancing at a few of the names and events occurring during the period.

Exploration: Vasco da Gama (1450), Christopher Columbus (1446), Ponce de Leon (1460), Ferdinand Magellan (1480), Discovery of America (1492), Fernando de Soto (1499), John Cabot (1451), Francisco de Coronado (1500), Magellan's voyage around the world (1519-1522), Sir Humphrey Gilbert (1539), Sir Francis Drake (1540), Sir Walter Raleigh (1552), John Smith (1580), Drake's trip around the world (1577-1580). *Art:* Leonardo da Vinci (1452), Michelangelo Buonarroti (1475), Raffaello Santi (Raphael) (1483). *Religion:* Martin Luther (1483), John Calvin (1509), Luther's Ninety-Five Theses (1517), Council of Trent (1545-1563). *Politics:* Queen Elizabeth I (1533). *Literature:* Edmund Spenser (1552), Sir Francis Bacon (1561), William Shakespeare (1564).

DEVELOPMENTS IN MUSIC. Great strides were also apparent in music. Heretofore music had been created chiefly for use in the church. Now a great volume of secular literature began to appear. The musician, like other creative artists of the period, did not adhere to the past but ventured into new paths of expression.

The main musical style of the period was vocal polyphony which involved the combining of two or more melodic lines, called voices, into harmonious agreement. The *mass* and the *motet* were the chief liturgical forms, the *madrigal* and the *canzona* the secular forms. These secular forms were sometimes light, gay, and witty, sometimes romantic or tragic. Their chief characteristic was a high degree of expressiveness. They paved the way for more dramatic vocal forms and for independent instrumental music.

The general trend toward secularism also manifested itself in a growing interest in instrumental music although as yet there were few instrumental forms, the instruments usually duplicating vocal parts. The *lute* was the principal instrument but the viol, harp, psaltry, dulcimer, oboe, recorder (flute), horn, bagpipe, trumpet, trombone, organ, clavichord, harpsichord, and various percussion instruments were in use. Toward the close of the sixteenth century, the violin as we know it today began to emerge, reaching its highest development during the seventeenth century under the Italian violin-maker Antonio Stradivari (1644-1737).

The Reformation and the rise of Protestantism further broadened musical horizons. Luther's strong convictions concerning the importance of music in religion, especially with congregational participation, brought about the development of the *chorale*. The limited vocal range and the simple melody and rhythm of the chorale made it easy to sing. The melody, which was in the upper voice, was sung in unison by the congregation; the harmony parts were sung by the choir. In style, the chorale was more harmonic than polyphonic.

IMPORTANT COMPOSERS. There were, of course, many composers during this period. The most significant are mentioned here.

Giovanni Pierluici da Palestrina (1525-1594) was the leading Italian composer of the period. His name was acquired from the village near Rome where he was born. He received his early musical training, and later served as organist. He composed over ninety masses and five hundred motets as well as hundreds of other pieces of a religious character. He also wrote over one hundred madrigals. Some of his shorter pieces are sung today by high school and college a cappella choirs.

Adrian Willaert (1485-1562) was born in Flanders but spent most of his creative life in Italy. He wielded a tremendous influence on the music of his day. He was choirmaster at St. Mark's in Venice for thirty-five years. The church has two organs each facing the other; this probably accounts for the double-choir effects which characterize some of Willaert's works. In addition to his many sacred works, Willaert also wrote a large number of madrigals and was a dominant influence in their development.

Other Italian composers are *Giovanni Gabrieli* (1557-1612); *Luca Marenzio* (1553-1599); and *Claudio Monteverdi* (1567-1643).

Tomas Luis de Victoria (1540-1611) was the leader in Spain. He was a friend of Palestrina and their styles are similar. Victoria confined his efforts to religious forms of which he wrote many volumes. Some of his works are sung today by college choirs.

Christobal Morales (1500-1553) was Victoria's teacher. His compositions were serious and religious in character.

Thomas Tallis (1505-1585) has been called the father of English cathedral music. He wrote for both the Anglican and the Roman Catholic Church and his works included many motets and anthems. He also wrote a few madrigals.

William Byrd (1543-1623) was the greatest English composer of the period and was comparable in stature to Palestrina and Lassus. He was an organist, composer, and publisher. Among his many works are masses, motets, psalms, anthems, madrigals, and instrumental compositions. A number of his works are performed today by high school and college choirs.

Orlando Gibbons (1583-1625), another of the outstanding English composers of the period, was organist at the Chapel Royal and at Westminster Abbey. His works were both religious and secular, some of the most outstanding of which were his madrigals and compositions for instruments.

Other English composers include *John Dowland* (1563-1626), who wrote only secular music; *John Kirbye* (1597-1634), who composed many fine madrigals; *Thomas Bateson* (1570-1630); *Thomas Ford* (1580-1646), and *Thomas Morley* (1557-1602).

The German and Austrian composers made notable contributions to music during the period:

Roland de Lassus or Orlando di Lasso (1532-1594), although not a German, spent most of his productive years in Munich where he was court choirmaster. Most of his works were for the Roman Catholic service—masses and motets. He was one of the most prolific writers of his day and his compositions rank with those of Palestrina.

Other German composers of note were *Johann Eccard*, (1553-1611), *Hieronymus Praetorius* (1560-1629); *Ludwig Senfl* (1490-1555); *Hans Leo Hassler* (1564-1612); and *Jacob Arcadelt* (1514-1570).

Records

RCA Victor, The History of Music in Sound, Vol. IV, LM-6092 (The Age of Humanism): Italian Madrigals; English Madrigals (Wilbye, Greaves, Weelkes, Morley); F. Chansons—16th Century; Tomas Luis de Victoria; Phillippe de Monte; Orlandus Lassus; Jacobus Gallus; Giovanni Pierluigi da Palestrina; Giovanni Gabrieli; English Church Music (Tallis, Byrd, Morley, Gibbons); Lutheran Church Music (Praetorious); Solo Songs (French, Spanish, and English); Instrumental Ensembles (Willaert, Gibbons, et al.); Keyboard Music (Virginal, Harpsichord, Organ—Bull, Gibbons, Frescobaldi, A. Gabrieli, Sweelinck, et al.); Early Opera (Monteverdi, Landi).

The Colonial Period (1607-1775)

America was a dream. Her discovery was a consequence of the feverish intellectual activity of the Renaissance; the desire to settle her was a result of political and religious conditions in the old countries, and the action which created her was an outgrowth of the idea of individual freedom and the tendency to break with the past. Here was a new land and here were people with new political and religious concepts. These two facts crystallized into a dream—a dream of a new nation where *idea* and *ideal* might join forces. The Separatists gave wings to the vision and the Colonial period culminated in the reality of the dream.

These hazardous adventures of the courageous settlers who sought religious and political freedom in the new land extended from 1607, the year Jamestown was founded, to 1775, the year of the Revolution. It was a period beset by perils and discouragements which culminated in at least some degree of security and an indomitable faith in the future. It was an era when a virgin wilderness felt the impact of civilized living. The culture of the old countries—churches, schools, courts, newspapers, books—was transplanted to this vast wilderness. Although the new environment had been inoculated with the old, it was strangely different in that the original dream of political and religious freedom did not die. The seeds of independence were already sprouting in the fertile soil of government by the people.

From the old country the colonists brought their hymns, carols, ballads, and dances. Many of these are still used today. Thus, traditional songs and ballads from Europe became the basis of American folk and art music.

The first music used in the new country was Henry Ainsworth's *Book of Psalms,* which was brought over on the Mayflower (1620) by the English Separatists. The book had been compiled for them some years earlier in Holland, where they had sought refuge from English terrorists. The thirty-nine psalm tunes were a collection of English, French, and Dutch melodies.

Another group of Puritans who had found exile in Geneva came to America ten years later (1630), bringing a different psalm book. The tunes in this English edition (published by John Day, 1562) were from the French. One of the hymns from this collection, of which we shall hear more later, is the familiar "Doxology" ("Old Hundredth"). Because of faulty translations in this psalm book, a new translation was prepared under the title of the *Bay Psalm Book.* This was published in 1640, the first book printed in New England and the second on the American continent.

The constant reference to the psalms is significant. Originally psalms were sung in Jewish Synagogues and later in early Christian churches. But the Reformation, under the leadership of Luther, produced many hymns or chorales which did not follow Biblical texts or even paraphrase them. Such hymns were frowned upon in England where the Puritans were following John Calvin, who preferred texts selected from the Scriptures. But whatever their source or nature, these early psalm tunes were a definite part of the Pilgrim way of life and expressive of the character of the early American colonists.

American interest in music in general is attested by the following:

1. The numerous editions of the *Bay Psalm Book.*

2. The publication and subsequent editions of a number of music instruction books.

3. The appearance of many instruments, brought over from Europe, and the beginning of concerts, particularly in Boston, Philadelphia, Bethlehem, and Charlestown. For example, the first opera in America was given in Charlestown in 1735. Other performances of opera soon were heard throughout the colonies.

4. The influx of European musicians and teachers to America and the beginning of concert tours, particularly by family groups.

5. The numerous singing schools which began to flourish toward the latter part of the period.

6. Singing of secular songs and ballads which the early settlers recalled from old country experiences.

As a final glance at the American scene, we should note the interest of the colonists in education, which was again expressive of their interest in religion. Harvard was founded in 1636, William and Mary in 1693, Yale in 1701, and Princeton in 1743. Each of these colleges was founded by a religious group for the purpose of training young men for the ministry. In this connection, it will be recalled that the Separatists or Puritans believed that the English Reformation had been too mild, and they therefore sought independence from the English Church. Their ambition was to evangelize the world, which may account, in part, for America's continued support of foreign missions.

Songs and Recordings

Old Hundredth. Based upon the Hundredth Psalm, this song of praise was sung by the Pilgrims as it is today in Protestant churches all over America. Conventionally known as the "Doxology," it was printed in the Bay Psalm Book, the first book published in New England. The melody (about 1550) is attributed to Louis Bourgeois, who was associated with John Calvin as editor of the German Psalter, compiled by Calvin for use in his church.

G. Singing Every Day, p. 73b
S. Music in Our Country, p. 25
F. Music Across Our Country, p. 99

Margaret Dodd Singers, New Records Inc., NRL 2007. This is a selection of songs from the *Bay Psalm Book* in which "lining out"—chanting of each line by the minister prior to the congregation's participation in song—is illustrated.

Psalm III. This song of strength and courage was one of the thirty-nine psalm tunes in the Ainsworth Psalter which was brought over on the Mayflower.

Burl Ives Song Book, p. 12
Haydn Society, HSL 2068 Hymns from the Ainsworth Psalter

Greensleeves. This beautiful song from England was a favorite
of early Americans, its popularity continuing to the present day.
In addition to the English version, the colonists used a text titled
"Young George Washington." Another very popular version is the
Christmas carol titled "What Child Is This," which may be found
in most school song books. The tune was used in 1727 by John Gay
in the *Beggar's Opera,* a ballad opera which was performed in
New York in 1750.

S. Music Around the World, p. 222r. This is a New Year's Carol.
  The text as used in the *Beggar's Opera* is on pp. 222 and 223.
Burl Ives Song Book, p. 34
Roger Wagner Chorale, Capitol PBR 8345
Burl Ives, Decca DL 5428 ("What Child Is This")

Barbara Allen. This old ballad from England and Scotland was
sung by the colonists and its popularity has never waned as attested by its over two hundred versions. ("Ken" means "know," and
"hone" means "yearn.")

Burl Ives Song Book, p. 50
American Songbag, Sandburg, p. 57
Roger Wagner Chorale, Capitol PBR 8345
Burl Ives, Decca DL5490
Burl Ives, Encyclopaedia Britannica, Album I

Little Mohee. This popular ballad concerns a love affair between
a white man and an Indian maiden, a romantic situation which
immediately reminds one of Captain John Smith and Pocahontas.
"Little Mohee" is derived from the English "The Indian Lass."
"My ain sweetheart" means "My own sweetheart."

While the song is of a serious nature, there is an undercurrent
of humor in each verse, revealing the human tendency to justify
questionable acts. The man who is telling the story implies that
he is innocent of encouraging the "sweet Indian lass" and certainly
not guilty of making any advances toward her. Being lonely and in
a strange land, he merely went out for a walk; *she* came and sat by
him; *she* introduced herself—that is, after proposing marriage.
But our "simon pure" spurned all of these advances, for he had his

"ain" sweetheart in his own country. Upon return to the old country, however, he found that the girl he had trusted had proved untrue, so he sailed back to his little Mohee.

G. Singing in Harmony, p. 61r
F. Voices of the World, p. 184
Burl Ives Song Book, p. 10 (Note that the middle portion of the melody is the same as "On Top of Old Smoky.")
Burl Ives, Columbia CL6058, Album II

Foggy, Foggy Dew. Although not appropriate for children, this song indicates a weakness in human flesh to which the Colonial period was not immune. It is another serious ballad with an undercurrent of humor. While no humor was intended by the weaver, it exists nevertheless in his attempts to justify his wrong deeds: the "only, only thing" that he did that was wrong "was to woo a fair young maid" and "to keep her from the foggy, foggy dew." She, like Little Mohee, made all the advances. Oh, that we had versions by the two girls!

Burl Ives Song Book, p. 60
The American Songbag, Sandburg, p. 14
Burl Ives, Decca DL5093, Vol. III
Burl Ives, Encyclopaedia Britannica, Album I

Robin. The wife, especially a lazy one, has long been the subject of folk wit. This was true during the Colonial period just as it is today.

Burl Ives Song Book, p. 64
Burl Ives, Columbia CL6144, Album III

Trip-A-Trop-A-Tronies. This song was brought over by the Dutch colonists and is a foot-riding song, a game which fathers played with their babies.

G. The First Grade Book, p. 61a

We Gather Together. This song was brought over by the Dutch colonists and has always been popular in school and church. It is particularly appropriate for the Thanksgiving season.

F. Music Across Our Country, p. 109
G. Singing Together, p. 109

S. Music Near and Far, p. 162
Roger Wagner Chorale, Capitol P8365 (Prayer of Thanksgiving)

The Twelve Days of Christmas. The twelve days of Christmas
are those between Christmas and January 6. The suitor endeavors
to prove his love for his sweetheart by bringing her a different gift
each day—gifts which are difficult to secure. The song may be
performed, as it often is, with hand motions representing the
various gifts.

G. Singing Together, p. 123
S. Music Around the World, p. 93
F. Music Through the Year, p. 70

The Wraggle Taggle Gypsies. An old English gypsy ballad.

S. Music in Our Country, p. 40

Lavender's Blue. This song was brought over by the English.

G. Singing On Our Way, p. 113*b*
S. Music in Our Town, p. 128
RCA Rhythm Album 3

Johnny Schomoker. This Pennsylvania Dutch song is enjoyed by
elementary school children, as well as by college men, as they
employ hand motions to imitate the playing of the various instruments.

G. Singing and Rhyming, p. 163*r*

F. Music Across Our Country, p. 112

Frog Went A-Courtin'. An animal song of Scottish origin.

G. Singing Every Day, p. 30*r*
F. Music Across Our Country, p. 130
RCA Primary Singing Album

Three Dukes Went A-Riding. An old English singing game.

G. Singing Together, p. 36
S. Music Now and Long Ago, p. 25

Paper of Pins. Another of the English singing games.

S. Music Now and Long Ago, p. 124*r*
Burl Ives Song Book, p. 40

Maple Sweet. A song of New England concerning a maple camp.

S. Music Near and Far, p. 178*a*

Bird's Courting Song. This is a favorite New England song which indicates the indirect method of parental instruction.

F. Voices of America, p. 143*r*

The Girl I Left Behind. This is an Irish and English song which, because of its application to early American life, was popular during the Colonial period. Later, the cowboys adapted their own version.

S. Music In Our Country, p. 38 (Irish version); p. 39 (cowboy)

Lord Lowell. Compare the final stanzas of this English ballad with those of "Barbara Allen."

S. Music Around the World, p. 208
Electra EHL 3, Frank Warner

Lord Randall. This is another of the English ballads which were popular during Colonial times and later on the concert stage.

Burl Ives Song Book, p. 58
Burl Ives, Columbia 2CL6058

The Lass With the Delicate Air. This song was written by the English composer Thomas Arne and is representative of the songs enjoyed by the more cultured settlers. It is more appropriate for solo voice than for group participation.

My Days Have Been So Wonderous Free. This song, one of the first published in the new country, was composed by Francis Hopkinson (1737-1791), a friend of Washington, Franklin, and Jefferson, a signer of the Declaration of Independence, and the first Secretary of the Navy. It was one of four songs written by Mr. Hopkinson. He also wrote seven pieces for the harpsichord and piano which were dedicated to George Washington, with copies going to Thomas Jefferson who was an outstanding amateur violinist. Hopkinson also wrote sacred music, was organist at his church, taught singing to the children of his church, and edited two hymn books which were used during the period. He might be considered one of America's first ministers of music.

Benjamin Franklin (1706-1790), who helped draft the Declaration of Independence and the Constitution, was another of America's early music enthusiasts. In addition to being America's first music critic, he played the guitar and the glassychord (glasses filled with water), a popular instrument of the day which Franklin improved. Mr. Franklin had many friends among the musicians in both Europe and America, and printed a great deal of the music of the time. In addition to folk music, he loved the great works of art.

Burl Ives Song Book, p. 108
Burl Ives, Encyclopaedia Britannica, Album II

In Europe—The Baroque Period (1600-1750)

In Europe this was an age of expansion in territory, trade, commerce and colonization, and a period of adjustment to rapidly changing political, religious, social, and economic conditions following the Protestant Reformation. There were serious conflicts between Catholics and Protestants. On the political front, the idea of freedom and the rights of the individual, as expressed by John Locke, were taking root. New organizations were being formed in business, commerce, trade, and banking. Because of this feverish activity, cultural achievement in general was not as great as it had been in the sixteenth century. Music and literature were exceptions and were greatly advanced.

Listed below are some of the great men of this period.

Religion: John Wesley (1703); Charles Wesley (1707). *Art:* Rembrandt van Rijn (1606). *Exploration:* Robert Cavelier La Salle (1643). *Philosophy:* John Locke (1632); François de Voltaire (1694). *Science:* Isaac Newton (1642); Isaac Watts (1674). *Literature:* John Milton (1608); John Bunyan (1628); John Dryden (1631); Daniel Defoe (1661); Jonathan Swift (1667); Henry Fielding

(1707); Samuel Johnson (1709); William Cowper (1731). *Government:* William Penn (1644). *Science, Literature, and Government:* Benjamin Franklin (1706).

In keeping with the revolutionary spirit of the times, many composers set out to explore new musical paths, and the musical principles of the Renaissance were left far behind. The period produced outstanding composers, among them Bach and Handel, two of the greatest composers of all time. It also produced such new forms as the oratorio, opera, overture, and orchestral suite.

Before proceeding with the musical achievements of the period, it is well to consider the characteristics of Baroque music. In general, the spirit of music was similar to that of architecture and painting, being characterized by elaboration, large-scale productions, spectacular and grandiose concepts. This suggests again further separation between sacred and secular music. The dramatic element, the paths of which had been marked out during the sixteenth century, had now definitely invaded the field, expressing itself in the development of opera, oratorio, and cantata, and in larger instrumental ensembles. The homophonic style, as contrasted with the polyphonic music of the past, dominated the period; solo melody prevailed over balanced interweaving of voices, and lower voices were subordinated. In other words, the harmonic or vertical concept of music was now replacing the horizontal or contrapuntal approach.

The Opera

Miracle and mystery plays were the forerunners of opera, and classic Greek drama was its model. The first operas showed these kinships. Later, the spectacular became characteristic. Because of the time required to make scenery changes, the *intermezzo* was introduced. Out of this grew the comic opera, called *opera buffa*, *opéra comique* or *singspiel*. In France, a particularly spectacular kind of opera developed, characterized by extensive and formalized choruses and ballets. The overture, later an important and independent instrumental form, became more elaborate and formal. It was the immediate forerunner of the symphony. The first opera house was built in Venice in 1637, initiating a movement which soon spread all over Europe.

The Oratorio, Cantata, and Passion

The early *oratorio* was similar to opera in being performed with scenery and costumes, the principal difference being the religious text of the oratorio. As time went on, a narrator presented dramatic details of the action and later this gave way to the *recitative* which, as in opera, followed the free rhythm of prose. The mature oratorios were large-scale dramatic productions with Biblical text, performed without costumes, scenery, or staging but with solo parts, chorus, and orchestra.

The *cantata* was a shorter, more lyrical form of oratorio and could have either a religious or a secular text.

The *passion* was a dramatic presentation dealing with the suffering of Christ on the cross and designed for the Easter season.

Instrumental Music

As has already been observed, music prior to 1600 was largely vocal. Instruments were used mainly to strengthen the vocal parts; purely instrumental forms had not been greatly developed. During the Baroque period, instrumental music came into its own, developing its own styles and forms at a pace unequaled in the history of music. Rapid development was possible because principles of composition had already been established in the vocal form. Important instrumental forms developed during this period were the overture, dance suites, the fugue, and the solo and ensemble sonata.

During this period instruments were greatly improved, and the virtuoso or concert artist developed. Because of its importance in the church, the organ had long been the leading instrument. Also in wide use were the clavichord and harpsichord, inheritances from the previous century, which the piano, invented during the first part of the eighteenth century, was soon to replace. The violin, too, had been greatly improved. Antonio Stradivari, the greatest violin-maker of all time, was born in 1644.

The orchestra continued its association with vocal music, particularly with opera and oratorio, and few large works for orchestra were written except the operatic overtures. Chamber music made a steady advance throughout the period. This was important to the development of orchestral music, for in using small ensembles composers learned the peculiarities of various instruments and how to combine their sounds.

Important Composers

Johann Sebastian Bach (1685-1750) was one of the greatest geniuses of all time, coming from a long line of distinguished German musicians. His work centered in the fields of church and instrumental music. Although he wrote masterfully for voices and other instruments, the organ works of Bach are perhaps the center of his expression. He was a virtuoso organ player. While Bach's music is often in a polyphonic style, it possesses a definite harmonic character. Very few of his compositions were published during his lifetime, the great majority remaining unpublished for one hundred years after his death. Over fifty large volumes of his works have been compiled. Being a devout Lutheran, he wrote over 200 motets and cantatas for use in the Lutheran service, as well as several passions and masses. The *St. John* and *St. Matthew* passions and the *B Minor Mass* are among his greatest choral works. Many of his choral works are performed today, as well as many of his instrumental compositions, especially those for keyboard instruments. His was mature music from a mature genius.

George Frederick Handel (1685-1759). Although German by birth and Italian by training, Handel is classified with the English composers because of his many creative years in England. His works show the influence of his cosmopolitan experience. His music is predominantly homophonic and is marked by strong rhythms and well defined phrases. Handel had a flair for the dramatic. He composed over 40 operas and about 20 oratorios. His fame and popularity, however, rest almost wholly upon a few of his oratorios, which he wrote during the later years of his life. His efforts were not confined to vocal forms. He composed

70 overtures and orchestral works. The oratorio "The Messiah" is one of the most universally known and loved of all musical compositions.

Handel and Bach make interesting contrasts. They were born the same year. Both were organists; Bach wrote much for the organ, Handel little. Bach was married twice and had twenty children; Handel never married. Bach cared little for dramatic forms; Handel wrote operas and oratorios. Bach's music was more polyphonic, Handel's more homophonic. Bach was born in Germany and spent his life there. Handel was born in Germany, received his training in Italy, and composed his greatest works in England. Bach had a long line of musical geniuses in his family; Handel had no musical ancestry. Both men spent their last years in blindness. Bach was buried in obscurity; Handel was buried in Westminster Abbey.

Other important German composers of the period were *Heinrich Schutz* (1585-1672); *Johann Hermann Schein* (1586-1630); *Samuel Scheidt* (1587-1654); *Johann Jakob Froberger* (1616-1667); *Dietrick Buxtehude* (1637-1707); and *Georg Phillipp Telemann* (1681-1767). The latter wrote mostly instrumental forms.

An English composer of great stature who wrote a wide variety of dramatic and instrumental music was *Henry Purcell* (1658-1695).

Claudio Monteverdi (1567-1643) made opera the most popular form of composition in Italy and was instrumental in establishing the first opera house which was built in Venice, 1637. This was the first of many opera houses which were to be built throughout Europe. In addition to his twelve musical dramas, Monteverdi wrote madrigals and sacred music.

Alessando Scarlatti (1659-1725), of Neapolitan and Roman fame, exerted a tremendous influence in dramatic music. He wrote no less than 115 operas, 200 masses, numerous madrigals, cantatas, chamber music for strings, and a number of oratorios. His son and pupil *Domenico Scarlatti* (1685-1757) also wrote dramatic and sacred music but made his most distinctive contributions through his works for keyboard instruments. The modern piano sonata is traceable directly to his innovations.

In France, the name of *Jean Baptiste Lully* (1632-1687) stands out because of his work in opera. Though an Italian by birth, he has been called the founder of French opera. As a court composer, he became the favorite of Louis XIV through his ballets. He wrote some 15 operas, 30 ballets, church music, violin solos, and other instrumental works. His place in the history of music is marked by his work with orchestra, opera, and ballet.

Other outstanding French composers of the period were *François Couperin* (1668-1733), famous as an organist and for his work with harpsichord, and *Jean Phillippe Rameau* (1683-1764), who was known for his operas, ballets, and keyboard music. His greatness is comparable to that of Bach and Handel and makes him possibly the foremost French composer of all time.

Records

RCA, The History of Music in Sound, Vol. V, LM6030 (Opera and Church Music): Italian Opera (Cavalli, Cesti, A. Scarlatti, Handel, *et al.*); French Opera (Lully, Rameau); English Opera (Blow); German Opera (Keiser); Italian Oratorio (Carissimi, Marcello); French Church Music (Rameau); Italian Church Music (A. Scarlatti); English Church Music; German Church Cantata (Schutz, Buxtehude, J. S. Bach); German Passion Music (Schutz, J. S. Bach); German Motet (J. S. Bach); German Mass (J. S. Bach).

RCA, The History of Music in Sound, Vol. VI, ML6031 (The Growth of Instrumental Music): English Ode (Purcell); English Oratorio (Handel); Solo Songs (Italian, English, and German); Solo Sonatas; Trio Sonatas (Corelli, Handel, *et al.*); Keyboard Music (Clavichord, Harpsichord, Organ); Orchestral Music (Purcell, Telemann); Concerto (Vivaldi).

The Beggar's Opera, Victor LM6048

Treasury of Harpsichord Music, Victor LM1217 (Wanda Landowska)

Messiah Highlights, Victor LM2088

CHAPTER II

A Nation Is Born

(1775-1820)

O beautiful for Pilgrim feet,
Whose stern, impassioned stress
A thoroughfare for freedom beat
Across the wilderness!
America! America!
God mend thine ev'ry flaw,
Confirm thy soul in self-control,
Thy liberty in law!

Written in 1893, these words were a voice in retrospect, vividly describing the purpose and determination of those who beat the paths of freedom across the wilderness of despotism and injustice. Certainly there would be flaws, but with self-control as the watchword, liberty under the law would be established and would be expressed simultaneously by the governing and the governed. This, then, was the period when the gold that was Americanism was refined in the American melting pot—a period of national gestation and birth—a period when a revolting people would declare their independence (1776) and then proceed to prove it (1812). It was a time when thirteen scattered colonies were forged into a nation out of the steel character and courage of the people.

It will be recalled that the Puritans' initial step toward freedom was taken when they came to America seeking religious and civil freedoms which had been denied them in Europe. The idea of freedom was far from new, for Aristotle and Plato had expounded it more than 300 years before the birth of Christ. Aristotle summed up the purpose of civilized society in these words: "The state comes into existence that man may live. It continues that man may live well." In his *Two Treatises on Civil Government*, written in the eighteenth century, John Locke said, "Men are, by nature, all free, equal, and independent." His ideas so powerfully affected the American colonists that they are embodied in the Declaration of Independence: "We hold these truths to be self-evident—that all men are created equal; that they are endowed by their Creator with certain inalienable rights; that among these are life, liberty, and the pursuit of happiness."

From the landing of the Pilgrims to the Declaration of Independence and the Revolutionary War, the all-prevailing passions were a revolt against tyranny and the establishment of freedom and justice. This period witnessed the birth of a nation. It was a time of momentous and epoch-making decisions, of invincible courage and dynamic action, of national consciousness and patriotic fervor—a time when a dream became a reality. But even with all this, only foundations could be built, for in the final analysis freedom and justice are developmental processes.

The term freedom has many connotations and is often used loosely. However broad its implications, it has never implied absence of restraint, for even governments, as stated in our Declaration of Independence, derive "their just powers from the consent of the governed." Individual freedom exists only under law, and is not a license to say, do, or act as one pleases, for it implies the responsibilities of good citizenship and judgment clothed in self-control and restraint, as expressed in "America the Beautiful."

Not only patriotic fervor, but also the total character and spirit of the American people are reflected in their many types of musical expression. Before looking at the music, it seems advisable to ask: "What are Americans like?"

American Characteristics

First, we are religious. From the time of the first Thanksgiving through practically every phase of our development as a nation, we have indicated a recognition of, and reverence for, God. In our frenzied efforts to establish and build we have, perhaps, developed a sense of urgency—we travel too fast for safety; we act before we think; we speak before we reflect; we preach more than we practice; we adore more than we worship. All of this may have caused us to seem ungrateful and unchristian, yet time and again we have been humbled by the great revivals which have swept our country. The Indian songs to the Great Spirit, the Negro spiritual, the white spiritual, the great hymns of faith, our pledge to the flag, the motto "In God We Trust," and the reference to God in our patriotic songs are indicative of our religious fervor.

Second, we are independent. While going our separate ways, we somehow manage to keep in step. We disagree and argue; we judge and condemn; we decry and belittle. But in individual or national crises, we join in a united spirit. We also unite in our enjoyment of the right to differ and in our hatred of those who would deny us this privilege.

Third, we are builders. We climbed the mountains and then tunneled through them; we forded the rivers and then bridged them; we endured the desert and then planted an oasis. Along the wayside we erected our homes, schools, and churches; we developed our natural resources and built industries. During one life-span, we built a network of steel across the continent and set boxes on grooved wheels for the exchange of our products. In one lifetime, we laid a web of concrete across the land and set air-conditioned trucks upon it to make our neighbors nearer. In one generation, we sent wings through the air to win the race with sound. Along our tracks and highways, we have strung wires for urgent messages, and through the air itself we have sent wireless waves of sight and sound into our homes.

Finally, we are humorists. One of our chief characteristics is the ability to find humorous elements in adversity. While we do not enjoy misfortune, we will endure it and make the most of it. Witness, for example, the humor which originated with our servicemen in two world conflicts. Or note the American humor personified by Will Rogers, who showed us how to chuckle at serious national and international situations. The following pioneer song illustrates a type of humor found in many folk songs and stories; it may be sung to the tune of the "Irish Washerwoman."

My name is Frank Boler, a bach'lor I am,
An' I'm keepin' ol' bach on an elegant plan,
For you'll find me out West in the county of Lane,
Just a-starvin' to death on my government claim.

Hurrah for Lane County, the land of the free,
The home of the grasshopper, gopher, and flea.
I sing loud her praises and boast of her fame,
While starvin' to death on my government claim.

My home it is built of the national soil,
An' the walls are erected accordin' to Hoyle,
An' the roof has no pitch but is level and plain,
An' I always get wet when it happens to rain.

How happy I am when I crawl into bed,
An' a rattlesnake rattles his tail at my head,
An' a gay little centipede void of all fear,
Crawls all over my pillow and into my ear.

It must be a ladybug cheerful and bright,
For she keeps me a-scratchin' far into the night,
An' a dear little flea that has teeth like a tack,
Plays 'Oh, why don't you scratch me' all over my back.

Stephen C. Foster struck a responsive chord with a characteristic type of American humor:

It rained all night the day I left,
The weather it was dry,
The sun so hot I froze to death;
Susanna don't you cry.

This type of humor which says the opposite of what it means is found in many other pioneer songs. Another example is "Polly-Wolly Doodle":

> *Oh, my Sal, she am a maiden fair,*
> *Sing Polly-Wolly Doodle all the day;*
> *With the curly eyes and laughing hair,*
> *Sing Polly-Wolly Doodle all the day.*

Early American Music

What has American character to do with American music? The answer is apparent: the characteristics of a people and the life they live are reflected in their songs. The songs of a nation are as expressive of its character as are its literature and history. In fact, songs of the people record historical events either directly or indirectly. For example, there were many "liberty songs" which followed the explosion at Bunker Hill, as well as songs about Washington, Adams, and Jefferson, the heroes of the day. The "Star-Spangled Banner" was penned during this period.

Highly expressive of the thoughts, feelings, and general spirit of the people during the Revolutionary War is the song "Chester." The words of this patriotic air were a bugle call of the Revolution. The text indicates contempt for the "haughty" British, trust in God, and faith in American youth. "Chester" was written by William Billings (1746-1800) of Boston, a friend of Samuel Adams and a champion of democracy. Billings' compositions were timely —even the character and imaginative qualities of his music were revolutionary. Although a tanner with little formal education, Billings exerted a tremendous influence on the sacred and patriotic music of his day, an influence which is felt even now. Billings created both text and music for the first all-American sacred collection, *The New England Psalm Singer* (1770). Five other collections followed, the last published in 1794. Although Billings' music was popular during his day, "Chester" was the most widely known, running a close second in popularity to "Yankee Doodle." In recent years, there has been a revival of interest in Billings' music, and a number of his sacred works are now being performed by high school and college choirs.

Westward Movement

Before we turn from the American scene, let us recall that the westward movement began during this period. After independence had become an established fact as a result of the War of 1812, the people began to turn away from the more densely settled areas along the coast to the western horizons. Mountains deflected the course of some English, Scotch, and Irish families who settled along the Appalachian and the Blue Ridge chains. Here we have found some of our richest treasures of folk song, for these mountain folk preserved many songs from their mother countries, some of which have remained unchanged through many generations. Of particular interest to elementary teachers are the nursery songs such as "A Frog Went A-Courting" and "The Frog and the Mouse."

Leaders of the Period

A list of the leading personalities suggests the achievements of the period. *Government and politics:* George Washington (1732); John Adams (1735); Patrick Henry (1736); John Hancock (1737); Thomas Paine (1737); Thomas Jefferson (1743); Alexander Hamilton (1757); James Monroe (1758); Andrew Jackson (1767); John Quincy Adams (1767); Napoleon Bonaparte (1769); Henry Clay (1777); Daniel Webster (1782); William Cullen Bryant (1794). *Literature:* Robert Burns (1759); Friedrich von Schiller (1759); William Wordsworth (1770); Sir Walter Scott (1771); Samuel Taylor Coleridge (1772); Charles Lamb (1775); Washington Irving (1783); John Keats (1795). *Exploration:* Daniel Boone (1735). *Science:* Robert Fulton (1765); Eli Whitney (1765). *Philosophy:* Arthur Schopenhauer (1788). *Business:* Cornelius Vanderbilt (1794). *Government, literature and science:* Benjamin Franklin (1706). *Other fields:* Betsy Ross (1752); Francis Scott Key (1780).

Songs and Recordings

Riflemen of Bennington. This was a well known song during the Revolution expressing the patriotism of the time.

S. Music in Our Country, p. 128r

Yankee Doodle (see patriotic songs)

Johnny Has Gone for a Soldier (To Be a Soldier). This is a lonesome song for the sweetheart, wife, or mother who was left behind to keep the home fires burning; it is a common theme for all wars. This song is the Revolutionary version of the Irish song "Shule Aroon."

Burl Ives Song Book, p. 98
Burl Ives, Encyclopaedia Britannica, Album II

In Good Old Colony Times. Reflecting back on the "good old days," this song continued to be sung long after the Revolution. It has a moral—crime doesn't pay.

S. Music in Our Country, p. 26

The Frog and the Mouse. This is a type of mountain song for the early settlers' children.

S. Music Now and Long Ago, p. 34r
F. Music Across Our Country, p. 131r

The Tailor's Mouse. Another children's favorite from early America, this song has remained popular through many generations.

G. Singing in Harmony, p. 32
Burl Ives, Columbia CL6115

Keemio Kimio. This is another of the songs for children used by early settlers; this one is from the southern Appalachians.

S. Music Around the World, p. 52

The Wee Cooper o'Fife. This song was brought over by the Scots and employs the lazy wife theme mentioned earlier.

S. Music in Our Country, p. 34
F. Voices of the World, p. 37
Burl Ives, Columbia

Rolly Trudum or *Lolly Too Dum.* This is a typical mountain song.

G. Singing in Harmony, p. 46r
Burl Ives, Decca, Vol. I

Down In The Valley. This is another mountain song, one with several variants.

The American Songbag by Sandburg lists nine verses.
F. Voices of America, p. 45
S. Music Near and Far, p. 69
Burl Ives, Decca, Vol. II

Young Man Who Wouldn't Hoe Corn. From the days of Captain John Smith, a lazy man was frowned upon, avoided by the ladies, and often the subject of folk wit. There simply was no place for a lazy man or woman among the early settlers.

G. Singing in Harmony, p. 34*ar*
Burl Ives, Encyclopaedia Britannica, Album V.

He's Gone Away. This is a beautiful example of the mountain songs. "Yondro" was probably the highest mountain in view; a "desrick" was a shack. Although of British origin, the song as we know it shows the influence of the Negro as well as the mountaineer.

Roger Wagner Chorale, Capitol P-8324 (Folk Songs of the New World)

Springfield Mountain. This is an Appalachian mountain ballad with a tragic ending.

F. Voices of America, p. 50*r*
Burl Ives Song Book, p. 68
Burl Ives, Columbia, Album II

Soldier, Soldier. An Appalachian courtship song, this has a touch of tragic humor.

S. Music in Our Country, p. 35
F. Voices of America, p. 49

Patriotic Songs

American patriotism is peculiar in that it seems to lie dormant, being awakened only in a time of national crisis. Nevertheless, it is there in great strength, a fact often overlooked by an envious enemy. We are very proud citizens, although we seldom express our pride, except in song. As we turn to examine our patriotic songs, we can easily feel the spirit of America—the spirit of the builder, the humorist, the independent, and the devout.

Yankee Doodle. This old tune, originally from nobody-knows-where, is America's first national song. Some claim it was first sung in England, while others declare it came from Holland, Germany, or Spain. It is appropriate that our first national song should be hybrid, like the people themselves.

It is definitely known that the tune was brought over by the British, who used it to poke fun at their ill-clad, ill-trained, ill-mannered backwoods allies in the war against the French in America. The words by Dr. Richard Shuckburg, a British army doctor, poet and musician, delighted the well-clad, well-trained Britishers who used every opportunity to sing it for the colonial troops. It is characteristic of Americans to laugh at their predicament and the ragged and tattered Yankees joined in the chorus.

The word *yankee* is thought by many to come from the Indian's pronunciation of English, *Yenglees,* or from an Indian chief, *Yankoo,* who fought with and lost to an early settler. *Doodle* means *do-little,* foolish, silly. But it was not a funny song at Bunker Hill and Lexington, or for Cornwallis who surrendered to its tune, October 19, 1781, or for the British who danced to its rhythm at the close of the war of 1812.

There are many verses to the song, most of them humorous but some serious. "And what they wasted ev'ry day, I wish it could be saved" is still the cry of many Americans. Read the words of the original song in the *Burl Ives Song Book,* page 72.

The Star-Spangled Banner. "Oh! say can you see?" was the question on the lips of Francis Scott Key all night in his anxious concern for the outcome of the battle for Fort McHenry. With the coming of dawn and the lifting fog, his concern was replaced by delight, for "the flag was still there."

The British were preparing to move against Baltimore and burn it as they had the city of Washington. First they must destroy Fort McHenry which defended the city and which was under the command of Joseph Nicholson, Key's brother-in-law.

The British were holding prisoner a distinguished American doctor and citizen, Dr. William Beanes. Francis Scott Key, a young Baltimore lawyer, armed with official papers from President Madison and a flag of truce, had been sent in a small boat to the British flagship to rescue the prisoner. The admiral agreed to release Dr. Beanes. The British were ready to open fire on Fort McHenry, and Mr. Key and party were not allowed to go ashore until the outcome of the battle was known.

All night long the prisoners strained their eyes for a glimpse of our flag, "And the rockets red glare, the bombs bursting in air, Gave proof thro' the night that our flag was still there." But after each glare the anxious question returned, "O say, does that Star-Spangled Banner yet wave?"

At dawn, Old Glory was still waving and Mr. Key knew that the British had lost the battle. He began to write the words of our national anthem on an envelope. The next day when Key's brother-in-law, Joseph Nicholson, saw the poem he was so delighted that he had a printer run off copies under the title "The Bombardment of Fort McHenry." Then it was observed that the words perfectly followed the hit tune of the day, an English drinking song entitled "To Anachreon in Heaven." The song was sung for the first time the following evening in a Baltimore tavern and met with great success. Although the tune is usually attributed to John Stafford Smith, some say the melody was also known in Scotland and Ireland.

Again the British had lost and in the defeat had given us the melody for another national song, this time the national anthem. Again the melody is thought to be a crossbreed. On March 3, 1931, one hundred and seventeen years after the poem was penned, "The Star-Spangled Banner" was officially made our national anthem.

Francis Scott Key is buried at Frederick, Maryland, and the Star-Spangled Banner is permitted to fly both night and day at his tomb. He is the only individual to be accorded such honor.

Hail Columbia. Although found in school and community song books, "Hail Columbia" is seldom sung and therefore is not as well known as our other patriotic songs. In the sense that both words and music were written by Americans, it is more American than other more popular national songs. Actually, this was "The President's March," written by Philip Phile for George Washington who became president in 1789.

The French Revolution broke out the year Washington became president and soon France was at war with England and Prussia. Since France had helped us gain independence, and since England was the mother country, American sympathies were divided between the two countries. President Washington favored neutrality. When the feeling was at its height, Joseph Hopkinson, son of Francis Hopkinson, wrote the words for "The President's March." This was done at the request of Gilbert Fox, a singer and actor friend of Hopkinson. Actually, Fox needed an audience for a benefit performance and felt that a patriotic text to the popular "President's March" would do the trick. Upon short notice, Joseph Hopkinson wrote the words. The announcement of this new song drew a large crowd for the performance. Since the tune was already popular and the patriotic text so timely, the song was an immediate success. But it did more than draw a crowd; it healed the wounds of political conflict, for both parties took the message of the song to heart.

> *Firm united let us be,*
> *Rallying around our Liberty,*
> *As a band of brothers joined*
> *Peace and Safety we shall find.*

The second verse seems an indirect plea for neutrality. The third and fourth verses are in praise of Washington, who was neutral.

A song had healed a rift between our leaders and perhaps helped keep us out of a war.

America. This is perhaps our most popular national song, which is probably due to its simplicity and its easy singing range. The tune is another of the nobody-knows-who-or-where variety, claimed by many nationalities.

The words are another matter. Lowell Mason had acquired some German song books. Since he did not read German, he asked his friend Samuel Francis Smith, who was studying for the ministry, to examine the texts of the songs. Mr. Smith found one

melody which strongly appealed to him and decided on the spur
of the moment to set patriotic words to the music. He did not
know at that time that the tune was England's "God Save the
King."

Mr. Mason was pleased and taught the song to a group of
children who sang it as a surprise for Mr. Smith. The fact that
Mr. Smith was a ministerial student accounts for the beautiful
prayer of the fourth verse. No portion of this song should be sung
without closing with this last verse.

It is interesting that so many peoples of the world have contributed to our most popular national songs and that America
and England share the same tune.

Columbia the Gem of the Ocean. The words and music of this
old favorite, often called "The Red, White, and Blue," were
written by an actor, Thomas A. Becket, at the request of another
actor, David T. Shaw, who needed a patriotic song for a benefit
performance. The song was written on the spur of the moment
and finished in one afternoon and evening. It was first sung in
Philadelphia in 1843.

The student will observe the use of many expressions characteristic of our early national songs, such as "The home of the brave
and free," "liberty," and "war's desolation." Compare the patriotic
pleas in the last verse of this song with the last verse of "The
Star-Spangled Banner."

Dixie. This "southern" song was written by an Ohioan and,
paradoxically, was used to inspire the Confederates into battle
during the Civil War. For this reason, it is usually classed among
our national airs.

Both words and music were written by Daniel Emmett, a professional minstrel. He was a popular member of Dan Bryant's
minstrels of New York shortly before the outbreak of the Civil
War. Mr. Bryant asked Dan Emmett to write a new *walk-around*
song. It was cold in New York at the time, a fact which may have
suggested the warmer climate of the South and the opening
words of the chorus, "I wish I was in Dixie." The song was an
immediate success, and its popularity has never waned. The song

moved to the South immediately before the Civil War and over-
night was a "hit." It was the song of the Confederates during
the war and since that time has been associated with the South.
The great variety in rhythmical patterns makes it a stirring tune
loved by both North and South. It was a favorite with President
Lincoln and was often requested by him.

Maryland, My Maryland. This song was written by a south-
erner during Civil War days. The words are by James Randall,
and the music is that of a German folk song. The North liked the
song too, but the northern version did not live, although both
versions were sung during the Civil War.

Randall was born in Baltimore, Maryland, and was sympathetic
with the South when the poem was written, although Maryland
remained in the Union. Mr. Randall had accepted a college position in New Orleans a short time before the Civil War and while
there read of a bloody mob affair in the streets of Baltimore.
Stirred by this news from his home town, he penned the words
of the song now sung throughout the country.

The Battle Cry of Freedom. George F. Root, a Chicago composer and publisher, wrote both the words and music of this song
as a rallying song for the recruiting officers of the Union. Mr.
Root also wrote other patriotic songs which became popular in
both the North and South. Probably the two best known are
"Just Before the Battle Mother" and "Tramp, Tramp, Tramp, the
Boys are Marching." He composed a number of hymns, too,
some of which are still sung today in Protestant churches.

The Battle Hymn of the Republic. This stirring song, written
by a great northern woman, has the power to break through the
opposing lines of conflict, as it did during the Civil War.

A contest was held in order to find a good patriotic song during the Civil War, but not one of over a thousand songs entered
was suitable. The honor for such a song, a song that can be sung
in time of war or peace, was to be bestowed upon a woman who
did not enter the contest. After visiting an army camp near
Washington where her husband was stationed, Julia Ward Howe

wrote the words of this famous song to the tune of "John Brown's Body." The poem was first published in the February issue of *The Atlantic Monthly*, 1862. The familiar melody of "John Brown's Body" helped it to become popular very quickly. Although Mrs. Howe wrote many magazine articles and books, "The Battle Hymn of the Republic" touched the mind and heart of the nation in a way that none of her other works did.

In recent years, several choral arrangements have been made of the hymn and have been sung by high school, college, and church choirs all over the land. The song will live as long as there is even a spark of patriotic fervor in our hearts.

America the Beautiful. Katherine Lee Bates, the author of this beautiful poem and instructor in English at Wellesley College, wrote the words while on a visit to Pike's Peak in 1893. One has only to experience this awe-inspiring view to understand how it could inspire a gifted person to express the very spirit of peacetime America. Every American should memorize the verses and meditate on their meaning, for there is no better description of our land and its people.

The music is by Samuel A. Ward. Although many composers tried to do a setting of the poem, none was successful. Miss Bates finally selected the well known church hymn by Mr. Ward as the best musical expression of her message.

"America the Beautiful" is the official song of the National Women's Clubs.

God Bless America. Irving Berlin's "God Bless America" became widely known shortly before World War II when Kate Smith introduced it on radio. It touched all Americans with its gratitude and patriotic fervor. All royalties from the song have gone to the Boy Scouts and Girl Scouts of America.

The Stars and Stripes Forever. Although not usually classed among our patriotic music, this song is often played on patriotic occasions and will probably find a permanent place in our national music. The music is by John Philip Sousa, the March King, who served under Presidents Hayes, Garfield, Arthur, Cleveland, and Harrison as director of the United States Marine Band. The melody for "The Stars and Stripes Forever" may be found in F. *Music Through the Year*, p. 150 and S. *Music Near and Far,* page 146.

The Marines' Hymn. This is the official song of the United States Marine Corps.

Caisson Song. This is the official song of the United States Field Artillery. It was written by Major Edmund Gruber while on duty in the Philippines, 1908.

The student should be familiar with "Reveille" and "Taps," Army bugle calls, which may be found in S. *Music Around the World,* page 73.

A number of our patriotic songs are recorded in the RCA Library for Elementary Children (Patriotic Album). The most familiar of these songs may be found in the various song series, and many of them are recorded by the publisher of the series.

In Europe—The Classical Period (1750-1820)

Due to the mental fermentation prior to and including the Colonial period in America, these years were marked by revolution (the French and the American) and war (the Napoleonic wars, the American Revolutionary War, and the War of 1812). It was a period when the individual in particular and people in general were elevated to a higher level of importance. The period saw the overthrow of the idea that society existed for the privileged classes and witnessed the adoption of the ideas of liberty and equality with new evaluation placed upon the individual. *Ideas* which had been expressed by writers and philosophers had now become the *ideals* of the common man.

This was a time of great mental development. Men began to question old paths of thought. Mathematics and science rose to new heights and scientific investigation by means of inductive reasoning began to take root. As a result, great strides were made in astronomy, chemistry, medicine, physics, geology, botany, and zoology. This was the so-called Age of Reason. Reason, it was thought, could solve all human problems and was pitted against faith.

Developments in Music

The style of the music of this period is usually described by the term classical. Much of the music was delicate, decorative, refined, and emotionally restrained. Forms were well defined, and composers were very interested in formal problems, as is evidenced by the establishment of the sonata form. Although counterpoint was still extensively employed, it was secondary to the harmonic approach.

It was during this period that instrumental music came into its own. Previous stress on the small instrumental ensemble had paved the way for the combination of instruments for special sound and tonal color effects. Modern orchestration and instrumentation were thus established, and the symphony orchestra was born. The instruments of the orchestra were grouped into choirs: string, woodwind, brass, and percussion. The basis of the classical symphony was the sonata form.

This development did not retard expression through solo instruments and small ensembles. Keyboard sonatas by Haydn, Mozart, and Beethoven and, to a lesser degree, violin sonatas, are proof of interest in and development of solo instruments. The string quartet, which employs two violins, a viola, and a 'cello, originated. Music written for these solo instruments, as well as for small ensembles, also followed the sonata form, which was established by Haydn and Mozart and reached its culmination in the work of Beethoven. The classical concerto underwent a development paralleling the forms mentioned. Concertos featuring almost every instrument were written—exploiting and developing individual possibilities. The small orchestra was also popular during this period, the form used being similar to the Baroque orchestral suite, which consisted of as many as ten movements, many of them dances. This form was variously known as *divertimento, cassation,* and *serenade (nachtmusik)*.

Opera, which had appeared in about 1600 and developed during the latter part of the seventeenth century, spread and flourished throughout Europe. Its popularity began to wane during the last half of the eighteenth century, due to complex and artificial plots. Christoph Gluck (1714-1787) attempted to reform the opera by improving the libretto, eliminating dry and pointless recitative, and integrating the chorus, orchestra, and ballet. Although Gluck represented the classical spirit in opera and is known for his leadership in opera reform, his works were not as successful as those of Mozart. We hear many beautiful arias from works of the period, but complete operas, except those by Mozart, are seldom performed today. Four of Mozart's best known and loved operas are *Die Zauberfloete* (*The Magic Flute*), *Le Nozze di Figaro* (*The Marriage of Figaro*), *Don Giovanni* (*Don Juan*) and *Cosi Fan Tutte* (*Women Are Like That*).

Overshadowed by the development of instrumental music and opera, sacred music, for the most part, marked time. However, some truly great sacred works were written during the period, such as *The Creation* and *The Seasons* by Haydn, *Requiem Mass* by Mozart and *Missa Solemnis* by Beethoven.

Important Composers

Christoph Willibald Gluck (1714-1787) was born near Nuremberg, Germany, the son of a forester. At the age of twelve, Christoph was enrolled in the Jesuit school at Komotau, where he studied violin, 'cello, clavier, organ, and voice. Moving to Prague at the age of eighteen, he taught and performed while continuing his studies. Four years later, he was introduced in Vienna by Prince Lobkowitz, and then Count Melzi took him to Milan to study with Sammartini. In Milan, at the age of twenty-seven, he wrote his first opera. His revolutionary ideas concerning opera made both friends and enemies in the capitals of Europe. He considered Vienna his home, and at the age of thirty-seven he was made conductor to Prince Frederick of that city. It was here that he composed many of his operas. His later career in Paris marked the peak of his musical life. He rewrote his greatest operas for

Parisian performances, casting them into their final and greatest forms. His works also include sacred and instrumental music, all of which was overshadowed by his operatic efforts.

Joseph Haydn (1732-1809), a poor peasant boy, was born in a small village on the Hungarian border not far from Vienna. His father was a wagon-maker. From the ages of eight to seventeen, he was a choir boy and received training in music, his general education being self-imposed. At seventeen, he was abruptly dismissed from the choir school, but friends gave him aid and encouragement. The relief from employment gave him time for creative efforts, and he soon began to write music which the world was to enjoy for generations to come. At the age of twenty-nine, he became assistant conductor on Prince Esterhazy's estate. The Prince was the head of a family widely known for its wealth, culture, and musical enthusiasm. Haydn spent the next thirty years of his life in this environment, composing and performing. The Prince died when Haydn was fifty-eight. Haydn went to London for a series of concerts, his first journey of any significance, and was received most enthusiastically. After two years, he returned to Vienna where he continued to compose and perform. He also taught, one of his students being the young Beethoven. Haydn's disposition was cheerful, generous, and lovable, and he possessed a rare sense of humor. A devout Catholic, he was an honorable and virile man, regarding his powers as a composer as a divine gift. Haydn was primarily a composer of chamber and orchestral music, about two-thirds of his works being for instruments. His vocal works include masses, oratorios, operas, and songs. In all, he wrote 125 symphonies, 30 trios, 77 quartets, 100 chamber pieces, 31 concertos, 175 solos, 100 sonatas, 14 masses, about 30 motets, 3 oratorios, 13 operas, several cantatas and operettas, and a large number of songs.

Wolfgang Amadeus Mozart (1756-1791) was born at Salzburg, the son of a violinist and composer. He began to play the piano at the age of four, to compose and perform in public at five, and to play the organ at six. At the age of seven, his first sonatas were published; at eight, his first symphony was composed; at ten, one part of an oratorio was written; at eleven, a musical comedy was composed; at twelve, an opera was written, and at fourteen, a grand opera. In addition to home instruction, Mozart's education was extended by travel in connection with concertizing which was carefully planned by his father. These trips took young Mozart away from home an aggregate of nine years during the first twenty-five years of his life—Munich, Vienna, Stuttgart, Heidelberg, Mannheim, Cologne, Paris, London, Lyons, Milan, Naples, the Low Countries, and Switzerland. From the standpoint of experience in performing and in meeting the leading composers of his time and hearing their music, these trips were definitely profitable, but financially they were failures. For a time, Mozart was a concertmaster in Vienna, but a change in administration brought about his dismissal. Thrown on his own resources, he had great difficulties, for there were no protecting copyright laws, and Mozart was not a businessman. During his short life, he composed 49 symphonies, 20 operas, 30 divertimenti, 26 quartets, 10 quintets, 15 masses, numerous sonatas, songs, and arias, and much chamber and sacred music.

Ludwig van Beethoven (1770-1827) was born at Bonn on the Rhine. His father and grandfather, particularly the latter, were musicians. His education was meager except in music but his great mind overcame this handicap. His life was marked by struggle, conflict, and tragedy which seem to have stimulated and vitalized his creative efforts. His precocity compares with Mozart's. His first meeting with Mozart in Vienna when Beethoven was seventeen prompted Mozart to prophesy that Beethoven would "make a noise in the world." The "noise" he made is still echoing. Later in Vienna, Beethoven studied with "Papa Haydn." Beethoven was a good student but was a revolutionary of the first rank. During his life, he made friends with many influential people upon whom he depended, and was able to hold their admiration despite his low origin, unaccountable moods, uncouth manners, and extreme sensitivity. His gratitude was expressed by the dedication of some fifty compositions to these individuals. Otherwise, Beethoven was independent, living alone in the world of his advanced ideas and unconventional innovations. Many times in love but never married, Beethoven was a lonely yet gigantic figure whose works have continued to astound the hearts and minds of men. It is difficult to classify Beethoven in history, for he was not the product of any school nor did he found one. The classical period culminates with him and he introduced the romantic spirit. Briefly, we may conclude that Beethoven was original and progressive, that he was a leader, a seer, an innovator, and an epoch-making genius. Listening to his music, one can feel the strength of this giant who conquered every hindrance, even the deafness which came at the height of his career. Beethoven wrote 9 symphonies, 32 piano sonatas, 12 overtures, 250 songs, 16 quartets, 1 opera, 1 oratorio, 2 masses, 10 cantatas, 5 concertos, 8 trios, 3 quartets, 9 violin sonatas, 5 'cello sonatas, and a host of smaller works.

Other classical composers of note were *Karl Philipp Emanuel Bach* (1714-1788), *Johann Christian Bach* (1735-1782), *Michael Haydn* (1737-1806), *François Gossec* (1734-1829), *Karl Ditters von Dittersdorf* (1739-1799), and *Luigi Boccherini* (1743-1805).

Records

HAYDN

Symphony No. 94 in G ("Surprise")   RCA Victor LM-1789
Symphony No. 40 in G Minor
"Surprise Symphony," RCA Elementary Library, WE-80
Andante "Clock Symphony," RCA Elementary Library WE-81

MOZART

Concerto No. 4 in D   RCA Victor LM-1030
Concerto No. 5 in A
Highlights from Marriage of Figaro, Victor LM-2053
March of the Priests from Magic Flute, RCA Elementary Library
    WE-75
Minuet, Don Giovanni, RCA Elementary Library WE-75
Gavotte, RCA Elementary Library WE-75
Symphony No. 39 in E Flat, RCA Elementary Library WE-74
Theme from Sonata in A, RCA Elementary Library WE-80

BEETHOVEN

Sonata No. 8 in C Minor (Pathetique)   Victor LM-1908
Sonata No. 23 in F Minor (Appassionata)
Symphony No. 5 in C Minor, Victor LM-1923
Country Dance, RCA Elementary Library WE-74
Sonata Op. 26, RCA Elementary Library WE-81

BOCCHERINI

Minuet, RCA Elementary Library WE-80

GLUCK

March, RCA Elementary Library WE-75
Minuet in F, RCA Elementary Library WE-75
Alceste, RCA Elementary Library WE-80

GOESSEC

Gavotte, RCA Elementary Library WE-80

CHAPTER 12

A Nation in Turmoil

—A Family Feud

(1820-1865)

The Common Man

Man's long struggle for liberty, self-government, and self-expression had finally been successful. He was now in the saddle, steadily reining his way toward political emancipation. Having achieved this goal, his American characteristics as religionist, independent, builder, and humorist now became strikingly apparent.

With individual initiative set free both in America and Europe, great advancements were made in science, literature, art, philosophy, government, and industry. Science took a new look at nature and began a concerted effort against disease; literature and art joined in the search for beauty and pleasure; philosophy joined with science in scrutinizing the universe and sought to diminish ignorance and suspicion; the invention of new machines powered by steam and electricity greatly accelerated the tempo of industry, which brought about new struggles and changes in the social and economic order. Royal absolutism had finally crumbled and now the popular demand was for complete political emancipation, individual liberty, representative government, and universal education. All of this resulted in a new spirit of nationalism, with the over-all stress upon man and nature, and an emotional approach toward life.

Encouraged by the Louisiana Purchase (1803) and the Lewis and Clark overland trek to the Pacific (1804-1806), many Americans moved farther and farther west. The Santa Fe trail to the Southwest, the Oregon trail to the Northwest, and the Mormon trail to Utah, had opened the great western areas. Spurred by the discovery of gold in California in 1848, the Western movement reached its peak the following year.

Slavery

But all this development was overshadowed by threats of secession and war over the question of slavery. Slavery had been abolished in most of the original states soon after the turn of the century, but had continued in other states. Great bitterness arose between the industrial North and the agricultural South. On one side were those who demanded outright abolition and on the other those who favored the right of each state to decide for itself. Soon after the election of Abraham Lincoln, eleven states seceded from the Union, and the bitter war began on April 12, 1861, with the bombardment of Fort Sumter in Charleston harbor. During the next four years, the country was economically, spiritually, and socially gutted. Brothers of the Union Blue and the Confederate Gray fought and died for the causes in which they believed. President Lincoln never wavered from his original purpose, which was to preserve the Union. This was clearly stated in his inaugural address and in the address at Gettysburg. Lincoln's determination in this matter and his just treatment of the losers was followed by the Thirteenth Amendment abolishing slavery in the United States. Thus freedom, the cornerstone of the American ideal, had been vindicated. From the War of 1812, America had gained freedom from external forces; from the Civil War, she had gained internal unity.

Entertainment

For the most part, the only form of entertainment for the settler and for those who boarded the westbound wagon and railroad trains was self-made—singing and dancing. Because of their light weight and compactness, the fiddle and harmonica were a part of the wagon cargo and became the popular accompaniment instruments. Many of the fiddle tunes had song texts so that they could be sung as well as played. "Skip to My Lou" is a good example.

The era also witnessed expanded river travel and trade. Following the first steamboat trip down the Mississippi in 1811, this great dividing stream between east and west became the main thoroughfare between North and South, with pleasure and commercial boats being a common sight along the river. Naturally, there were many songs about rivers.

As a result of river travel a new type of entertainment, exclusively American, was born—the minstrel show. This came about as a result of the white man's effort to imitate the singing and dancing of the Negro. At first these shows flourished along the river routes and in the larger cities of the east; in time they made their way west along the inland trails established by the Western movement. One of the best known of the minstrel songs is "Dixie."

Because of increased activities on the sea—the fishing industry along our own shores and trade with other countries—many songs about the sea, such as "Blow the Man Down," grew in popularity. Sailors, like other groups, sang about their work and had recreational songs as well. The working chanties celebrated the outward and homeward journeys, and the recreational songs were forecastle (foc'sle) songs.

The opening of the Erie Canal in 1825 produced recreational and working songs along the Canal route, such as "Buffalo Gals" and "The Erie Canal." Then, too, there were songs about the miner and his work, and the lumberjack and his experiences.

Influenced by both the white man and the Negro, Stephen C. Foster (1826-1864) captured the thoughts and feelings of the people in his immortal songs. Such songs as his are known as composed folk songs. Foster wrote over 200 songs, many of which are popular today. Although from a wealthy and influential Pittsburgh family, a family of outstanding professional men, Stephen, the black sheep of the group, is the one member who is loved and remembered today. His songs are so well known that no comment on individual songs seems necessary.

Religion

During this period of tremendous and courageous activity, religion was not forgotten, for revivals were common all over the country, especially in the South. Influenced by these and by the Negro's sacred music, many white spirituals in the Negro idiom appeared. Among these are "Wondrous Love" and "Jesus Walked this Lonesome Valley." Oliver Holden (1765-1844) composed some of the great hymns of the church, such as the coronation hymn "All Hail the Power of Jesus' Name." Lowell Mason (1792-1872), a singing school teacher and father of public school music in America, wrote many hymns which are favorites today. Characteristic of these are "My Faith Looks Up to Thee," "Nearer My God to Thee" and "From Greenland's Icy Mountains." Thomas Hastings (1784-1872) wrote "Rock of Ages," which is a favorite hymn of Protestant groups. Associated with Mr. Mason and his schools was George Webb (1803-1887), who wrote "Stand Up, Stand Up for Jesus." William Bradbury (1816-1868) was another composer whose hymns ("He Leadeth Me," "Just As I Am," "Sweet Hour of Prayer," and "Savior, Like A Shepherd Lead Us") are favorites today.

Songs and Recordings

Sourwood Mountain. There are many versions of this Kentucky song; it is also popular as a dance tune.

G. Singing Together, p. 50a
S. Music Around the World, p. 133
F. Voices of America, p. 44r
Burl Ives, Encyclopaedia Britannica, Album VI

Captain Jinks. A typical dance tune of the period.

F. Voices of America, p. 99
S. Music Around the World, p. 184
G. Singing Together, p. 35*r*

Cindy. A southern mountain tune of fiddle and banjo fame;
it has a humorous text.

G. Singing Together, p. 92
S. Music Around the World, p. 56
F. Voices of America, p. 63
Capitol P-8324 (Roger Wagner Chorale)

On Top of Old Smoky. Another beautiful mountain song, this
one from Kentucky.

S. Music Around the World, p. 57
Roger Wagner Chorale, Capitol P-8324
Burl Ives, Columbia, Album I

Skip to My Lou. This is another of the fiddle tunes with a
text for singing. *Lou* is a Tennessee term for *sweetheart.* The
song is of the play party type, and continues to be popular
with all ages.

F. Music Across Our Country, p. 125*r*
S. Music Through the Day, p. 68*a*
G. Singing and Rhyming, p. 44
Roger Wagner Chorale, Capitol P-8324

Pop Goes the Weasel. This is an ever popular singing game
and square-dance tune.

S. Music Now and Long Ago, p. 122
G. Singing Every Day, p. 50*b*
F. Music Across Our Country, p. 104*b*

Paw-paw Patch. Another favorite singing game and fiddle
tune.

G. Singing Every Day, p. 51*r*
S. Music Through the Day, p. 14*a*
F. Music Through the Year, p. 15*r*

Billy Boy. This is a courtship song of English origin; there is also an Irish version.

G. Singing Every Day, p. 76
S. Music Now and Long Ago, p. 94
F. Music Across Our Country, p. 141r
Burl Ives Song Book, p. 168 (English); p. 170 (Irish)
Burl Ives, Encyclopaedia Britannica, Album I

The Deaf Woman's Courtship. This is another song of the courtship type, but, unlike "Billy Boy," this one is humorous.

F. Voices of America, p. 41

Sweet Betsy from Pike. Very few of the early songs were about women, but this one indicates the courage of the pioneer woman. It describes the hardships of the forty-niners, who crossed the desert, rivers, and mountains to the California gold fields. This is an example of American fortitude and courage in the face of discouragement. For obvious reasons, the school song books have substituted "husband" for "lover." Burl Ives and Carl Sandburg print the text as it was originally sung.

G. Singing Together, p. 91r
Burl Ives Song Book, p. 234
The American Songbag, Sandburg, p. 107
Burl Ives, Columbia, Album I

Clementine. Originating in California during the gold rush days, this was one of the social songs of the forty-niners.

F. Voices of America, p. 27

Sacramento. This is another gold rush song based upon Stephen Foster's minstrel song "Camp Town Races."

S. Music in Our Country, p. 105
Burl Ives, Encyclopaedia Britannica, Album IV

Cutting Down the Pines. This is a typical lumberjack song.

S. Music Near and Far, p. 74r

The Jam on Gerry's Rocks. This is a lumberman's song from Maine.

S. *Music Near and Far*, p. 76

My Sweetheart's the Mule in the Mine. This miner's song from Pennsylvania is typical of songs originating in the mines throughout the new country. Mules were used to pull the ore carts. Marriageable women were scarce.

F. *Voices of America*, p. 154
S. *Music in Our Country*, p. 63

Down in the Coal Mines. Here is another miner's song from Pennsylvania. The lad who tells this story gives an analysis of himself and exposes his philosophy of life.

S. *Music in Our Country*, p. 62

Blow the Man Down. Whether in San Francisco or New York, this song was sung by all young men who followed the sea. This song originated with those who worked on the Black Ball line, the first to establish regular passenger service. "Kicking" Jack Williams was captain of one of the ships.

G. *Singing in Harmony*, p. 76*a*
S. *Music Around the World*, p. 107
F. *Music Across Our Country*, p. 102
Burl Ives, Encyclopaedia Britannica, Album IV

Rio Grande or *Away, Rio.* This is a capstan chantey (outward bound).

G. *Singing in Harmony*, p. 78
F. *Voices of America*, p. 158
Burl Ives, Encyclopaedia Britannica, Album IV

Cape Cod Chantey. This is a song to the girls at home.

G. *Singing Together*, p. 64*b*
S. *Music Near and Far*, p. 107
F. *Voices of the World*, p. 181

Shenandoah. Here is a mournful short-haul chantey of great beauty and a favorite of sailors everywhere. Judging from the geographical references and the mention of the Indian maid (in some versions), it was probably a land song originally but moved to the river and finally to the sea.

G. Singing in Harmony, p. 76*br*
S. Music in Our Country, p. 109*r*
F. Music Across Our Country, p. 78*r*
Burl Ives, Encyclopaedia Britannica, Album IV
Roger Wagner Chorale, Capitol P-8324

The Erie Canal. This is a work song relating to the driver and his mule who towed barges on the Canal. References to the mule are reminiscent of the miner's song "My Sweetheart's the Mule in the Mines." Both songs imply a shortage of women.

G. Singing Together, p. 62*r*
S. Music in Our Country, p. 94
Burl Ives, Encyclopaedia Britannica, Album IV

Buffalo Gals. This was originally a minstrel song: "Luby Fan, Woncha Come Out Tonight." It was popular with the pioneers, and was later adapted by cowboys. Since marriageable girls were scarce, the singers indicated no particular preference for Buffalo Gals, but for gals in any town through which they might pass. However, "Buffalo Gals" as a title stuck. Its popularity as a song and fiddle square-dance tune has never waned.

S. Music in Our Country, p. 84*r*
Burl Ives, Encyclopaedia Britannica, Album V

Old Dan Tucker. Sung by many mothers to their babies, this minstrel song was written by Dan Emmett, composer of "Dixie."

G. Singing Every Day, p. 80*r*
F. Voices of America, p. 59
Burl Ives, Encyclopaedia Britannica, Album III

Polly-Wolly-Doodle. This is another minstrel song which has survived. Because of its popularity on college campuses, it is often listed as a college song.

G. Singing Every Day, p. 8
F. Voices of America, p. 30

Dixie. A minstrel song (see "Patriotic Songs")
Wayfaring Stranger. A white spiritual.

S. Music Around the World, p. 154*r*
F. Voices of the World, p. 183

Burl Ives, Columbia, Album I
Roger Wagner Chorale, Capitol P-8324

The Promised Land (On Jordan's Stormy Banks I Stand). White spiritual.

S. Music in Our Country, p. 110

Wondrous Love. White spiritual.

F. Voices of America, p. 66r

How I Love My Home. White spiritual.

F. Music Through the Year, p. 128r

Stephen Foster Songs:

Old Folks at Home, G. Singing and Rhyming, p. 65
Oh! Susanna, G. Singing Every Day, p. 77r; S. Music in Our Country, p. 112
Ring, Ring the Banjo, G. Singing Together, p. 183r
Old Kentucky Home, G. Singing in Harmony, p. 91
The Glendy Burke, S. Music Near and Far, p. 112; F. Voices of America, p. 60
Nelly Bly, S. Music Around the World, p. 48
Some Folks Do, F. Music Across Our Country, p. 143
Camptown Races, F. Voices of the World, p. 10
Open Thy Lattice, Love
Beautiful Dreamer
Katy Bell
Oh! Lemuel
I Dream of Jeannie With the Light Brown Hair
Old Black Joe
Roger Wagner Chorale, Capitol P-8267 (Album contains all titles mentioned above.)
Turkey in the Straw, arr. Guion, Victor 4390

The Negro

Another type of folk music which has been closely identified with America since its inception is Negro songs, with their delightfully different rhythms and melodies. Beginning in 1619, Negroes arrived on slave ships from Africa. Their spirituals and work songs have touched the heart of America and greatly influenced both her popular and serious music. This influence, however, has been relatively recent, for although the greatest songs were created under slavery, they remained in local areas until after the Civil War. They were introduced to the country at large by Negro singers from such schools as Fisk University, Hampton Institute, and Tuskegee Institute. In 1871, Fisk University sent out a choir to raise money for the school. Choir tours from other Negro schools followed. Audiences were charmed by their music, but no one paid particular attention to the uniqueness of its rhythms and melodies until Dvorak's visit to America in 1892. Before his departure in 1895, the Bohemian composer said, "Here, in the music you have neglected, even despised, is something spontaneous, sincere and different, native to your own country."[1] After hearing Dvorak's *Symphony From the New World,* which was strongly influenced by the Negro folk idiom, other composers and arrangers became interested. Today there is an abundance of Negro folk music arranged for all levels and media. Performance of these folk songs ranges from the grade school to the concert stage.

Like other peoples, the Negro had his work, play, and social songs, his lullabies and ballads, but most important of all are his spirituals, or religious songs. Nowhere is there a more spontaneous outpouring of religious fervor in song. Under the enforced burden of slavery and poverty, religion was the Negro's source of consolation and refuge. Even though his plight might seem unbearable, his faith was sustained by the promise and hope expressed so poignantly in the spirituals.

Since the spirituals are so readily understood, no detailed analysis is necessary. It does seem advisable, however, to point up some of the chief characteristics of these songs as a basis for understanding, appreciation, and interpretation.

1. *The spirituals were created by groups of people and are therefore especially adaptable to group participation.* The "lead off" singer set the tempo and mood—much as the early minister "lined out" the Psalms—and the group responded on the refrain (example—"You Can't Get to Heaven").

---

[1] *Harper's Magazine,* February 1895.

2. *The Negro has a unique way of applying the spiritual message directly to himself.* For example, "Not the preacher nor the deacon, but it's *me*, O Lord, standin' in the need o' prayer"; or "*I* looked over Jordan and what did *I* see. A band of angels comin' after *me*, comin' for to carry *me* home." "He's got the whole wide world in His hand" concludes with "He's got *me* in His hand." Even "Were You There" becomes meditatively personal: "Oh! Sometimes it causes *me* to tremble."

The personal application might also be indirect, which makes it no less effective. A comparison of his political situation with that of the Israelites in Egypt would, of necessity, take the indirect approach:

> *When Israel was in Egypt's Land,*
> *Let my people go!*
> *Oppress'd so hard they could not stan',*
> *Let my people go!*

Another excellent example of personal implication—this one a secular song—is the "Blue Tail Fly" (Roger Wagner Chorale, Capitol P-8324). Whether originally a minstrel show or slave song, it reveals by implication and mixed emotion a slave's resentment of his lazy master's demands for service. The first portion of the song indicates regret clothed in pity because of his master's death, but the nonsensical refrain expresses relief and is definitely joyous: "Jimmie crack corn and I don't care, my master's gone away."

3. *The Negro spiritual expresses universal thought and feeling.* This is indicated in such songs as: "Sometimes I Feel Like a Motherless Child, A Long Ways From Home"; "Goin' to Set Down an' Rest Awhile, When My Good Lord Calls Me"; "I'm Troubled in Mind"; "Sometimes I Feel Like I Wanna Go Home"; "When De Storm of Life is Ragin', Stan' by Me"; and "Trouble's Gwine Ter Weigh Me Down."

4. *The Negro spiritual is dramatic.* Consider: "My Lord, what a mornin' when the stars begin to fall"; "Get on Board, little children"; "Swing low, sweet chariot"; "Were you there?" and

Oh, wasn't that a pity an' a shame?
An' He never said a mumbelin' word.
They carried Him to Pilates bar,
An' He never said a mumbelin' word;
Not a word, not a word, not a word.

5. *Finally, these songs express faith and hope for ultimate victory.* This is evident in most spirituals, but a few examples are "Goin' to shout"; "Nobody knows the trouble I see, Glory Hallelujah."

Negro Music

G. Singing in Harmony, pp. 89, 114r, 116r, 117, 118r
G. Singing Every Day, p. 71ar
G. Singing Together, p. 82
S. Music Through the Day, pp. 73r, 114a
S. Music in Our Town, pp. 28, 62, 105r
S. Music Now and Long Ago, pp. 68r, 76r
S. Music Near and Far, pp. 28, 29r, 165
S. Music Around the World, pp. 6, 26r, 89, 156r
F. Music Across Our Country, p. 134r, 170
F. Voices of the World, pp. 11, 179
F. Voices of America, pp. 70r, 71, 72, 73r, 74r

Dorothy Maynor Sings Spirituals and Sacred Songs. (Includes 9 spirituals and 6 sacred selections from the great works of music.) Victor Cal-344
Marion Anderson Sings Spirituals. (Includes 11 spirituals.) Victor LM-2032
Roger Wagner Chorale, Were You There? Capitol P-8365.
Juba Dance—Dett, RCA Elementary Library WE-76

Art Music

The folk idiom did not completely satisfy the taste of the more cultured class, and so oratorio societies developed and opera performances were frequent. Accomplished musicians who had studied under the old masters of Europe came to America to teach and concertize. Ole Bull, a Norwegian violinist, visited this country a number of times and delighted American audiences with his masterful performances. The popular and beloved "Swedish Nightingale," Jenny Lind, was brought to America by

P. T. Barnum of circus fame. Her two-year visit in the new country won her many friends, and she made many friends for good music.

Leaders of the Period

The mention of personalities (first half of the nineteenth century) suggests the many achievements of the time.

Exploration: David Crockett (1786), Sir William Parry (1790), Thomas Cooke (1808), Kit Carson (1809), David Livingstone (1813).

Religion: Alexander Campbell (1788), Brigham Young (1801), Joseph Smith (1805), Frank Newman (1805), Henry Ward Beecher (1813), Charles Spurgeon (1834), Phillips Brooks (1835), Dwight L. Moody (1837).

Education: Horace Mann (1796), William H. McGuffey (1800), Mark Hopkins (1802), Charles W. Eliot (1834).

Philosophy: Arthur Schopenhauer (1788), David R. Locke (1833).

Literature: Lord Byron (1788), James Fenimore Cooper (1789), John Howard Payne (1792), Percy B. Shelley (1792), William Cullen Bryant (1794), Thomas Carlyle (1795), Honore de Balzac (1799), Thomas Macaulay (1800), Victor Hugo (1802), Leonard Bacon (1802), Ralph Waldo Emerson (1803), Nathaniel Hawthorne (1804), George Sand (1804), Hans Christian Andersen (1805), Elizabeth Browning (1806), Henry Wadsworth Longfellow (1807), James G. Whittier (1807), Oliver Wendell Holmes Sr. (1809), Edgar Allan Poe (1809), Alfred Lord Tennyson (1809), Horace Greeley (1811), William M. Thackeray (1811), Robert Browning (1812), Charles Dickens (1812), Harriet Beecher Stowe (1812), Henry David Thoreau (1817), Julia Ward Howe (1819), James Russell Lowell (1819), Walt Whitman (1819), Henrik Ibsen (1828), Samuel L. Clemens (1835).

Industry: Cornelius Vanderbilt (1794), George Peabody (1795), Charles Goodyear (1800), Cyrus H. McCormick (1809), William Vanderbilt (1821), Andrew Carnegie (1837), Jay Gould (1839), J. P. Morgan, Sr. (1837), John Wanamaker (1830), John D. Rockefeller (1839).

Government: Stephen F. Austin (1792), Sam Houston (1793), John Brown (1800), Jefferson Davis (1808), Abraham Lincoln (1809), Prince Otto von Bismarck (1850), James A. Garfield (1831), Grover Cleveland (1837).

Law: William E. Gladstone (1809), Robert Ingersoll (1833).

Military: Matthew Perry (1794), Robert E. Lee (1807), Thomas "Stonewall" Jackson (1824).

Science and Medicine: Thomas Bell (1792), Charles Darwin (1809), Herbert Spencer (1820), Hermann von Helmholtz (1821), Louis Pasteur (1822), Thomas Huxley (1825).

In Europe—The Romantic Period (1820-1900)

The Romantic period includes the era covered in this and the following chapter. Because of the large number of important composers in this era, only choral works can be treated here. Instrumental music will be discussed in the next chapter.

Like other areas of expression, the music of the Romantic period was marked by individualism, emotionalism, and nationalism. The orchestra and the piano were spotlighted, placing choral music in the shadows. Program music (descriptive) was more important than at any time before or since. In general, melodies were warm expressing deep personal feeling; harmony was advanced by the use of new and altered chords; counterpoint played a secondary role; stress was placed upon the small forms, especially in piano and song literature.

Although mentioned in the classical period, Beethoven belongs also to the Romantic era. Until middle life, his music was classical in style, showing the influence of his teacher, Haydn. When mature, however, his individualism came to the surface and he began to discard the artificial restraints of the classical form. It might be said of Beethoven that he mastered the past, conquered the present, and took complete command of the future. Thus he opened new paths of freedom and initiated musical Romanticism.

The Opera

Opera, which had begun in Italy in the early seventeenth century, reached its peak during the latter portion of the nineteenth century. Although Italy continued as a leader in this field, she now began to share the spotlight with Germany and France. Because of their country's original and continued leadership in dramatic music, the Italian composers are mentioned first.

Gioachino Rossini (1792-1868), a successful comic opera composer, was born at Pesaro where his father was a civil official. His mother was a singer in comic opera. At the age of fifteen, Rossini entered the conservatory and from the beginning showed little interest in strict composition. By nature he was vivacious and witty so that his efforts were limited to comic opera. In addition to 40 dramatic works, he wrote 10 cantatas, his chief sacred work being the *Stabat Mater*. His best known operas are *L'Italiana in Algeri* ("The Italian Girl in Algiers"), *Il Barbiere di Sivilia* ("The Barber of Seville") and *Guillaume Tell* ("William Tell").

Gaetano Donizetti (1797-1848) was born at Bergamo, the son of a weaver. He received a good education and his father insisted that he should study law or teaching. To avoid these, Donizetti joined the army and wrote his first three operas while stationed at Venice. After release from army duties at the age of twenty-five, he gave full time to composition. In addition to 65 operas, he wrote a number of masses, string quartets, and songs. His best known opera is *Lucia di Lammermoor*.

Vincenzo Bellini (1801-1835) was born at Catania, the son of an organist who was his first teacher. At eighteen, he went to Naples to study and remained there until the age of twenty-six. During his short life, his musical activities centered around Naples and Milan. His melodies, which influenced Chopin, were warm and sentimental. His principal operas are *La Sonnambula, Norma* and *I Puritani*.

Giuseppe Verdi (1813-1901) was the greatest Italian composer of the period. His flare for the dramatic, his ability as a melodist, and his mastery of vocal and instrumental expressions enabled him to produce works of lasting quality and popularity. His best known operas are *Rigoletto, Il Trovatore, La Traviata, Aida, Otello* and *Falstaff*.

Born at Busseto in an innkeeper's family, his musical tendencies were noted at an early age. At ten, he was the village organist. Encouraged by a local merchant who later became his father-in-law, Verdi went to Milan for study at the age of sixteen. By the time he was twenty, he was composing in various forms. He returned to Busseto, married, and became the leading musician of the village. Later he moved to Milan where he began his opera composing career, a career which took him to some of the largest cities and musical centers of Europe. Although primarily a composer of opera, this generous, warm-hearted Italian patriot wrote one *Requiem* which made a lasting impression.

Other Italian operatic composers of note are Ruggiero Leoncavallo (1858-1919), who wrote *I Pagliacci;* Giacomo Puccini (1858-1924), who composed *La Boheme, Madam Butterfly,* and *Tosca;* and Pietro Mascagni (1863-1945), who wrote *Cavalleria Rusticana.*

In France, the traditional comic opera held sway until about the middle of the century, when its characteristics began to merge with those of grand opera. The latter had developed during the first half of the nineteenth century and, because it featured extravagant and heroic characters, demons, grandiose effects, great choral masses and ballet was often called "grand spectacle opera."

Giacomo Meyerbeer (1791-1864) was born at Berlin of wealthy and cultured Jewish parents who gave him every opportunity for development. His early training was under the leading German teachers of the day, but in order to realize more fully his ambition in dramatic composition, he went to Venice for further training. While there he wrote five Italian and one German opera. The latter was produced by Rossini in Paris in 1826, which led to Meyerbeer's going there to live. Having been a student of French opera literature, he now turned to

French opera. Among his best known operas are *Les Huguenots* and *L'Africaine*.

Charles Gounod (1818-1893), who began his career in sacred music and later turned to the dramatic field, left two operas of note, *Faust* and *Romeo et Juliette*.

In connection with French opera mention should also be made of Thomas' *Mignon*, Massenet's *Manon*, Bizet's *Carmen*, Berlioz' *Les Troyens*, Delibes' *Le Roi l'a Dit* and *Lakme*, Offenbach's *Les Contes d'Hoffman*, Saint-Saens' *Samson et Dalila*.

In Germany, the Romantic opera was characterized by the use of German folk song style, with subjects drawn from folk lore and legend.

Carl Maria von Weber (1786-1826) was the chief predecessor of Wagner and suggested a fusion of the arts which Wagner carried out. He also paved the way for the enlargement of the orchestra and more colorful orchestral effects.

Weber was born at Eutin where his father was choirmaster. During the first twenty-five years of his life, Weber traveled extensively and became acquainted with the leading theatres and theatrical productions of his day. Settling down for a time at Salzburg, he studied composition with Michael Haydn. Although gifted as pianist and concert artist, his greatest contribution was in opera and orchestral music. His principal operas are *Der Freischütz, Euryanthe,* and *Oberon*.

Richard Wagner (1813-1883) was the most important figure in German opera and one of the greatest geniuses of all time. Wagner conceived of dramatic art as a fusion of the arts—poetry, stage craft, and vocal and instrumental music. He wrote his own libretti and innovated the use of a musical theme associated with a particular character, place, situation, or mood. Wagner increased the size of the orchestra and made it a definite part of the dramatic expression.

Wagner was born at Leipzig. His grandfather and father were civil officers interested in the theatre. After his father's early death and his mother's re-marriage, he was reared by his stepfather in Dresden. He received a good education and was especially fond of Greek, German poetry, and tragic drama. It was only after his return to Leipzig (at about eighteen years of age) for further study, that he became interested in music, especially the orchestral works of Beethoven. After some experience as chorusmaster at the theatre where his brother was tenor, he became conductor of a theatrical troupe which went bankrupt and then of another which also failed. After some months in Dresden, he was named director at Riga where he began dramatic composition in earnest. When his contract expired, he left Riga along with his debts and set out for Paris, where he met Meyerbeer and Berlioz. After three years in Paris, where he supported himself largely by writing essays, he returned to Dresden, where he became court choirmaster. Here several of his operas were produced, but because of his uncompromising attitude, Wagner gained few friends and many enemies. At the age of thirty-six, he was forced to flee the country, finally settling at Zurich, where he remained for the next fifteen years, creating literary and musical works. He was partly supported by Liszt. The exile proved a blessing in disguise, for these were productive years. Finally, he received a summons from Ludwig II of Bavaria to settle in Munich, where he would receive ample support for his dramatic ambitions. Gradually the tide of criticism subsided, and his mastery was acknowledged with enthusiasm.

His operas include *Rienzi, Der fliegende Hollander, Tannhäuser, Lohengrin, Tristan und Isolde, Die Meistersinger, Parsifal* and the four which together form *Der Ring des Nibelungen: Das Rheingold, Die Walküre, Siegfried,* and *Götterdämmerung.*

Martha by Fredrick von Flotow and *The Merry Wives of Windsor* by Otto Nicolai are well known German operas of the period.

Representative Russian operas of the period are *A Life for the Tsar* and *Russlan et Ludmilla* by Michail Glinka; *Boris Godunov* by Modest Moussorgsky; *May Night, Snow Maiden, Mlada, Sadko, Tsar's Bride,* and *Tsar Saltan* by Nicolai Rimsky-Korsakoff.

The Bartered Bride by Friedrich Smetana and *Rusalka* by Anton Dvorak are representative of Bohemian opera.

Opera in England was of little consequence except for the humorous satires created by Gilbert and Sullivan. Typical of these clever English operettas are *H.M.S. Pinafore, The Pirates of Penzance, Trial by Jury, Patience, Iolanthe, The Yeomen of the Guard, The Gondoliers,* and *The Mikado.*

The Art Song

One of the most important developments during the Romantic period was that of the solo or art song. Two factors contributed to this development: (1) the rise of the Romantic poets, whose works were especially adaptable to song, and (2) the development of the piano, which was ideal as an accompanying instrument.

In contrast to the plan in folk song where the music is the same for each stanza, most art songs are *through-composed;* that is, the music is changed for each stanza in keeping with the mood of the text.

Franz Schubert (1797-1828) was among the greatest composers of the art song. Although he lived less than thirty-two years, he wrote over 1100 works, 600 of which were songs. He was one of the greatest melodists of all time and his song accompaniments are as sensitive as the poetic text.

Schubert was born in a suburb of Vienna. His father was a music-loving schoolmaster who encouraged him and instructed him in music. Schubert sang in church choir and later played first violin in his school orchestra. His musical training was meager although he had short periods of good instruction. Due to his peculiar personality, his life was filled with material misfortune and social isolation. This was not a handicap to his creative activities, but his genius went unobserved until after his death, except by an obscure circle of admirers. Being shy and awkward, Schubert avoided high society, spending his mornings in composing and his evenings with a rough student group whose ways he loved. He loved poetry and his song texts are drawn from over 100 poets, including 70 from Goethe, 50 from Schiller and over 40 from Müller. He worked with great rapidity and made no preliminary sketches and very few revisions. He wrote for pleasure and had little idea of the value of his work. Besides his many songs and his orchestral works, his compositions include about 60 part-songs, 6 masses, 2 cantatas, 24 piano sonatas, 20 string quartets, a number of overtures and many smaller pieces such as impromptus, dances, and marches.

Other outstanding song composers of the period were *Hugo Wolf, Robert Franz, Felix Mendelssohn, Robert Schumann, Johannes Brahms, Charles Gounod, Claude Debussy, Michail Glinka, Peter Tschaikovsky, Sergei Rachmaninoff,* and *Modest Moussorgsky.*

Choral Music

Even though opera, art song, orchestra, and piano were the chief media of expression during the Romantic period, there were a few notable contributions in the choral field. These, whether oratorio, cantata, or smaller forms, embraced the Romantic style and feeling.

Felix Mendelssohn (1809-1847) was the greatest nineteenth century composer of oratorio. His superior instrumentation for the orchestra and his skill as a melodist gave his works high and lasting quality. *Elijah* and *St. Paul* are his greatest oratorios. Mendelssohn was definitely romantic, but clung closer to the classical style than many others of his generation. Due to his intellect, social leadership, and organizational abilities, his was a picturesque and influential career. He was much sought after by students and musicians, and his ideas were the ideals of many. He was instrumental in introducing the works of J. S. Bach to a music world which had been ignorant of Bach's greatness.

Mendelssohn was born at Hamburg of wealthy and intellectual Jewish parents who later adopted Christianity. Mendelssohn had the finest tutors of his day and was constantly surrounded by choice social, literary, and artistic influences. He traveled and concertized widely in Europe and was popular wherever he went. None of this affected him adversely or retarded his creative efforts.

In addition to *Elijah* and *St. Paul,* Mendelssohn wrote many other works of lasting quality, among which were 4 symphonies, 7 concert overtures, a violin concerto, 2 piano concertos, many songs, and a great deal of chamber, piano, and organ music.

Other notable composers of choral music were Beethoven (*Christ On the Mount of Olives* and *Missa Solemnis*), Sphor (*The Last Judgment*), Berlioz (*Damnation de Faust, Requiem, Te Deum*), Schumann (*Das Paradies und die Peri, Mass in C Minor*), Liszt (*St. Elizabeth*), Stainer (*The Crucifixion, Hungarian Coronation Mass*), Parry (*Judith, Job*), Elgar (*The Kingdom*), Brahms (*Requiem*), Cherubini (*Mass in D Minor*), Schubert (*6 Latin Masses*), Faure (*Requiem*), Bruckner (*Te Deum, Mass in F Minor*), Franck (*Les Beatitudes*), Verdi (*Requiem*).

Records

Treasury of Grand Opera, Victor LM-1148
Treasury of Grand Opera, Victor, LM-1847
Songs for Male Chorus (Schubert), Shaw Chorale, Victor, LM-1800
Brahms Liebeslieder Waltzes and German Folk Songs (Roger Wagner Chorale), Capitol P-8176
Mass in G (Schubert), Robert Shaw Chorale, Victor LM-1784
How Lovely Are the Messengers (Mendelssohn), RCA Elementary Library, WE-86

CHAPTER 13

The Solidification

of a Nation

(1865-1900)

Jim Cooper

Although named The Reconstruction Period in American history, we might also think of the period following the Civil War as a continuation of the Age of the Common Man. For whether we focus upon the era immediately before or after the war, the common man was in command. No introduction to the period is more fitting than the following poem by Dr. Everett A. Gillis:[1]

---

[1] Used by permission of the author and *The Kaleidograph Press*. Dr. Gillis is professor of English at Texas Technological College and is an authority on Southwest literature and a recognized poet.

Jim Cooper, American

I was sired by a father with fiery eyes,
Under a lucky planet,
For he gave me a temper with a trigger edge,
And his character of granite.

His jeans were made of homespun stuff,
And he wrote with a turkey feather;
He taught me the heft of an axe aloft
And its ring in the frosty weather.

He taught me the feel of a rifle stock
And the trick of a fiddle merry;
And he gave me his Bible and saddle bags
When I left for the rolling prairie.

Jim Cooper came from Kentucky's woods
To the green and rolling prairie,
With a Bible in his saddle bags
And a fiddle to make him merry.

He built him a cabin of cedar wood
And pledged it in Kentucky brandy,
And he planted his crops in the fear of God,
But he kept his rifle handy.

And he found my heart at a husking bee
With the starlight glittering over,
And he won my heart with a handsome phrase,
And a sprig of buffalo clover.

He raised his boys in the American way,
To fortitude and daring,
He gave the seventh son to the Lord
For his mother died in the bearing.

And he left his peace for a battle cry
And the saber's ruthless rattle;
And he stood like a rock wall by his flag
In the bitter siege of the battle.

Faith, hope, and charity define
The pattern of his story—
One with the men who made his times
A legend and a glory.

When Dr. Gillis was asked who Jim Cooper was, he replied: "His name is not in a history book, on a map, or in the portrait galleries of the great, but in the running legends of the land—in the forests and the prairies, in the deserts and the mountains —at Shiloh, Bull Run, Gettysburg. For his boots made the roads and lanes, and his plow and his cattle the homes and farms. Where his hands dug the water holes, or with his neighbors he built the crossroad stores and the churches, there are the cities and the towns—solid and substantial as granite, simple and warming as a handclasp. But his shadow makes a legend in the land. This was Jim Cooper, American."

Jim Cooper and the thousands like him who went west to build their homes, churches, and schools did not find life uninteresting, for the whole country was teeming with activity. The Pony Express spurred its way from Saint Joseph to Sacramento in 1860; the telegraph spun its way from coast to coast in 1861; the Civil War blasted the Mason-Dixon line, 1861-1865; and the Central Pacific and the Union Pacific joined rails at Ogden, Utah, in 1869. These gigantic undertakings within the span of nine years are indications of the spirit and activities at the beginning of the period and were a perfect setting for the Homestead Act of 1862. Jim Cooper and his friends took full advantage of this act, pre-empted public land, and farming soon became a dominant economic force in the wide open spaces. Wherever the Jim Coopers went, they took their fiddles, guitars, mandolins, harmonicas, frenchharps, banjos and songs to make their labor lighter and their lives happier. Their experiences, their thoughts, and their feelings are recorded in song.

Ranching was then, as now, a giant industry. Cattle trails such as the Chisholm trail cut their meandering paths across the country toward the railroad tracks. The pistol-totin', law-unto-himself character was both hero and villain of the wild west dramatic saga.

The cowboy was by no means the jolly carefree ki-yi yip-pi-yay character so often portrayed. Actually he was a lonesome fellow a long way from home, and his trail was long and arduous. Except at the end of the trail, he was not the "rip-roaring" character as often portrayed, riding his horse at "break-neck" speed. On the contrary, his horse was his working companion and cattle were not to be excited. His songs to his horse and the "dogies" are expressive of his feelings toward them: "Good-Bye, Old Paint" and "Git Along, Little Dogie." Since he lived close to nature, many of his songs reflect its beauty, and the rhythm seems to picture rolling prairies or the rhythmic movement of a horse. Another poem by Dr. Gillis describes a Texas cattle drive in simple yet vivid language:

Cattle Drive[2]

We headed them north three thousand head
Of rangy, longhorn cattle,
As tough as rawhide, fleet as deer,
With a noise like thunder's rattle.

We pointed them out at the break of spring
When the grass was lush and green,
From the Rio Grande and the Gulf-coast plains
Up the trail to Abilene.

Our outfit was brisk, all seasoned hands,
At point and flank and swing,
And a "techy cook" on the chuck wagon gear,
And a trail boss to make us sing.

We lived with those longhorns from dawn to dusk,
And a bit of night watch too,
And sang for a lullaby, "sleep, little dogies,
Or you'll be a son-o-gun stew!"

And we herded them up out of Texas—
Dry drive or clover trail—
Indian Territory through into Kansas,
Our dust like a smoky gale.

Three months it was, sweating and swearing,
And our ponies hardly alive—
We reached trail's end on the Fourth of July,
With not a lost steer on the drive.

---

[2] From *Sunrise in Texas.* Used by permission of the author.

*And we stormed into town for the big celebration
And shot up the place for a joke,
And squandered our pay in the gambling halls,
Then started for Texas—plum broke!*

If the reader has wondered why there were so few pioneer songs in praise of women, he may recall that prior to the twentieth century this was a man's world. For the most part men made the songs and sang them; they did the entertaining; they wrote the books and edited the periodicals; they engaged in politics; they voted. A woman's place was in the home. But with the spotlight focusing more and more on women's suffrage and education for the female, the themes of songs turned more and more toward the fairer sex. The songs which did appear made a lasting impression. Some of these are Lorena, Anna Lee, Yellow Rose of Texas, Jeannie With the Light Brown Hair, Beautiful Dreamer, Sweet Adeline, Down By the Old Millstream, Dear Old Girl, and Sweet Betsy from Pike.

Thus it was that following the Civil War the new country began to expand, to settle, and to acquire maturity—a maturity necessary for later development in the arts. While folk songs and dances, minstrel songs, fiddle tunes, and great hymns of faith were the companions of those who traveled through or settled in the west, great works of music were appearing in the more cultured centers, a fact which eventually led to America's ascent as a musical nation. The majority of those who pioneered in serious American music were accomplished musicians who had studied under the leading masters of Europe.

Musical Leaders in America

Theodore Thomas (1835-1905), who came from Germany in 1845, is credited with creating an interest in orchestral music and in establishing the first permanent orchestras in New York and Chicago. The first New York concert was given in 1862.

Leopold Damrosch (1832-1885), soon after his arrival in America, organized the Oratorio Society of New York, giving his first concert—Handel's *Samson*—in 1873. The following year, he gave Handel's *Messiah,* which he conducted annually until his death. In 1878, Mr. Damrosch, a bitter rival of Mr. Thomas, organized his own orchestra which later merged with the Philharmonic. For years to come, the name of Damrosch—first Leopold and then his son, Walter—was synonymous with the New York Symphony and the Metropolitan Opera.

The interest in orchestral music created by Mr. Thomas and Dr. Damrosch during the War Between the States was soon to spread to other metropolitan areas, where some of the greatest symphony orchestras of the world were to be established.

The leading teachers and composers were as follows:

John Paine (1839-1906) was the first important native composer to be recognized abroad. He became the first music instructor at Harvard (1862) and established the Harvard School of Music. Since Harvard, the first college in America, was used as a model by other colleges, new music schools were founded in rapid succession: Oberlin, 1865; New England Conservatory, 1867; Cincinnati Conservatory of Music, 1867; Chicago Musical College, 1867; Peabody Institute, 1868; and American Conservatory, 1868.

Dudley Buck (1839-1909), a native of Connecticut who had extensive training under the leading teachers of Europe, probably made his greatest contribution as a composer of sacred music. Although he pioneered in the larger choral forms, his anthems, which remain popular today, are his most permanent contribution to American music.

George Chadwick (1854-1931) was born in Lowell, Massachusetts. He, too, studied in Europe. Soon after his return to America, he was made instructor of music at the New England Conservatory (1882), a position he held until his death. He was known as a teacher and author but most of all for his twenty major works for orchestra.

Horatio Parker (1863-1919) was born at Auburndale, Massachusetts. After studying with Mr. Chadwick and later in Europe, he became organist at St. Andrews and taught at the National Conservatory. Later he accepted an invitation to be organist at Trinity Church, Boston, where Phillips Brooks was pastor. In

1894, he became head of the Music Department at Yale and while there organized the New Haven Symphony. Although he wrote a number of instrumental works, he is best known for his choral compositions, the most famous being the cantata *Hora Novissima.*

Mrs. H. H. A. Beach (1867-1944) is of special interest as the first outstanding composer among American women. Although she composed a number of large works, she is best known for her settings of Browning's "Ah, Love But A Day" and "The Year's at the Spring."

Edward MacDowell (1861-1908) was a native of New York who spent the formative years of his life in Europe as a student and teacher. Grieved by the death of his friend Franz Liszt, he returned to America in 1886 and settled in Boston. He was known as a teacher, composer, and concert pianist. Although MacDowell wrote several major works, he is best known for the little pieces found in his *Woodland Sketches,* such as "To a Water Lily" and "To a Wild Rose." In later life he spent eight years as head of the Music Department at Columbia University, but resigned as a result of a disagreement with the administration. MacDowell was one of the first to use Indian melodies as themes, as he did in his second *Indian Suite.* After his death, Mrs. MacDowell spent the remainder of her life carrying out her husband's wish to establish a retreat for creative artists on the MacDowell farm at Peterboro, New Hampshire. This is known today as the MacDowell Colony.

Leaders of the Period

Again it is profitable to list the names of outstanding personalities who dominated the American and European scenes during the period. This list mentions those who were active during the last half of the century.

Literature: Thomas Hardy (1840), Charles W. Stoddard (1843), Eugene Field (1850), Guy de Maupassant (1850), Robert Louis Stevenson (1850), Henry Van Dyke (1852), James Whitcomb Riley (1853), Elbert Hubbard (1856), Oscar Wilde (1856), Leonard

Huxley (1861), Edward K. Bok (1863), Rudyard Kipling (1865),
H. G. Wells (1866), William S. Porter (O. Henry) (1867), Winston
Churchill (1871), Paul Lawrence Dunbar (1872).

Government: William McKinley (1843), Henry Cabot Lodge
(1850), Woodrow Wilson (1856), William Howard Taft (1857),
Theodore Roosevelt (1858), William Jennings Bryan (1860),
Charles Curtis (1860), Warren G. Harding (1865), Calvin Cool-
idge (1872), Dwight Morrow (1873).

Science: Alexander Graham Bell (1847), Thomas A. Edison
(1847), Luther Burbank (1849), Walter Reed (1851), Sigmund
Freud (1856), Wilbur Wright (1867), Orville Wright (1871),
Guglielmo Marconi (1874).

Industry: George Westinghouse (1846), F. W. Woolworth
(1852), Andrew H. Mellon (1855), Charles W. Schwab (1862),
Henry Ford (1863), J. Pierpont Morgan (1867).

Education: Booker T. Washington (1859), John Dewey (1859),
Nicholas Murray Butler (1862), George Washington Carver
(1864).

Law: Clarence Darrow (1857), Charles Evans Hughes (1862).

Songs and Recordings

When Johnny Comes Marching Home. Being particularly
appropriate to war-time, the popularity of this song waxes and
wanes. Although it was sung to some extent during the War
Between the States as "We All Went Down to New Orleans," it
attained greater popularity during the Spanish American War, in
1898. It was revived again during World Wars I and II.

G. Singing in Harmony, p. 160

The Little Old Sod Shanty. This was a favorite of the early
and lonely "sodbuster," who created this song about the house
he built on his pre-empted one hundred and sixty acres of
government land. It is another example of American humor,
reflecting our ability to laugh at uncomfortable situations. In
timbered areas, the words were changed to "The little old log
cabin in the lane." Read the complete text in *The American*

Songbag by Carl Sandburg. A religious text has also been set to this tune under the title of "The Lily of the Valley," which is sung widely throughout the South, giving it the flavor of a white spiritual. "Little Joe the Wrangler" is also sung to this tune.

S. Music in Our Country, p. 118
Burl Ives Song Book, p. 250
Burl Ives, Encyclopaedia Britannica, Album V
Roger Wagner Chorale, Capitol P-8332 (Little Joe the Wrangler)

A Shuckin' of the Corn. This is a folk song of the Tennessee farmer. After the corn was harvested, the farmers would gather at their neighbors for a corn-shucking party, sometimes called a "shucking bee." The ladies might engage in a "quilting bee." Out of such occasions grew songs of this type.

S. Music Near and Far, p. 10
G. Singing in Harmony, p. 183r

Pick a Bale o' Cotton. This is a work song of the southern farm where cotton is one of the chief crops.

F. Music Across Our Country, p. 49
S. Music Near and Far, p. 11

Cotton Needs Picking. Another of the cotton-picking songs of the southern farmer.

G. Singing in Harmony, p. 82b
F. Music Across Our Country, p. 133r

Boll Weevil. The boll weevil is one of the cotton farmer's worst enemies, and until recently developed insecticides appeared, the farmer was at its mercy. According to this song, the weevil migrated from Mexico with his family, squatted on Texas soil, and like a good Texan, fell in love with the place. No matter what adversities he might be forced to endure he would "stan' it like a man." The weevil tells the story, which is the farmer's indirect way of expressing his ability to laugh at adversity. Read the text in *The American Songbag* by Carl Sandburg.

G. Singing Together, p. 54*r*
S. Music in Our Country, p. 66
Burl Ives, Encyclopaedia Britannica, Album VI

Pat on the Railroad. Pat and many of his Irish kin furnished much of the labor for the new railroads that were being built throughout the country. This is one of his more melancholy songs.

S. Music Around the World, p. 108
Burl Ives Song Book, p. 232
Burl Ives, Encyclopaedia Britannica, Album VI

I've Been Working on the Railroad. This railroad working song from who-knows-where was, and is, sung all over the country whether or not a railroad is near. Texans have adopted their own text: "The Eyes of Texas Are Upon You."

S. Music Near and Far, p. 123
G. Singing Every Day, p. 35*r*
F. Voices of America, p. 26*a*
Capitol P-8324 (Roger Wagner Chorale)

Drill Ye Terriers, Drill. A composed song originating in New York City, this song is a favorite of laborers everywhere.

S. Music in Our Country, p. 97
G. Singing in Harmony, p. 10
Burl Ives, Encyclopaedia Britannica, Album VI

John Henry. This song concerns the competition between human labor and mechanized power, a competition which has long been the concern of labor organizations.

S. Music in Our Country, p. 144
Burl Ives, Encyclopaedia Britannica, Album VI

God of Our Fathers. This great hymn was written for the celebration of the hundredth anniversary of the Declaration of Independence.

F. Voices of America, p. 11
S. Music Around the World, p. 25

Red River Valley. When this song went west, it became a cowboy love song.

G. Singing in Harmony, p. 58
S. Music Around the World, p. 111

Goodbye, Old Paint. This is the farewell song of a cowboy to his favorite horse.

G. Singing Every Day, p. 38r
F. Music Across Our Country, p. 55
S. Music in Our Town, p. 121
Burl Ives, Columbia Records, Album III
Roger Wagner Chorale, Capitol P-8332

Night Herding Song. The cowboy sang this lullaby as he slowly rode night watch around the herd, quieting the cattle for the night. He maintained his lonely vigil under the stars while the cattle and his companions rested.

S. Music in Our Country, p. 79
G. Singing Every Day, p. 40ar
F. Voices of the World, p. 180
Roger Wagner Chorale, Capitol P-8332

Git Along, Little Dogies. This trail song was sung to the dogies, or calves, and expresses the cowboy's liking for cattle and for his work.

F. Voices of America, p. 151r
Roger Wagner Chorale, Capitol P-8332
Burl Ives, Encyclopaedia Britannica, Album V

Goin' to Leave Old Texas Now. Another of the cowboy farewell songs.

G. Singing Together, p. 58r
F. Music Across Our Country, p. 46r
S. Music in Our Country, p. 78

The Old Chisholm Trail. This is a cowboy song concerning experiences on one of the most famous of the cattle trails.

G. Singing in Harmony, p. 72
S. Music in Our Country, p. 119

Burl Ives, Encyclopaedia Britannica, Album V
Roger Wagner Chorale, Capitol P-8332

My Home's in Montana. A typical cowboy melody and text. This melody is used by Morton Gould in his *Cowboy Rhapsody.*

S. Music Now and Long Ago, p. 56
G. Singing Together, p. 9
F. Music Across Our Country, p. 53

Cowboy's Lament or *Streets of Laredo.* This is one of the most popular of the cowboy songs and is an adaptation of a British ballad about a young man (or woman) who went wrong. There is also an Irish version which concerns a young soldier who followed the path to degradation. Each of these is on the general theme of "from rum to ruin." The influence of the soldier and the woman is clearly seen in the verse from the cowboy version which reads:

> *O, beat the drum slowly and play the fife lowly* } soldier
> *Play the dead march as they carry me along,*
> *Put bunches of roses all over my coffin,* } woman
> *Roses to deaden the clods as they fall.*

S. Music Around the World, p. 116
Burl Ives Song Book, p. 206
Burl Ives, Columbia, Album I
Burl Ives, Encyclopaedia Britannica, Album VI
Roger Wagner Chorale, Capitol P-8324

Trail to Mexico. This is another of the wonderfully descriptive trail songs of the American cowboy.

G. Singing in Harmony, p. 73r
Roger Wagner Chorale, Capitol P-8332

The Lone Star Trail. A cattle trail ballad in which the cowboy determines to quit cow punching.

S. Music in Our Town, p. 120r
F. Music Across Our Country, p. 47r

I Ride an Old Paint. Here is a soothing song about the cowboy's horse, the last verse being something of a will. In contrast to "Bury Me Not on the Lone Prairie," this cowboy prefers to die on the prairie.

    S. Music Around the World, p. 119

Home On the Range. This is the cowboy's pastoral, reflecting the quiet and peace of the rolling prairie. The rhythm, melody, and words are quiet, restful, serene, and secure. The song is an excellent prescription for those who suffer from "modern" complexes. It is probably the best known and loved of the cowboy songs.

    S. Music in Our Country, p. 82
    G. Singing in Harmony, p. 11
    F. Music Through the Year, p. 10r
    Roger Wagner Chorale, Capitol P-8332

Other Records

Songs of the North and South (Burl Ives), Encyclopaedia Britannica, Vol. II

The Confederacy, Columbia ML-4927 (Includes General Lee's Grand March; All Quiet Along the Potomac Tonight; Lorena; Bonnie Blue Flag; The Yellow Rose of Texas; Somebody's Darling; We All Went Down to New Orleans; Lee's Farewell Order to the Army of Northern Virginia; The Conquered Banner; Dixie's Land with Quickstep and Interlude; Year of Jubilo)

    The Lincoln Portrait by Aaron Copland, Columbia ML-2042
    The Lonesome Train by Robinson and Corwin, Decca ML-5054
    Cowboy Rhapsody by Gould, Columbia ML-4218
    Cowboy Ballads, Folkways F-222
    When Johnny Comes Marching Home Again, arr. Harris, Victor-8629
    Pop Goes the Weasel, Victor-4397
    Arkansas Traveler, Victor-22131
    Saturday Night Barn Dance by Siegmeister, Columbia ML-2123
    Irish Washerwoman, arr. Soweby, Victor-22131
    The Plow That Broke the Plains by Thompson, Victor M-1116
    Rodeo Ballet Suite by Copland, Victor LM-32
    Billy the Kid, Ballet Suite by Copland, Columbia ML-2167

In Europe—The Romantic Period (Continued)

The Romantic period covers the Age of the Common Man and the Reconstruction period in American history. Having discussed the choral works of the Romantic period in the preceding chapter, we will now consider the instrumental music of the era.

The Piano

The piano, which had been in a developmental stage for some time, reached maturity during the nineteenth century and probably attracted more attention than any other medium of musical expression. Composers and performers turned to the piano for their individual and national expressions.

Frederic Chopin (1810-1849), the tone-poet, wrote almost exclusively for the piano. His music is lyrical in quality, consisting of beautiful song-like melodies with decorations particularly appropriate for the instrument.

Chopin was born in Warsaw, the son of a businessman and teacher. He received a fair general and musical education, but left the Lyceum at the age of seventeen. At twenty-two, he began concertizing and developing as a composer. He moved to Paris and was associated with France and French music for the rest of his life. His concert career was virtually ended at the age of twenty-five by tuberculosis. During the few remaining years of his life, he devoted himself almost exclusively to composition except for an occasional recital or concert.

His devotion to Poland and his resentment of the Russian invasion of that country caused much of his music to show strong national feeling. His works consist of 50 mazurkas, 15 waltzes, 19 nocturnes, 25 preludes, 27 etudes, 3 impromptus, 3 fantasias, 3 variations, 4 sonatas, 2 piano concertos, and a number of polonaises.

Franz Liszt (1811-1886) was born at Raiding, a small town in western Hungary near Vienna. His father was an amateur musician and manager of one of the Esterhazy estates. Liszt's

talent was so marked that when he was nine years old a group
of noblemen presented him with an annual scholarship for six
years. His father took him at once to Vienna for study under
leading teachers. Later he was taken to Paris for further instruction. The stipend ceased at the time Liszt was fifteen, and the
elder Liszt died the following year, forcing Franz to choose a
pianist's career. From the age of twenty-eight on, his time was
largely occupied by concert tours through Europe. Wherever
he played, his audience was captivated by his superb interpretation and his technical mastery. His large financial income was
matched by his generosity.

His piano works include 14 rhapsodies, 2 concertos, etudes,
and transcriptions and arrangements from Bach, Beethoven,
Weber, Mendelssohn, Meyerbeer, Rossini, Berlioz, Wagner, Raff,
Glinka, Arcadelt, Mozart, and Schubert.

Robert Schumann (1810-1856) is difficult to classify, for his
compositions extended into all idioms except church music. None
of his works, however, is more expressive of the Romantic style
than his works for piano. He was also a supreme master of the
art-song form.

Schumann was born at Zwickau where his father was a book-
seller, author, and translator. His mother was the daughter of
a physician. At an early age Robert indicated a strong interest
in literature and music, the fields to which he devoted his life.
His father died when Robert was sixteen and his mother sent
him to Leipzig to study law. Musical influences proved too
strong for him to continue in law, and at twenty he began to
study music in earnest. His ambition was to become a concert
pianist, but due to an injury to his right hand this was not
possible. He then turned to composition and music criticism, the
latter appearing in *Neue Zeitschrift fur Musik,* a musical journal
which he founded. Clara, his wife, was a talented composer and
the leading pianist of Europe. Their life together was ideal in
every respect. His brilliant career, and finally his life, ended as
a result of a nervous breakdown.

His works for piano comprise a long list including etudes,
sonatas, papillions, a toccata, and a concerto. There were also

works for piano and strings, trios, quartets, and other chamber works. For orchestra there were 4 symphonies and 4 concert-overtures; for voice, about 250 songs and a number of choral works.

Among other notable composers of piano music should be mentioned Franz Schubert, Johannes Brahms, Edward Grieg, Edward MacDowell, and the immortal Ludwig Beethoven.

Orchestral Music

As suggested elsewhere, the orchestra and orchestration were enlarged and greatly improved by Weber and Wagner. The popular forms were the symphony, concerto, symphonic suite, symphonic poem, and concert overture.

Johannes Brahms (1833-1897), born at Hamburg, the son of a musician, is usually considered the greatest symphonic composer of the nineteenth century. His compositions are so original, so intellectual, and so carefully worked out as to place him among the greatest composers of all time. He developed first as a pianist and concertized at an early age, but settled in Vienna at the age of twenty-nine. Although away from Vienna for two or more extended periods, most of his life was spent in the secluded pursuit of artistic ideals. His friendship with the Schumanns began when Brahms was twenty and continued through the years. Clara Schumann was one of the greatest interpreters of his music.

Brahms wrote 4 symphonies, 2 symphonic overtures, a concerto for violin and 'cello, 2 serenades, 2 piano concertos, 1 violin concerto, symphonic variations, 3 string quartets, 2 string quintets, 3 piano quartets, 3 piano trios, a piano and clarinet quintet, a horn trio, a clarinet trio, 2 clarinet sonatas, 3 violin sonatas, 2 'cello sonatas, and 2 sextets. In addition to these, he wrote many superb songs, a number of choral works including the well-loved *Requiem*, and several organ works.

In addition to Brahms, other German composers are:

Richard Strauss (1864-1949). His principal orchestral works are the symphonic poems *Don Juan, Don Quixote* (variations for 'cello and orchestra), *Symphonia Domestica, Til Eulenspiegel, "Thus Spake Zarathustra,"* and *A Hero's Life.* He was also an important composer of operas.

Johann Strauss (1825-1899) is noted for his very popular Viennese waltzes.

Gustav Mahler (1860-1911) wrote 10 symphonies of great length which are orchestrated in a Wagnerian style.

Anton Bruckner (1824-1896) wrote 10 symphonies which in style have an affinity with Schubert's.

Franz Schubert (1797-1828) wrote 8 symphonies and 8 overtures.

Felix Mendelssohn (1809-1847) wrote 5 symphonies, 2 piano concertos, concert overtures, and a violin concerto.

Hector Berlioz (1803-1869), born at Lyons, was the leading French symphonist of the first half of the nineteenth century. His father, a physician, sent him to Paris to study medicine, but much to his father's disgust the youth turned to music. He made a definite contribution with his colorful orchestration and wrote a treatise on the subject which has had wide influence on composers of orchestral works. Like Schumann, Berlioz was noted as a brilliant music critic.

Among his works are 5 concert overtures and 4 symphonies, several operas, and several cantatas.

In addition to Berlioz, other French composers are:

Camelle Saint-Saens (1835-1921) wrote 5 symphonies, 4 symphonic poems, 2 orchestral suites, 5 piano concertos, 10 operas (*Samson et Dalila*), cantatas, masses, and chamber music.

Cesar Franck (1822-1890). *Symphony in D Minor* is his most popular orchestral work.

Vincent d' Indy (1851-1931) wrote 3 symphonic overtures, program symphonies, symphonic poems, and a few operas.

George Bizet (1838-1875). The *L'Arlesienne Suite* is his most popular orchestral work. Of his operas, *Carmen* is the best known.

Jules Massenet (1842-1912). In addition to a large number of operas, Massenet wrote several orchestral suites and fantasias.

Claude Debussy (1862-1918) wrote symphonic suites, cantatas, operas, and many smaller works. His piano music is important.

Peter Tschaikovsky (1840-1893), a Russian, produced a mass of orchestral works. They have enjoyed sustained popularity. Tschaikovsky wrote 6 symphonies, 7 orchestral suites, 5 symphonic poems, 7 overtures, 10 operas, 3 piano concertos, much chamber music, 3 ballets, and a large number of songs and piano pieces.

Other Russian composers of instrumental ensemble music are:

Niccolai Rimski-Korsakoff (1844-1908) wrote 3 symphonies and many other orchestral works, the most popular being the orchestral suite *Scheherazade*. He also wrote about a dozen operas, several cantatas, and many songs.

Modest Moussorgsky (1839-1881). *Night on Bald Mountain,* a symphonic poem, and the suite *Pictures at an Exhibition* are his most popular works. In addition, he wrote 3 operas, several choral works, piano pieces, and songs.

Mention should also be made of other composers who, during the Romantic period, contributed to orchestral literature. Among them are *Anton Dvorak* (1841-1904)—5 symphonies, the best known being *Symphony from the New World*—and *Edvard Grieg* (1843-1907)—3 orchestral suites, an overture, piano and violin concertos, 3 violin sonatas, and many smaller but notable works. His *Peer Gynt Suite* has long been a favorite.

Records

Chopin Mazurkas and Polonaises, Victor LM2049

Etudes (Chopin and Schumann), Victor LM6000

Concerto No. 1 in E-Flat; No. 2 in C Minor (Liszt), Victor LM2068

Liebestraum No. 3; Valse Impromptu (Liszt), Victor ERA298

Les Preludes (Liszt), Victor LM1775

Hungarian Rhapsody No. 1 in E-Flat (Liszt); Hungarian Rhapsody No. 2 in C-Sharp; Hungarian Dances Nos. 2 and 3 (Brahms), Victor LM6038

Concerto for Piano and Orchestra in A Minor (Schumann), Victor LM1050

Symphony No. 3 in E-Flat (Schumann), Victor LM1125

Roman Carnival Overture (Berlioz), Victor LM1834

Symphonie Fantastique (Berlioz), Victor LM1900

Auroras Wedding, Humoresque, Solitude (Tschaikovsky), Victor LM1774

1812 Overture (Tschaikovsky), Victor LM1999

Nutcracker Suite (Tschaikovsky), Victor LM2052

Symphony No. 5 in E Minor (Tschaikovsky), Victor LM1947

Concerto No. 1 in A Minor (Saint-Saens), Victor LM2016

Symphony in D Minor (Franck), Victor LM1852

Music from Carmen (Bizet), Victor LM1069

Symphony No. 1 in C; L'Arlesienne Suites Nos. 1 and 2 (Bizet), Victor LM1706

Death and Transfiguration (R. Strauss), Victor LM2077

Highlights from Die Fledermaus (J. Strauss), Victor LM1114

Tales from Vienna Woods; The Blue Danube (J. Strauss), Victor LM1809

Symphony No. 2 in B-Flat; Symphony No. 8 in B Minor, "Unfinished" (Schubert), Victor LM9032

Concerto in E Minor; Concerto in D Minor (Mendelssohn), Victor LM1720

Songs Without Words Nos. 1 to 49 (Mendelssohn), Victor LM6128

Minuet in G (Beethoven); Thäis (Massenet); Meditation (Grieg); Traumerei (Schumann), Victor ERA29

Peer Gynt Suite; Lyric Suite (Grieg), Victor LM2125

Encores by Horowitz, Victor LM1171

Music to Remember (Chopin, Tschaikovsky, Paderewski, Schumann), Victor LM1981

World Wide Favorites (Debussy, Liszt, Beethoven, Schumann, Saint-Saens), Victor LM1967

Scheherazade Symphonic Suite (Rimsky-Korsakoff), Victor LM1956

Pictures at an Exhibition (Moussorgsky), Victor LM2201

Slavonic Dances Nos. 1 to 10 (Dvorak), Victor LM2096

Symphony No. 5 in E Minor "From the New World" (Dvorak), Victor LM1778

Liebeslieder Waltzes (Brahms)—Roger Wagner Chorale, Capitol P8176 (sung in English)

German Folk Songs (Brahms)—Roger Wagner Chorale, Capitol P8176 (sung in English)

Also see RCA Elementary Record Library

CHAPTER 14

Modern Idioms

This chapter deals briefly with modern idioms in musical expression. No longer is there a need to parallel the American and the European scenes. Modern transportation and communication have, in a very real sense, made us *one world*. Nothing happens anywhere without all peoples immediately becoming aware of it; any innovation is instantly known to the world community.

The first half of the twentieth century was marked by political, economic, and social upheavals of national and international scope. Beginning with the Spanish-American War (1898), there followed two major wars, World War I (1914-1918) and World War II (1939-1945). Instability and economic chaos marked the depression of the 1930's. A short list of personalities who influenced the twentieth century suggests the spirit of the times. Leonard Huxley (1860), Rudyard Kipling (1865), Charles Steinmetz (1865), H. G. Wells (1866), Frank Lloyd Wright (1869), Theodore Dreiser (1871), Winston Churchill (1874), Guglielmo

Marconi (1874), Thomas Mann (1875), Will Rogers (1879), Joseph Stalin (1879), Pablo Picasso (1881), Franklin Delano Roosevelt (1882), Benito Mussolini (1883), David Lawrence (1885), Sinclair Lewis (1885), Humbert Wolfe (1885), Chiang Kai-Shek (1886), Eugene O'Neill (1888), Adolf Hitler (1889), Ernest Hemingway (1898), John Steinbeck (1902).

Among the teeming activities in all areas of the world was a tremendous development in science, particularly in physics and chemistry. Radio, the automobile, the airplane, radar, atomic energy, and plastics appeared during this period. Although science has led the parade in the march of human endeavor, it has been accompanied in the search for new and seemingly radical forms of expression by forward movements in art, architecture, literature, and music. As in the past, the revolt was away from old patterns in thought and expression, and the changes have come with confusing rapidity.

With the one-world concept brought about by transportation, communication, and the world-wide development of science, it would seem that greater understanding among nations would result. Unfortunately, such is not the case. In fact, the gulf between the ideologies of democracy and communism has widened and deepened. Envy, strife, selfishness, distrust, and fear still dominate human relations. The solution to this dilemma will not be found in might and destructive forces, but through constructive efforts and a world consciousness of, and concern for, human welfare. Perhaps the best approach to the problem is through an exchange of constructive creative efforts such as music.

Before proceeding to serious modern idioms of musical expression, let us look briefly at developments in other areas. During the latter part of the nineteenth century, Edison had invented the talking machine and vaudeville had replaced the minstrel show as the established form of entertainment. These developments played an important part in the development of a popular music which reflected the spirit of the times and forecast the advent of modern jazz. Furthermore, the phonograph and vaudeville were primarily responsible for the switch to songs about the fairer sex, such as My Wild Irish Rose, Love Me and the World is Mine, When Irish Eyes are Smiling, I'll Take You Home Again

Kathleen, In the Evening by the Moonlight, After the Ball, Bicycle Built for Two, and Melancholy Baby. Today high fidelity record players and stereophonic sound have replaced the phonograph and musical comedy has replaced vaudeville. The record business is a multi-million-dollar industry.

Closely related to the phonograph are radio, the motion picture, and television. All of these media stimulated the spread of popular music and provided opportunities for the dissemination of serious forms of expression.

There were other highly important events which indicated a wide and genuine interest in music and which were initial steps toward making America a world leader in musical affairs. A few of these are listed below.

1. Dvorak's visit to America and the interest in our folk music which his *New World Symphony* aroused.

2. The establishment of symphony orchestras in Boston and New York, and later in St. Louis, Chicago, Cleveland, Pittsburgh, Philadelphia, San Francisco, and Los Angeles.

3. The visit to America of the waltz king, Johann Strauss, and the popularity of his waltzes.

4. The national and international attention which Edward MacDowell (1861-1908) attracted with his *Indian Suite* and *Woodland Sketches*.

5. The American concert tours of such popular European artists as Caruso and Paderewski.

6. The influx of numerous European teachers, conductors, and composers.

7. The leadership of Patrick Gilmore, John Philip Sousa, and Edwin Franko Goldman in creating an interest in band music.

8. The influence of F. Melius Christiansen and John Finley Williamson on college, high school, and church choral music.

9. The establishment of conservatories of music in leading cities, and the establishment of schools of music in colleges and universities.

10. The growth of old, and the establishment of new publishing and music equipment houses all over the land.

11. The teaching of music in the public schools.

Today there are in the United States approximately one thousand community orchestras; many thousands of communities sponsor concert series; hardly a high school is without a band, choir, or orchestra. This interest and growth in orchestras, bands, and choirs has encouraged composers to write and to make transcriptions and arrangements for these groups.

This grass roots interest and development came as a result of the teaching of music in public schools. The people in general, and educators and school boards in particular, should be credited with the cultural development which they have promoted through music.

The Operetta and Broadway Musical

Forerunners of the broadway musical were the minstrel show and vaudeville. The dominant figure in operetta was *Victor Herbert* (1859-1924), who wrote over thirty such works, some of the most popular being *The Fortune Teller, Babes in Toyland, The Red Mill, Naughty Marietta, Sweethearts,* and *Eileen.*

Although not as popular as Herbert, *Reginald De Koven* (1859-1920) wrote a number of operettas including *The Highwayman* and *Red Feather.* He will long be remembered for "Oh Promise Me," which is used extensively at weddings.

Rudolf Friml (1881) and *Sigmund Romberg* (1887-1951) produced a number of scores which have enjoyed sustained popularity. Some have been made into successful movies. They include *Firefly, Rose Marie,* and *The Vagabond King* by Friml, and *May Time, Blossom Time, The Student Prince, The Desert Song,* and *New Moon* by Romberg.

The term *broadway musical* immediately brings to mind the name of *Jerome Kern* (1885-1945), who wrote a number of successful shows, the most popular being *Showboat,* which contains such long-time favorites as "Old Man River," "Make Believe," "Can't Help Lovin' That Man of Mine," and "Why Do I Love You?"

One of the most prolific and popular Broadway writers of musicals is *Irving Berlin* (1888). Among his most successful popular songs are "Oh, How I Hate to Get Up in the Morning," "Alexander's Ragtime Band," "When My Baby Smiles at Me," "Always," "What'll I Do," "Blue Skies," "Remember," "The Girl That I Marry," "God Bless America," and "White Christmas." Probably his most successful show is *Annie Get Your Gun.*

Cole Porter (1892) is another of the successful writers of musical shows. Some of the most popular have been *Fifty Million Frenchmen, Kiss Me Kate,* and *Silk Stockings.* He will long be remembered for his songs "Night and Day," "Rosalie," and "Begin the Beguine."

The name of *Richard Rodgers* (1902) is well known to the American public because of his many successful musical shows. The first of these were in collaboration with *Lorenz (Larry) Hart* who wrote the lyrics. After Mr. Hart's death in 1943, *Oscar Hammerstein, Jr.,* joined with Mr. Rodgers to produce such successful hits as *Oklahoma, Carousel, South Pacific,* and *The King and I.*

Contemporary competitors of Rodgers and Hammerstein are *Frederick Loewe* (1904), composer, and *Alan Lerner* (1918), librettist, whose *Brigadoon* and *Paint Your Wagon* and, more recently, *My Fair Lady* have been highly successful.

Other composers of highly successful musicals are: *Vincent Youmans, No! No! Nanette* and *Hit the Deck; Kurt Weill, Knickerbocker Holiday* and *Lady in the Dark; Frank Loesser, Guys and Dolls* and *Most Happy Fella; Harold Arlen, The Wizard of Oz* and *Bloomer Girl* (known also for his songs "Stormy Weather" and "Over the Rainbow").

Ragtime, Blues, and Jazz

On the lighter side, yet wielding an unmistakable influence on serious music, is what is commonly known as "popular" music. Such music is probably another outgrowth of the minstrel show. *Ragtime* began in New Orleans around the turn of the century with Negro musicians improvising ragtime melodies. Another popular style which originated with the Negro is the *blues*. W. C. Handy's "Memphis Blues" and "St. Louis Blues" are characteristic. Influenced by both ragtime and blues, *jazz* appeared soon after the turn of the century. Jazz is usually associated with the dance band which features percussion instruments, brasses (trumpets and trombones), woodwinds (saxophone and clarinet), guitar, vibra-harp, string bass, and piano. In recent years a more profound type of jazz has appeared which employs a wider instrumentation and adopts dissonant harmonies used by serious composers. *Swing* can best be described as improvisation around a given tune, reminiscent of ragtime practice.

Some of the finest examples of jazz in more serious music are George Gershwin's *An American in Paris, Rhapsody in Blue, Concerto in F for Piano, Of Thee I Sing* (musical comedy), and his major work, the opera *Porgy and Bess*. In these works, art and popular music were successfully fused. Long to be remembered are such songs as "Bess, You is My Woman Now," "It Ain't Necessarily So," "I Got Plenty of Nothin'," and "Summertime."

Other good examples of the jazz influence on serious music are: Morton Gould, *Chorale and Fugue in Jazz;* Stravinsky, *Rite of Spring;* Carpenter, *Skyscrapers;* Ravel, *Concerto for Piano;* Gruenberg, *Daniel Jazz;* and Shostakovitch, *Suite for Jazz Orchestra.*

Modern Art Music

The first half of the twentieth century has been marked by revolutionary tendencies comparable to that of the early Baroque era. During this time, as in other revolutionary periods, there is manifest a revolt against accepted practices of the immediate past. Such rebellion is usually accompanied by wide and sometimes radical experimentation which often clouds the real and influential forces. In their efforts to express the spirit of the times, many composers seem lost in a fog of confusion. Others seem to know exactly what they want. Be this as it may, the fact is that music, like literature, art and architecture, has experienced tremendous changes in these modern times.

One of the greatest revolts has been away from conventional chord construction and progression toward a freer treatment of dissonant material. For example, instead of building chords by thirds, as had been customary, at least since the beginning of the Baroque era, chords are now being built by fourths, fifths, sevenths, and seconds. Adjacent scale tones sounded together are known as *tone clusters*.

Another important aspect of modern music has been the breaking down of conventional tonal structure and the substituting of successions of remotely related chords, the employment of two or more keys at the same time, and at times the complete abandonment of tonal feeling.

Then, too, there has been a return to the aurally unfamiliar old church modes, a departure from the use of the established major and minor scale structure, and the employment of the whole tone scale (whole steps between each tone of the scale).

Other notable changes have been a return to counterpoint (the emphasis being placed upon the independent melodic line rather than on the total harmonic effect), a greater variety of rhythmic patterns and complex rhythmic structure, and a wide use of measures of different lengths within the same composition.

But even in the confusion of extreme experimentation and rapid changes in harmony, tonality, modes and rhythms, there have emerged three distinct movements of expression. The first of these was *impressionism,* which originated in France under the leadership of *Claude Debussy* (1862-1918), *Albert Roussel* (1869-1937), and *Maurice Ravel* (1875-1937). Such music is characterized by a vague, atmospheric type of expression—an "impression" —rather than a detailed, clear-cut picture. The second is *expressionism* which aims at the expression of the subconscious or inner self (in contrast to impressionism where the external is emphasized). *Arnold Schoenberg* (1874-1951) was a leading exponent of this school. The third classification is *neoclassicism* which is a return to the objectivity of the classical point of view. Characteristic of neoclassicism is a simplification and clarification of form, together with the assimilation of the modern trends mentioned above. Leaders in this type of expression are *Igor Stravinsky* (1882), *Serge Prokofiev* (1891-1953), and *Paul Hindemith* (1895).

A complete list of modern composers and their recorded works would be of great length and highly impractical for the elementary teacher and student. For this reason, a limited list of composers and recordings, which will serve as an introduction to modern music, is given below. Because of its practicality for teachers and students, American music is stressed.

CLAUDE DEBUSSY
    Children's Corner, Columbia ML4366
    La Mer, Angel 35081

MAURICE RAVEL
    Mother Goose Suite, Victor LM 1012
    Rhapsodie Espagnole, Angel 35081
    Le Tombeau de Couperin, Remington RLP-149-17
    Bolero, Victor DM 552

PAUL DUCAS
    The Sorcerer's Apprentice, Victor LM 1118

IGOR STRAVINSKY
    Firebird Suite, Columbia 4 ML 4700
    The Rite of Spring, Victor LM 2085

MODEST MOUSSORGSKY
    Pictures at an Exhibition, Columbia 4 ML 4700
                                      Victor LM 2201

SERGE PROKOFIEV
    Peter and the Wolf, Victor M 477
                         Columbia ML 4038

JOHN ALDEN CARPENTER
    Skyscrapers, Victor M 130

EDWARD MACDOWELL
    Indian Suite, Mercury 50082
    Woodland Sketches, MGM 3182

FERDE GROFE
    Grand Canyon Suite, Capitol T 272
                         Victor LM 1004 or 36095
    Death Valley Suite, Columbia CL 763 or M 463
                         Capitol 271
    Mississippi Suite,   Capitol P 8347
                         Victor 35859
    Hudson River Suite, Capitol P8347

GEORGE GERSHWIN
> Rhapsody in Blue, Columbia CL 700 or ML 4026
> > Victor LM 2017
> > Decca 8024
> > Capitol H 4302
> An American in Paris, Decca 8024
> > Columbia ML 4026
> Music of George Gershwin, Columbia CL 770
> Porgy and Bess (excerpts), Decca 7006
> Porgy and Bess (symphonic picture), Victor LM 6003

ROY HARRIS
> Abraham Lincoln Walks at Midnight, MGM 3210
> Fantasy for Piano and Orchestra, MGM 3210

VIRGIL THOMSON
> The Plow that Broke the Plains, Decca 7527
> Acadian Songs and Dances (from Louisiana Story), Decca 9616
> Filling Station, Vox PL 9050

RANDALL THOMPSON
> The Testament of Freedom, Mercury 50073

AARON COPLAND
> Billy the Kid, Capitol P 8238
> > Victor LM 1934
> Rodeo, Capitol P 8196 or Capitol L 8198
> > Victor LM 1934
> Appalachian Spring, Victor LCT 1134

WILLIAM SCHUMAN
> George Washington Bridge, Mercury 50079

MORTON GOULD
> Ballad for Band, Mercury 50079

GIAN CARLO MENOTTI
> Amahl and the Night Visitors, Victor LM 1701
> The Telephone ⎫ Columbia OSL 154
> The Medium ⎭

HOWARD HANSON
> Song of Democracy, Mercury 50150

DEEMS TAYLOR
> Through the Looking Glass, Mercury 50081

CHARLES GRIFFES
> The Pleasure Dome of Kubla Khan, Mercury 50085

RUDOLF FRIML
> The Firefly (excerpts), MGM E-3080
> The Vagabond King (excerpts), Capitol 219

Don Gillis
>   Saga of a Prairie School, London LL 176
Victor Herbert
>   Music of Herbert, Columbia CL 765
Jerome Kern
>   Music of Jerome Kern, Columbia CL 776
Richard Rodgers
>   Music of Rodgers, Columbia CL 810
>   Oklahoma (excerpts), Capitol 2-595
>   Carousel (excerpts), Victor LPM 1048
>   South Pacific (excerpts), Victor LOC 1032

Bibliography

Affelder, Paul. *How to Build a Record Library*. New York: E. P. Dutton, 1947.

Andrews, Frances M. and Clara E. Cockerille. *Your School Music Program*. Englewood Cliffs, New Jersey: Prentice-Hall, Inc., 1958.

Andrews, Gladys. *Creative Rhythmic Movement for Children*. Englewood Cliffs, New Jersey: Prentice-Hall, Inc., 1954.

Baldwin, Lillian E. *Music for Young Listeners* (Green Book, Crimson Book, and Blue Book). New York: Silver Burdett, 1951.

Burrows, Raymond and Bessie C. Redmond. *Symphony Themes*. New York: Simon & Schuster, 1942.

Coleman, Satis. *Creative Music in the Home*. New York: John Day Co., 1939.

Copland, Aaron. *What to Listen for in Music*, Rev. ed., New York: McGraw-Hill Book Co., 1957.

Ellison, Alfred. *Music with Children*. New York: McGraw-Hill Book Co., 1959.

Geri, Frank. *Illustrated Games and Rhythms for Children: Primary Grades*. Englewood Cliffs, New Jersey: Prentice-Hall, Inc., 1955.

Harris, Jane, Anne Pittman, and Marlys Swenson. *Dance a While*. Minneapolis: Burgess Publishing Co., 1950.

Hood, Marguerite and E. J. Schultz. *Learning Music Through Rhythms*. Boston: Ginn & Co., 1949.

Howard, John T. and George K. Bellows. *A Short History of Music in America*. New York: The Cornwall Press, Inc., 1957.

Hughes, Dorothy T. *Rhythmic Games and Dances*. New York: American Book Co., 1942.

Leonard, Charles and Robert W. House. *Foundation and Principles of Music Education*. New York: McGraw-Hill Book Co., 1959.

Leavitt, Helen S. and Warren S. Freeman. *Recording for the Elementary School*. New York: Oliver Durrell, Inc., 1949.

Machlis, Joseph. *The Enjoyment of Music*. New York: W. W. Norton & Co., Inc., 1957.

McKinney, Howard D. and W. R. Anderson. *Music in History*, 2nd ed., New York: American Book Co., 1957.

McMillan, L. Eileen. *Guiding Children's Growth Through Music*. Boston: Ginn & Co., 1959.

Morgan, Russell Van Dyke and Hazel N. Morgan. *Music Education in Action*. Chicago: Neil A. Kjos Music Co., 1954.

Mursell, James L. *Human Values in Music*. New York: Silver Burdett Co., 1934.

———— *Music Education Principles and Programs*. New York: Silver Burdett Co., 1956.

Myers, Louise K. *Teaching Children Music in the Elementary School*, 2nd ed., Englewood Cliffs, New Jersey: Prentice-Hall, Inc., 1956.

Nye, Robert E. and Vernice T. Nye. *Music in the Elementary School*. Englewood Cliffs, New Jersey: Prentice-Hall, Inc., 1957.

Pierce, Anne E. *Teaching Music in the Elementary School*. New York: Henry Holt & Co., 1959.

Ratner, Leonard G. *Music: The Listener's Art*. New York: McGraw-Hill Book Co., Inc., 1957.

Sheehy, Emma D. *There's Music in Children*, Rev. ed., New York: Henry Holt & Co., 1952.

Stringham, Edwin John. *Listening to Music Creatively*, 2nd ed., Englewood Cliffs, New Jersey: Prentice-Hall, Inc., 1959.

Tischler, Hans. *The Perceptive Listener*. Englewood Cliffs, New Jersey: Prentice-Hall, Inc., 1955.

Toose, Ruth and Beatrice P. Krone. *Literature and Music*. Englewood Cliffs, New Jersey: Prentice-Hall, Inc., 1955

INDEX

INDEX FOR SONGS
AND DANCES